THE CRIMSON FAIRY BOOK

Edited by

ANDREW LANG

With Numerous Illustrations by
H. J. Ford

DOVER PUBLICATIONS, INC.
NEW YORK

Published in Canada by General Publishing Company, Ltd., 30 Lesmill Road, Don Mills, Toronto, Ontario.

Published in the United Kingdom by Constable and Company, Ltd., 10 Orange Street, London WC 2.

This Dover edition, first published in 1967, is an unabridged republication of the work orginally published by Longmans, Green and Company, London, in 1903.

Standard Book Number: 486-21799-X

Library of Congress Catalog Card Number: 67-17988

Manufactured in the United States of America
Dover Publications, Inc.
180 Varick Street
New York, N. Y. 10014

PREFACE

EACH Fairy Book demands a preface from the Editor, and these introductions are inevitably both monotonous and unavailing. A sense of literary honesty compels the Editor to keep repeating that he *is* the Editor, and not the author of the Fairy Tales, just as a distinguished man of science is only the Editor, not the Author of *Nature*. Like nature, popular tales are too vast to be the creation of a single modern mind. The Editor's business is to hunt for collections of these stories told by peasant or savage grandmothers in many climes, from New Caledonia to Zululand; from the frozen snows of the Polar regions to Greece, or Spain, or Italy, or far Lochaber. When the tales are found they are adapted to the needs of British children by various hands, the Editor doing little beyond guarding the interests of propriety, and toning down to mild reproofs the tortures inflicted on wicked stepmothers, and other naughty characters.

These explanations have frequently been offered already; but, as far as ladies and children are concerned, to no purpose. They still ask the Editor how he can invent so many stories—more than Shakespeare, Dumas, and Charles Dickens could have invented in a century. And the Editor still avers, in Prefaces, that he did not invent one of the stories; that nobody knows, as a rule, who invented them, or where, or when. It is only plain that, perhaps a hundred thousand years ago, some savage grandmother told a tale to a savage granddaughter; that the granddaughter told it in her turn; that various tellers made changes to suit their taste, adding or omitting features and incidents; that, as the world grew civilised, other alterations were made, and that, at last, Homer composed the 'Odyssey,' and somebody else composed the Story of Jason and the Fleece of Gold, and the enchantress Medea, out of a set of wandering popular tales, which are still told among Samoyeds and Samoans, Hindoos and Japanese.

All this has been known to the wise and learned for centuries, and especially since the brothers Grimm wrote in the early years of the Nineteenth Century. But children remain unaware of the facts, and so do their dear mothers; whence the Editor infers that they do not read his prefaces, and are not members of the Folk-Lore Society, or students of Herr Köhler and M. Cosquin, and M. Henri Guidoz and Professor Child, and Mr. Max Müller. Though these explanations are not attended to by the Editor's customers, he makes them once more, for the relief of his conscience. Many tales in this book are translated, or adapted, from those told by mothers and nurses in Hungary; others are familiar to Russian nurseries; the Servians are responsible for some; a rather peculiarly fanciful set of stories are adapted from the Roumanians; others are from the Baltic shores; others from sunny Sicily; a few are from Finland, and Iceland, and Japan, and Tunis, and Portugal. No doubt many children will like to look out these places on the map, and study their mountains, rivers, soil, products, and fiscal policies, in the geography books. The peoples who tell the stories differ in colour, language, religion, and almost everything else; but they all love a nursery tale. The stories have mainly been adapted or translated by Mrs. Lang, a few by Miss Lang and Miss Blackley.

CONTENTS

ILLUSTRATIONS

COLOURED PLATES

[*between pages 212 and 213*]

FULL-PAGE PLATES

IN TEXT

LOVELY ILONKA

THERE was once a king's son who told his father that he wished to marry.

'No, no!' said the king; 'you must not be in such a hurry. Wait till you have done some great deed. My father did not let me marry till I had won the golden sword you see me wear.'

The prince was much disappointed, but he never dreamed of disobeying his father, and he began to think with all his might what he could do. It was no use staying at home, so one day he wandered out into the world to try his luck, and as he walked along he came to a little hut in which he found an old woman crouching over the fire.

'Good evening, mother. I see you have lived long in this world; do you know anything about the three bulrushes?'

'Yes, indeed, I've lived long and been much about in the world, but I have never seen or heard anything of what you ask. Still, if you will wait till to-morrow I may be able to tell you something.'

Well, he waited till the morning, and quite early the old woman appeared and took out a little pipe and blew in it, and in a moment all the crows in the world were flying about her. Not one was missing. Then she asked if they knew anything about the three bulrushes, but not one of them did.

The prince went on his way, and a little further on he found another hut in which lived an old man. On being questioned the old man said he knew nothing, but begged the prince to stay overnight, and the next morning the old man called all the ravens together, but they too had nothing to tell.

The prince bade him farewell and set out. He wandered so far that he crossed seven kingdoms, and at last, one evening, he came to a little house in which was an old woman.

'Good evening, dear mother,' said he politely.

'Good evening to you, my dear son,' answered the old woman. 'It is lucky for you that you spoke to me or you would have met with a horrible death. But may I ask where are you going?'

'I am seeking the three bulrushes. Do you know anything about them?'

'I don't know anything myself, but wait till to-morrow. Perhaps I can tell you then.' So the next morning she blew on her pipe, and lo! and behold every magpie in the world flew up. That is to say, all the magpies except one who had broken a leg and a wing. The old woman sent after it at once, and when she questioned the magpies the crippled one was the only one who knew where the three bulrushes were.

Then the prince started off with the lame magpie. They went on and on till they reached a great stone wall, many, many feet high.

'Now, prince,' said the magpie, 'the three bulrushes are behind that wall.'

The prince wasted no time. He set his horse at the wall and leaped over it. Then he looked about for the three bulrushes, pulled them up and set off with them on his way home. As he rode along one of the bulrushes happened to knock against something. It split open and, only think! out sprang a lovely girl, who said: 'My heart's love, you are mine and I am yours; do give me a glass of water.'

But how could the prince give it her when there was

THE FIRST BULRUSK-MAIDEN FLIES AWAY

no water at hand? So the lovely maiden flew away. He split the second bulrush as an experiment and just the same thing happened.

How careful he was of the third bulrush! He waited till he came to a well, and there he split it open, and out sprang a maiden seven times lovelier than either of the others, and she too said: 'My heart's love, I am yours and you are mine; do give me a glass of water.'

This time the water was ready and the girl did not fly away, but she and the prince promised to love each other always. Then they set out for home.

They soon reached the prince's country, and as he wished to bring his promised bride back in a fine coach he went on to the town to fetch one. In the field where the well was, the king's swineherds and cowherds were feeding their droves, and the prince left Ilonka (for that was her name) in their care.

Unluckily the chief swineherd had an ugly old daughter, and whilst the prince was away he dressed her up in fine clothes, and threw Ilonka into the well.

The prince returned before long, bringing with him his father and mother and a great train of courtiers to escort Ilonka home. But how they all stared when they saw the swineherd's ugly daughter! However, there was nothing for it but to take her home; and, two days later, the prince married her, and his father gave up the crown to him.

But he had no peace! He knew very well he had been cheated, though he could not think how. Once he desired to have some water brought him from the well into which Ilonka had been thrown. The coachman went for it and, in the bucket he pulled up, a pretty little duck was swimming. He looked wonderingly at it, and all of a sudden it disappeared and he found a dirty looking girl standing near him. The girl returned with him and managed to get a place as housemaid in the palace.

Of course she was very busy all day long, but whenever she had a little spare time she sat down to spin.

Her distaff turned of itself and her spindle span by itself and the flax wound itself off; and however much she might use there was always plenty left.

When the queen—or, rather, the swineherd's daughter—heard of this, she very much wished to have the distaff, but the girl flatly refused to give it to her. However, at last she consented on condition that she might sleep one night in the king's room. The queen was very angry, and scolded her well; but as she longed to have the distaff she consented, though she gave the king a sleeping draught at supper.

Then the girl went to the king's room looking seven times lovelier than ever. She bent over the sleeper and said: 'My heart's love, I am yours and you are mine. Speak to me but once; I am your Ilonka.' But the king was so sound asleep he neither heard nor spoke, and Ilonka left the room, sadly thinking he was ashamed to own her.

Soon after the queen again sent to say that she wanted to buy the spindle. The girl agreed to let her have it on the same conditions as before; but this time, also, the queen took care to give the king a sleeping draught. And once more Ilonka went to the king's room and spoke to him; whisper as sweetly as she might she could get no answer.

Now some of the king's servants had taken note of the matter, and warned their master not to eat and drink anything that the queen offered him, as for two nights running she had given him a sleeping draught. The queen had no idea that her doings had been discovered; and when, a few days later, she wanted the flax, and had to pay the same price for it, she felt no fears at all.

At supper that night the queen offered the king all sorts of nice things to eat and drink, but he declared he was not hungry, and went early to bed.

The queen repented bitterly her promise to the girl, but it was too late to recall it; for Ilonka had already entered the king's room, where he lay anxiously waiting for something, he knew not what. All of a sudden he saw a lovely maiden who bent over him and said: 'My dearest love, I am yours and you are mine. Speak to me, for I am your Ilonka.'

At these words the king's heart bounded within him. He sprang up and embraced and kissed her, and she told him all her adventures since the moment he had left her. And when he heard all that Ilonka had suffered, and how he had been deceived, he vowed he would be revenged; so he gave orders that the swineherd, his wife and daughter should all be hanged; and so they were.

The next day the king was married, with great rejoicings, to the fair Ilonka; and if they are not yet dead—why, they are still living.

[From *Ungarische Mährchen.*]

LUCKY LUCK

ONCE upon a time there was a king who had an only son. When the lad was about eighteen years old his father had to go to fight in a war against a neighbouring country, and the king led his troops in person. He bade his son act as Regent in his absence, but ordered him on no account to marry till his return.

Time went by. The prince ruled the country and never even thought of marrying. But when he reached his twenty-fifth birthday he began to think that it might be rather nice to have a wife, and he thought so much that at last he got quite eager about it. He remembered, however, what his father had said, and waited some time longer, till at last it was ten years since the king went out to war. Then the prince called his courtiers about him and set off with a great retinue to seek a bride. He hardly knew which way to go, so he wandered about for twenty days, when, suddenly, he found himself in his father's camp.

The king was delighted to see his son, and had a great many questions to ask and answer; but when he heard that instead of quietly waiting for him at home the prince was starting off to seek a wife he was very angry, and said: 'You may go where you please but I will not leave any of my people with you.'

Only one faithful servant stayed with the prince and refused to part from him. They journeyed over hill and dale till they came to a place called Goldtown. The King of Goldtown had a lovely daughter, and the prince, who soon heard about her beauty, could not rest till he saw her.

He was very kindly received, for he was extremely good-looking and had charming manners, so he lost no

THE FAITHFUL SERVANT & THE THREE EAGLES

time in asking for her hand and her parents gave her to him with joy. The wedding took place at once, and the feasting and rejoicings went on for a whole month. At the end of the month they set off for home, but as the journey was a long one they spent the first evening at an inn. Everyone in the house slept, and only the faithful servant kept watch. About midnight he heard three crows, who had flown to the roof, talking together.

'That's a handsome couple which arrived here to-night. It seems quite a pity they should lose their lives so soon.'

'Truly,' said the second crow; 'for to-morrow, when midday strikes, the bridge over the Gold Stream will break just as they are driving over it. But, listen! whoever overhears and tells what we have said will be turned to stone up to his knees.'

The crows had hardly done speaking when away they flew. And close upon them followed three pigeons.

'Even if the prince and princess get safe over the bridge they will perish,' said they; 'for the king is going to send a carriage to meet them which looks as new as paint. But when they are seated in it a raging wind will rise and whirl the carriage away into the clouds. Then it will fall suddenly to earth, and they will be killed. But anyone who hears and betrays what we have said will be turned to stone up to his waist.'

With that the pigeons flew off and three eagles took their places, and this is what they said:

'If the young couple does manage to escape the dangers of the bridge and the carriage, the king means to send them each a splendid gold embroidered robe. When they put these on they will be burnt up at once. But whoever hears and repeats this will turn to stone from head to foot.'

Early next morning the travellers got up and breakfasted. They began to tell each other their dreams. At last the servant said:

'Gracious prince, I dreamt that if your Royal Highness would grant all I asked we should get home safe and sound; but if you did not we should certainly be lost. My dreams never deceive me, so I entreat you to follow my advice during the rest of the journey.'

'Don't make such a fuss about a dream,' said the prince; 'dreams are but clouds. Still, to prevent your being anxious I will promise to do as you wish.'

With that they set out on their journey.

At midday they reached the Gold Stream. When they got to the bridge the servant said: 'Let us leave the carriage here, my prince, and walk a little way. The town is not far off and we can easily get another carriage there, for the wheels of this one are bad and will not hold out much longer.'

The prince looked well at the carriage. He did not think it looked so unsafe as his servant said; but he had given his word and he held to it.

They got down and loaded the horses with the luggage. The prince and his bride walked over the bridge, but the servant said he would ride the horses through the stream so as to water and bathe them.

They reached the other side without harm, and bought a new carriage in the town, which was quite near, and set off once more on their travels; but they had not gone far when they met a messenger from the king who said to the prince: 'His Majesty has sent your Royal Highness this beautiful carriage so that you may make a fitting entry into your own country and amongst your own people.'

The prince was so delighted that he could not speak. But the servant said: 'My lord, let me examine this carriage first and then you can get in if I find it is all right; otherwise we had better stay in our own.'

The prince made no objections, and after looking the carriage well over the servant said: 'It is as bad as it is smart'; and with that he knocked it all to pieces, and they went on in the one that they had bought.

At last they reached the frontier; there another

messenger was waiting for them, who said that the king had sent two splendid robes for the prince and his bride, and begged that they would wear them for their state entry. But the servant implored the prince to have nothing to do with them, and never gave him any peace till he had obtained leave to destroy the robes.

The old king was furious when he found that all his arts had failed; that his son still lived and that he would have to give up the crown to him now he was married, for that was the law of the land. He longed to know how the prince had escaped, and said: 'My dear son, I do indeed rejoice to have you safely back, but I cannot imagine why the beautiful carriage and the splendid robes I sent did not please you; why you had them destroyed.'

'Indeed, sire,' said the prince, 'I was myself much annoyed at their destruction; but my servant had begged to direct everything on the journey and I had promised him that he should do so. He declared that we could not possibly get home safely unless I did as he told me.'

The old king fell into a tremendous rage. He called his Council together and condemned the servant to death.

The gallows was put up in the square in front of the palace. The servant was led out and his sentence read to him.

The rope was being placed round his neck, when he begged to be allowed a few last words. 'On our journey home,' he said, 'we spent the first night at an inn. I did not sleep but kept watch all night.' And then he went on to tell what the crows had said, and as he spoke he turned to stone up to his knees. The prince called to him to say no more as he had proved his innocence. But the servant paid no heed to him, and by the time his story was done he had turned to stone from head to foot.

Oh! how grieved the prince was to lose his faithful servant! And what pained him most was the thought that he was lost through his very faithfulness, and he

THE FAITHFUL SERVANT TURNS INTO STONE

determined to travel all over the world and never rest till he found some means of restoring him to life.

Now there lived at Court an old woman who had been the prince's nurse. To her he confided all his plans, and left his wife, the princess, in her care. 'You have a long way before you, my son,' said the old woman; 'you must never return till you have met with Lucky Luck. If he cannot help you no one on earth can.'

So the prince set off to try to find Lucky Luck. He walked and walked till he got beyond his own country, and he wandered through a wood for three days but did not meet a living being in it. At the end of the third day he came to a river near which stood a large mill. Here he spent the night. When he was leaving next morning the miller asked him: 'My gracious lord, where are you going all alone?'

And the prince told him.

'Then I beg your Highness to ask Lucky Luck this question: Why is it that though I have an excellent mill, with all its machinery complete, and get plenty of grain to grind, I am so poor that I hardly know how to live from one day to another?'

The prince promised to inquire, and went on his way. He wandered about for three days more, and at the end of the third day saw a little town. It was quite late when he reached it, but he could discover no light anywhere, and walked almost right through it without finding a house where he could turn in. But far away at the end of the town he saw a light in a window. He went straight to it and in the house were three girls playing a game together. The prince asked for a night's lodging and they took him in, gave him some supper and got a room ready for him, where he slept.

Next morning when he was leaving they asked where he was going and he told them his story. 'Gracious prince,' said the maidens, 'do ask Lucky Luck how it happens that here we are over thirty years old and no lover has come to woo us, though we are good, pretty, and very industrious.'

The prince promised to inquire, and went on his way.

Then he came to a great forest and wandered about in it from morning to night and from night to morning before he got near the other end. Here he found a pretty stream which was different from other streams as, instead of flowing, it stood still and began to talk: 'Sir prince, tell me what brings you into these wilds? I must have been flowing here a hundred years and more and no one has ever yet come by.'

'I will tell you,' answered the prince, 'if you will divide yourself so that I may walk through.'

The stream parted at once, and the prince walked through without wetting his feet; and directly he got to the other side he told his story as he had promised.

'Oh, do ask Lucky Luck,' cried the brook, 'why, though I am such a clear, bright, rapid stream I never have a fish or any other living creature in my waters.'

The prince said he would do so, and continued his journey.

When he got quite clear of the forest he walked on through a lovely valley till he reached a little house thatched with rushes, and he went in to rest for he was very tired.

Everything in the house was beautifully clean and tidy, and a cheerful honest-looking old woman was sitting by the fire.

'Good-morning, mother,' said the prince.

'May Luck be with you, my son. What brings you into these parts?'

'I am looking for Lucky Luck,' replied the prince.

'Then you have come to the right place, my son, for I am his mother. He is not at home just now, he is out digging in the vineyard. Do you go too. Here are two spades. When you find him begin to dig, but don't speak a word to him. It is now eleven o'clock. When he sits

THE COMPLAINT OF THE THREE MAIDENS

down to eat his dinner sit beside him and eat with him. After dinner he will question you, and then tell him all your troubles freely. He will answer whatever you may ask.'

With that she showed him the way, and the prince went and did just as she had told him. After dinner they lay down to rest.

All of a sudden Lucky Luck began to speak and said: 'Tell me, what sort of man are you, for since you came here you have not spoken a word?'

'I am not dumb,' replied the young man, 'but I am that unhappy prince whose faithful servant has been turned to stone, and I want to know how to help him.'

'And you do well, for he deserves everything. Go back, and when you get home your wife will just have had a little boy. Take three drops of blood from the child's little finger, rub them on your servant's wrists with a blade of grass and he will return to life.'

'I have another thing to ask,' said the prince, when he had thanked him. 'In the forest near here is a fine stream but not a fish or other living creature in it. Why is this?'

'Because no one has ever been drowned in the stream. But take care, in crossing, to get as near the other side as you can before you say so, or you may be the first victim yourself.'

'Another question, please, before I go. On my way here I lodged one night in the house of three maidens. All were well-mannered, hard-working, and pretty, and yet none has had a wooer. Why was this?'

'Because they always throw out their sweepings in the face of the sun.'

'And why is it that a miller, who has a large mill with all the best machinery and gets plenty of corn to grind is so poor that he can hardly live from day to day?'

'Because the miller keeps everything for himself, and does not give to those who need it.'

The prince wrote down the answers to his questions, took a friendly leave of Lucky Luck, and set off for home.

When he reached the stream it asked if he brought it any good news. 'When I get across I will tell you,' said he. So the stream parted; he walked through and on to the highest part of the bank. He stopped and shouted out:

'Listen, oh stream! Lucky Luck says you will never have any living creature in your waters until someone is drowned in you.'

The words were hardly out of his mouth when the stream swelled and overflowed till it reached the rock up which he had climbed, and dashed so far up it that the spray flew over him. But he clung on tight, and after failing to reach him three times the stream returned to its proper course. Then the prince climbed down, dried himself in the sun, and set out on his march home.

He spent the night once more at the mill and gave the miller his answer, and by-and-by he told the three sisters not to throw out all their sweepings in the face of the sun.

The prince had hardly arrived at home when some thieves tried to ford the stream with a fine horse they had stolen. When they were half-way across, the stream rose so suddenly that it swept them all away. From that time it became the best fishing stream in the country-side.

The miller, too, began to give alms and became a very good man, and in time grew so rich that he hardly knew how much he had.

And the three sisters, now that they no longer insulted the sun, had each a wooer within a week.

When the prince got home he found that his wife had just got a fine little boy. He did not lose a moment in pricking the baby's finger till the blood ran, and he brushed it on the wrists of the stone figure, which shuddered all over and split with a loud noise in seven parts and there was the faithful servant alive and well.

When the old king saw this he foamed with rage, stared wildly about, flung himself on the ground and died.

The servant stayed on with his royal master and served him faithfully all the rest of his life ; and, if neither of them is dead, he is serving him still.

[From *Ungarische Mährchen.*]

THE HAIRY MAN

SOMEWHERE or other, but I don't know where, there lived a king who owned two remarkably fine fields of rape, but every night two of the rape heaps were burnt down in one of the fields. The king was extremely angry at this, and sent out soldiers to catch whoever had set fire to the ricks; but it was all of no use—not a soul could they see. Then he offered nine hundred crowns to anyone who caught the evil-doer, and at the same time ordered that whoever did not keep proper watch over the fields should be killed; but though there were a great many people, none seemed able to protect the fields.

The king had already put ninety-nine people to death, when a little swineherd came to him who had two dogs; one was called 'Psst,' and the other 'Hush'; and the boy told the king that he would watch over the ricks.

When it grew dark he climbed up on the top of the fourth rick, from where he could see the whole field. About eleven o'clock he thought he saw someone going to a rick and putting a light to it. 'Just you wait,' thought he, and called out to his dogs: 'Hi! Psst, Hush, catch him!' But Psst and Hush had not waited for orders, and in five minutes the man was caught.

Next morning he was brought bound before the king, who was so pleased with the boy that he gave him a thousand crowns at once. The prisoner was all covered with hair, almost like an animal; and altogether he was so curious to look at that the king locked him up in a strong room and sent out letters of invitation to all the

The Prince lets out the Hairy Man

other kings and princes asking them to come and see this wonder.

That was all very well; but the king had a little boy of ten years old who went to look at the hairy man also, and the man begged so hard to be set free that the boy took pity on him. He stole the key of the strong room from his mother and opened the door. Then he took the key back, but the hairy man escaped and went off into the world.

Then the kings and princes began to arrive one after another, and all were most anxious to see the hairy man; but he was gone! The king nearly burst with rage and with the shame he felt. He questioned his wife sharply, and told her that if she could not find and bring back the hairy man he would put her in a hut made of rushes and burn her there. The queen declared she had had nothing to do with the matter; if her son had happened to take the key it had not been with her knowledge.

So they fetched the little prince and asked him all sorts of questions, and at last he owned that he had let the hairy man out. The king ordered his servants to take the boy into the forest and to kill him there, and to bring back part of his liver and lungs.

There was grief all over the palace when the king's command was known, for he was a great favourite. But there was no help for it, and they took the boy out into the forest. But the man was sorry for him, and shot a dog and carried pieces of his lungs and liver to the king, who was satisfied, and did not trouble himself any more.

The prince wandered about in the forest and lived as best he could for five years. One day he came upon a poor little cottage in which was an old man. They began to talk, and the prince told his story and sad fate. Then they recognised each other, for the old fellow was no other than the hairy man whom the prince had set free, and who had lived ever since in the forest.

The prince stayed here for two years; then he wished

to go further. The old man begged him hard to stay, but he would not, so his hairy friend gave him a golden apple out of which came a horse with a golden mane, and a golden staff with which to guide the horse. The old man also gave him a silver apple out of which came the most beautiful hussars and a silver staff; and a copper apple from which he could draw as many foot soldiers as ever he wished, and a copper staff. He made the prince swear solemnly to take the greatest care of these presents, and then he let him go.

The boy wandered on and on till he came to a large town. Here he took service in the king's palace, and as no one troubled themselves about him he lived quietly on.

One day news was brought to the king that he must go out to war. He was horribly frightened for he had a very small army, but he had to go all the same.

When they had all left, the prince said to the housekeeper:

'Give me leave to go to the next village—I owe a small bill there, and I want to go and pay it'; and as there was nothing to be done in the palace the housekeeper gave him leave.

When he got beyond the town he took out his golden apple, and when the horse sprang out he swung himself into the saddle. Then he took the silver and the copper apples, and with all these fine soldiers he joined the king's army.

The king saw them approach with fear in his heart, for he did not know if it might not be an enemy; but the prince rode up, and bowed low before him. 'I bring your Majesty reinforcements,' said he.

The king was delighted, and all dread of his enemy at once disappeared. The princesses were there too, and they were very friendly with the prince and begged him to get into their carriage so as to talk to them. But he declined, and remained on horseback, as he did not know at what moment the battle might begin; and whilst they were all talking together the youngest princess, who was also the loveliest, took off her ring, and her sister tore her handkerchief in two pieces, and they gave these gifts to the prince.

Suddenly the enemy came in sight. The king asked whether his army or the prince's should lead the way; but the prince set off first and with his hussars he fought so bravely that only two of the enemy were left alive, and these two were only spared to act as messengers.

The king was overjoyed and so were his daughters at this brilliant victory. As they drove home they begged the prince to join them, but he would not come, and galloped off with his hussars.

When he got near the town he packed his soldiers and his fine horse all carefully into the apple again, and then strolled into the town. On his return to the palace he was well scolded by the housekeeper for staying away so long.

Well, the whole matter might have ended there; but it so happened that the younger princess had fallen in love with the prince, as he had with her. And as he had no jewels with him, he gave her the copper apple and staff.

One day, as the princesses were talking with their father, the younger one asked him whether it might not have been their servant who had helped him so much. The king was quite angry at the idea; but, to satisfy her, he ordered the servant's room to be searched. And there, to everyone's surprise, they found the golden ring and the half of the handkerchief. When these were brought to the king he sent for the prince at once and asked if it had been he who had come to their rescue.

'Yes, your Majesty, it was I,' answered the prince.

'But where did you get your army?'

'If you wish to see it, I can show it you outside the city walls.'

And so he did; but first he asked for the copper apple from the younger princess, and when all the soldiers were drawn up there were such numbers that there was barely room for them.

The king gave him his daughter and kingdom as a reward for his aid, and when he heard that the prince was himself a king's son his joy knew no bounds. The prince packed all his soldiers carefully up once more, and they went back into the town.

Not long after there was a grand wedding; perhaps they may all be alive still, but I don't know.

TO YOUR GOOD HEALTH!

LONG, long ago there lived a king who was such a mighty monarch that whenever he sneezed every one in the whole country had to say 'To your good health!' Every one said it except the shepherd with the staring eyes, and he would not say it.

The king heard of this and was very angry, and sent for the shepherd to appear before him.

The shepherd came and stood before the throne, where the king sat looking very grand and powerful. But however grand or powerful he might be the shepherd did not feel a bit afraid of him.

'Say at once, "To my good health!"' cried the king.

'To my good health!' replied the shepherd.

'To mine—to *mine*, you rascal, you vagabond!' stormed the king.

'To mine, to *mine*, your Majesty,' was the answer.

'But to *mine*—to my own,' roared the king, and beat on his breast in a rage.

'Well, yes; to mine, of course, to my own,' cried the shepherd, and gently tapped his breast.

The king was beside himself with fury and did not know what to do, when the Lord Chamberlain interfered:

'Say at once—say this very moment: "To your health, your Majesty"; for if you don't say it you'll lose your life,' whispered he.

'No, I won't say it till I get the princess for my wife,' was the shepherd's answer. Now the princess was sitting on a little throne beside the king, her father, and she looked as sweet and lovely as a little golden dove. When she heard what the shepherd said she could not help laughing, for there is no denying the fact that this young shepherd with the staring eyes pleased her very much; indeed he pleased her better than any king's son she had yet seen.

But the king was not as pleasant as his daughter, and he gave orders to throw the shepherd into the white bear's pit.

The guards led him away and thrust him into the pit with the white bear, who had had nothing to eat for two days and was very hungry. The door of the pit was hardly closed when the bear rushed at the shepherd; but when it saw his eyes it was so frightened that it was ready to eat itself. It shrank away into a corner and gazed at him from there, and, in spite of being so famished, did not dare to touch him, but sucked its own paws from sheer hunger. The shepherd felt that if he once removed his eyes off the beast he was a dead man, and in order to keep himself awake he made songs and sang them, and so the night went by.

Next morning the Lord Chamberlain came to see the shepherd's bones, and was amazed to find him alive and well. He led him to the king, who fell into a furious passion, and said: 'Well, you have learned what it is to be very near death, and *now* will you say "To my good health"?'

But the shepherd answered: 'I am not afraid of ten deaths! I will only say it if I may have the princess for my wife.'

'Then go to your death,' cried the king; and ordered him to be thrown into the den with the wild boars. The wild boars had not been fed for a week, and when the shepherd was thrust into their den they rushed at him to tear him to pieces. But the shepherd took a little flute out of the sleeve of his jacket and began to play a merry tune, on which the wild boars first of all shrank shyly away, and then got up on their hind legs and

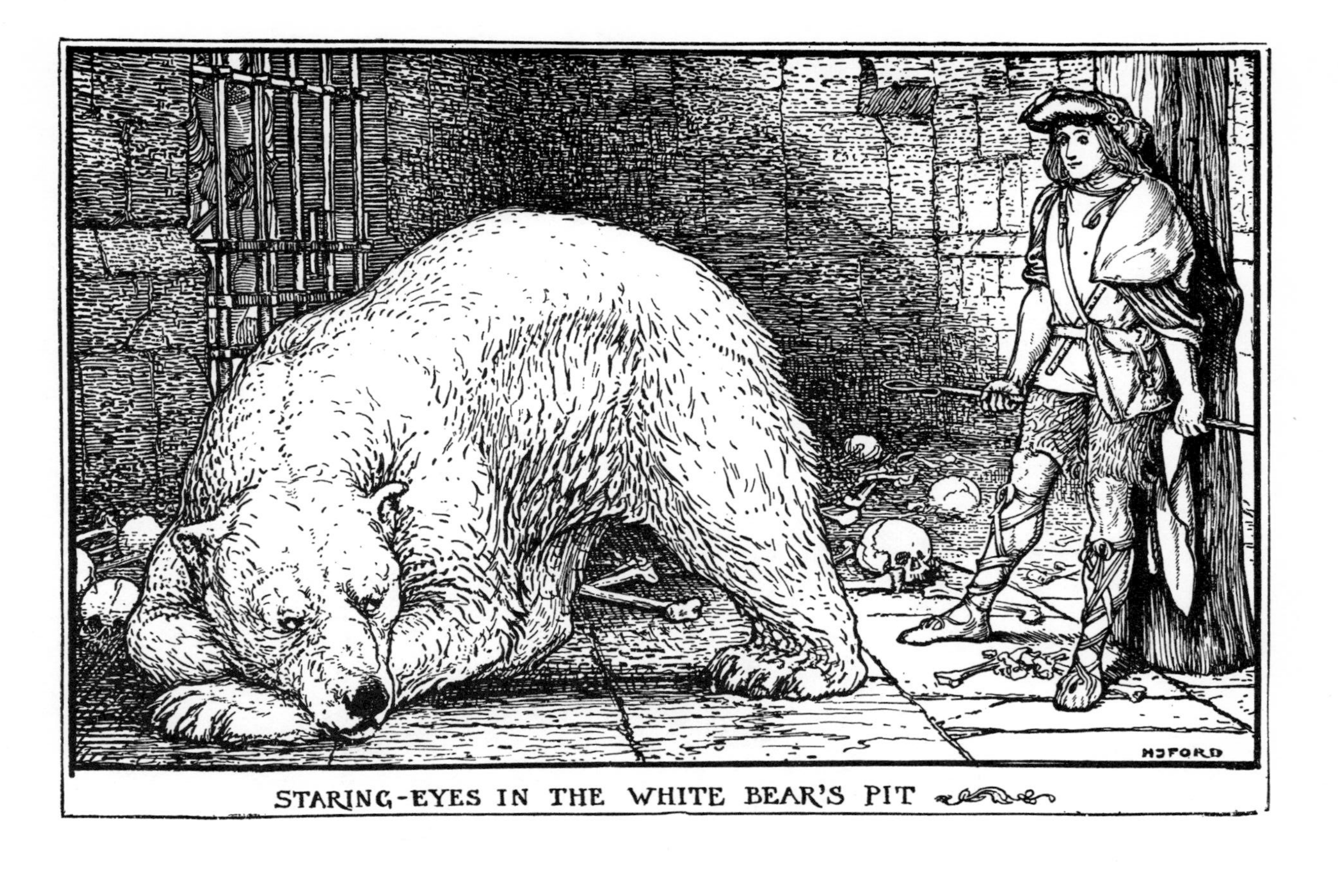

STARING-EYES IN THE WHITE BEAR'S PIT

danced gaily. The shepherd would have given anything to be able to laugh, they looked so funny; but he dared not stop playing, for he knew well enough that the moment he stopped they would fall upon him and tear him to pieces. His eyes were of no use to him here, for he could not have stared ten wild boars in the face at once; so he kept on playing, and the wild boars danced very slowly, as if in a minuet, then by degrees he played faster and faster till they could hardly twist and turn quickly enough, and ended by all falling over each other in a heap, quite exhausted and out of breath.

Then the shepherd ventured to laugh at last; and he laughed so long and so loud that when the Lord Chamberlain came early in the morning, expecting to find only his bones, the tears were still running down his cheeks from laughter.

As soon as the king was dressed the shepherd was again brought before him; but he was more angry than ever to think the wild boars had not torn the man to bits, and he said: 'Well, you have learned what it feels to be near ten deaths, *now* say "To my good health!"'

But the shepherd broke in with, 'I do not fear a hundred deaths, and I will only say it if I may have the princess for my wife.'

'Then go to a hundred deaths!' roared the king, and ordered the shepherd to be thrown down the deep vault of scythes.

The guards dragged him away to a dark dungeon, in the middle of which was a deep well with sharp scythes all round it. At the bottom of the well was a little light by which one could see if anyone was thrown in whether he had fallen to the bottom.

When the shepherd was dragged to the dungeons he begged the guards to leave him alone a little while that he might look down into the pit of scythes; perhaps he might after all make up his mind to say 'To your good health' to the king. So the guards left him alone and he stuck up his long stick near the well, hung his cloak round the stick and put his hat on the top. He also hung his knapsack up inside the cloak so that it might seem to have some body within it. When this was done he called out to the guards and said that he had considered the matter but after all he could not make up his mind to say what the king wished. The guards came in, threw the hat and cloak, knapsack and stick all down the well together, watched to see how they put out the light at the bottom and came away, thinking that now there really was an end of the shepherd. But he had hidden in a dark corner and was laughing to himself all the time.

Quite early next morning came the Lord Chamberlain, carrying a lamp and he nearly fell backwards with surprise when he saw the shepherd alive and well. He brought him to the king, whose fury was greater than ever, but who cried:

'Well, now you have been near a hundred deaths; will you say: "To your good health"?'

But the shepherd only gave the same answer:

'I won't say it till the princess is my wife.'

'Perhaps after all you may do it for less,' said the king, who saw that there was no chance of making away with the shepherd; and he ordered the state coach to be got ready, then he made the shepherd get in with him and sit beside him, and ordered the coachman to drive to the silver wood. When they reached it he said: 'Do you see this silver wood? Well, if you will say, "To your good health," I will give it to you.'

The shepherd turned hot and cold by turns, but he still persisted:

'I will not say it till the princess is my wife.'

The king was much vexed; he drove further on till they came to a splendid castle, all of gold, and then he said:

'Do you see this golden castle? Well, I will give you that too, the silver wood and the golden castle, if only you will say that one thing to me: "To your good health."'

The shepherd gaped and wondered and was quite dazzled, but he still said:

'No; I will *not* say it till I have the princess for my wife.'

This time the king was overwhelmed with grief, and gave orders to drive on to the diamond pond, and there he tried once more.

'Do you see this diamond pond? I will give you that too, the silver wood and the golden castle and the diamond pond. You shall have them all—all—if you will but say: "To your good health!"'

The shepherd had to shut his staring eyes tight not to be dazzled with the brilliant pond, but still he said:

'No, no; I will not say it till I have the princess for my wife.'

Then the king saw that all his efforts were useless, and that he might as well give in, so he said:

'Well, well, it's all the same to me—I will give you my daughter to wife; but, then, you really and truly must say to me: "To your good health."'

'Of course I'll say it; why should I not say it? It stands to reason that I shall say it then.'

At this the king was more delighted than anyone could have believed. He made it known all through the country that there were to be great rejoicings, as the princess was going to be married. And everyone rejoiced to think that the princess, who had refused so many royal suitors, should have ended by falling in love with the staring-eyed shepherd.

There was such a wedding as had never been seen. Everyone ate and drank and danced. Even the sick were feasted, and quite tiny new-born children had presents given them.

But the greatest merry-making was in the king's palace; there the best bands played and the best food was cooked; a crowd of people sat down to table, and all was fun and merry-making.

And when the groomsman, according to custom, brought in the great boar's head on a big dish and placed it before the king so that he might carve it and give everyone a share, the savoury smell was so strong that the king began to sneeze with all his might.

'To your very good health,' cried the shepherd before anyone else, and the king was so delighted that he did not regret having given him his daughter.

In time, when the old king died, the shepherd succeeded him. He made a very good king and never expected his people to wish him well against their wills; but, all the same, everyone did wish him well, for they all loved him.

[From *Russische Mährchen.*]

THE STORY OF THE SEVEN SIMONS

Far, far away, beyond all sorts of countries, seas and rivers, there stood a splendid city where lived King Archidej, who was as good as he was rich and handsome. His great army was made up of men ready to obey his slightest wish; he owned forty times forty cities, and in each city he had ten palaces with silver doors, golden roofs, and crystal windows. His council consisted of the twelve wisest men in the country, whose long beards flowed down over their breasts, each of whom was as learned as a whole college. This council always told the king the exact truth.

Now the king had everything to make him happy, but he did not enjoy anything because he could not find a bride to his mind.

One day, as he sat in his palace looking out to sea, a great ship sailed into the harbour and several merchants came on shore. Said the king to himself: 'These people have travelled far and beheld many lands. I will ask them if they have seen any princess who is as clever and as handsome as I am.'

So he ordered the merchants to be brought before him, and when they came he said: 'You have travelled much and visited many wonders. I wish to ask you a question, and I beg you to answer truthfully.

'Have you anywhere seen or heard of the daughter of an emperor, king, or a prince, who is as clever and as handsome as I am, and who would be worthy to be my wife and the queen of my country?'

The merchants considered for some time. At last the eldest of them said: 'I have heard that across many seas, in the Island of Busan, there is a mighty king, whose daughter, the Princess Helena, is so lovely that she can certainly not be plainer than your Majesty, and so clever that the wisest greybeard cannot guess her riddles.'

'Is the island far off, and which is the way to it?'

'It is not near,' was the answer. 'The journey would take ten years, and we do not know the way. And even if we did, what use would that be? The princess is no bride for you.'

'How dare you say so?' cried the king angrily.

'Your Majesty must pardon us; but just think for a moment. Should you send an envoy to the island he will take ten years to get there and ten more to return—twenty years in all. Will not the princess have grown old in that time and have lost all her beauty?'

The king reflected gravely. Then he thanked the merchants, gave them leave to trade in his country without paying any duties, and dismissed them.

After they were gone the king remained deep in thought. He felt puzzled and anxious; so he decided to ride into the country to distract his mind, and sent for his huntsmen and falconers. The huntsmen blew their horns, the falconers took their hawks on their wrists, and off they all set out across country till they came to a green hedge. On the other side of the hedge stretched a great field of maize as far as the eye could reach, and the yellow ears swayed to and fro in the gentle breeze like a rippling sea of gold.

The king drew rein and admired the field. 'Upon my word,' said he, 'whoever dug and planted it must be good workmen. If all the fields in my kingdom were as well cared for as this, there would be more bread than my people could eat.' And he wished to know to whom the field belonged.

Off rushed all his followers at once to do his bidding,

and found a nice, tidy farmhouse, in front of which sat seven peasants, lunching on rye bread and drinking water. They wore red shirts bound with gold braid, and were so much alike that one could hardly tell one from another.

The messengers asked: 'Who owns this field of golden maize?' And the seven brothers answered: 'The field is ours.'

'And who are you?'

'We are King Archidej's labourers.'

These answers were repeated to the king, who ordered the brothers to be brought before him at once. On being asked who they were, the eldest said, bowing low:

'We, King Archidej, are your labourers, children of one father and mother, and we all have the same name, for each of us is called Simon. Our father taught us to be true to our king, and to till the ground, and to be kind to our neighbours. He also taught each of us a different trade which he thought might be useful to us, and he bade us not neglect our mother earth, which would be sure amply to repay our labour.'

The king was pleased with the honest peasant, and said: 'You have done well, good people, in planting your field, and now you have a golden harvest. But I should like each of you to tell me what special trades your father taught you.'

'My trade, O king!' said the first Simon, 'is not an easy one. If you will give me some workmen and materials I will build you a great white pillar that shall reach far above the clouds.'

'Very good,' replied the king. 'And you, Simon the second, what is your trade?'

'Mine, your Majesty, needs no great cleverness. When my brother has built the pillar I can mount it, and from the top, far above the clouds, I can see what is happening in every country under the sun.'

'Good,' said the king; 'and Simon the third?'

'My work is very simple, sire. You have many ships built by learned men, with all sorts of new and clever improvements. If you wish it I will build you quite a simple boat—one, two, three, and it's done! But my plain little home-made ship is not grand enough for a king. Where other ships take a year, mine makes the voyage in a day, and where they would require ten years mine will do the distance in a week.'

'Good,' said the king again; 'and what has Simon the fourth learnt?'

'My trade, O king, is really of no importance. Should my brother build you a ship, then let me embark in it. If we should be pursued by an enemy I can seize our boat by the prow and sink it to the bottom of the sea. When the enemy has sailed off, I can draw it up to the top again.'

'That is very clever of you,' answered the king; 'and what does Simon the fifth do?'

'My work, your Majesty, is mere smith's work. Order me to build a smithy and I will make you a cross-bow, but from which neither the eagle in the sky nor the wild beast in the forest is safe. The bolt hits whatever the eye sees.'

'That sounds very useful,' said the king. 'And now, Simon the sixth, tell me your trade.'

'Sire, it is so simple I am almost ashamed to mention it. If my brother hits any creature I catch it quicker than any dog can. If it falls into the water I pick it up out of the greatest depths, and if it is in a dark forest I can find it even at midnight.'

The king was much pleased with the trades and talk of the six brothers, and said: 'Thank you, good people; your father did well to teach you all these things. Now follow me to the town, as I want to see what you can do. I need such people as you about me; but when harvest time comes I will send you home with royal presents.'

THE SIXTH SIMON CATCHES THE EAGLE

The brothers bowed and said: 'As the king wills.' Suddenly the king remembered that he had not questioned the seventh Simon, so he turned to him and said: 'Why are you silent? What is your handicraft?'

And the seventh Simon answered: 'I have no handicraft, O king; I have learnt nothing. I could not manage it. And if I *do* know how to do anything it is not what might properly be called a real trade—it is rather a sort of performance; but it is one which no one—not the king himself—must watch me doing, and I doubt whether this performance of mine would please your Majesty.'

'Come, come,' cried the king; 'I will have no excuses, what is this trade?'

'First, sire, give me your royal word that you will not kill me when I have told you. Then you shall hear.'

'So be it, then; I give you my royal word.'

Then the seventh Simon stepped back a little, cleared his throat, and said: 'My trade, King Archidej, is of such a kind that the man who follows it in your kingdom generally loses his life and has no hopes of pardon. There is only one thing I can do really well, and that is—to steal, and to hide the smallest scrap of anything I have stolen. Not the deepest vault, even if its lock were enchanted, could prevent my stealing anything out of it that I wished to have.'

When the king heard this he fell into a passion. 'I will *not* pardon you, you rascal,' he cried; 'I will shut you up in my deepest dungeon on bread and water till you have forgotten such a trade. Indeed, it would be better to put you to death at once, and I've a good mind to do so.'

'Don't kill me, O king! I am really not as bad as you think. Why, had I chosen, I could have robbed the royal treasury, have bribed your judges to let me off, and built a white marble palace with what was left. But though I know how to steal I don't do it. You yourself asked me my trade. If you kill me you will break your royal word.'

'Very well,' said the king, 'I will not kill you. I pardon you. But from this hour you shall be shut up in a dark dungeon. Here, guards! away with him to the prison. But you six Simons follow me and be assured of my royal favour.'

So the six Simons followed the king. The seventh Simon was seized by the guards, who put him in chains and threw him in prison with only bread and water for food. Next day the king gave the first Simon carpenters, masons, smiths and labourers, with great stores of iron, mortar, and the like, and Simon began to build. And he built his great white pillar far, far up into the clouds, as high as the nearest stars; but the other stars were higher still.

Then the second Simon climbed up the pillar and saw and heard all that was going on through the whole world. When he came down he had all sorts of wonderful things to tell. How one king was marching in battle against another, and which was likely to be the victor. How, in another place, great rejoicings were going on, while in a third people were dying of famine. In fact there was not the smallest event going on over the earth that was hidden from him.

Next the third Simon began. He stretched out his arms, once, twice, thrice, and the wonder-ship was ready. At a sign from the king it was launched, and floated proudly and safely like a bird on the waves. Instead of ropes it had wires for rigging, and musicians played on them with fiddle bows and made lovely music. As the ship swam about, the fourth Simon seized the prow with his strong hand, and in a moment it was gone—sunk to the bottom of the sea. An hour passed, and then the ship floated again, drawn up by Simon's left hand, while in his right he brought a gigantic fish from the depth of the ocean for the royal table.

Whilst this was going on the fifth Simon had built his forge and hammered out his iron, and when the king returned from the harbour the magic cross-bow was made.

His Majesty went out into an open field at once, looked up into the sky and saw, far, far away, an eagle flying up towards the sun and looking like a little speck.

'Now,' said the king, 'if you can shoot that bird I will reward you.'

Simon only smiled; he lifted his cross-bow, took aim, fired, and the eagle fell. As it was falling the sixth Simon ran with a dish, caught the bird before it fell to earth and brought it to the king.

'Many thanks, my brave lads,' said the king; 'I see that each of you is indeed a master of his trade. You shall be richly rewarded. But now rest and have your dinner.'

The six Simons bowed and went to dinner. But they had hardly begun before a messenger came to say that the king wanted to see them. They obeyed at once and found him surrounded by all his court and men of state.

'Listen, my good fellows,' cried the king, as soon as he saw them. 'Hear what my wise counsellors have thought of. As you, Simon the second, can see the whole world from the top of the great pillar, I want you to climb up and to see and hear. For I am told that, far away, across many seas, is the great kingdom of the Island of Busan, and that the daughter of the king is the beautiful Princess Helena.'

Off ran the second Simon and clambered quickly up the pillar. He gazed around, listened on all sides, and then slid down to report to the king.

'Sire, I have obeyed your orders. Far away I saw the Island of Busan. The king is a mighty monarch, but full of pride, harsh and cruel. He sits on his throne and declares that no prince or king on earth is good enough for his lovely daughter, that he will give her to none, and that if any king asks for her hand he will declare war against him and destroy his kingdom.'

'Has the king of Busan a great army?' asked King Archidej; 'is his country far off?'

'As far as I could judge,' replied Simon, 'it would take you nearly ten years in fair weather to sail there. But if the weather were stormy we might say twelve. I saw the army being reviewed. It is not so *very* large—a hundred thousand men at arms and a hundred thousand knights. Besides these, he has a strong bodyguard and a good many cross-bowmen. Altogether you may say another hundred thousand, and there is a picked body of heroes who reserve themselves for great occasions requiring particular courage.'

The king sat for some time lost in thought. At last he said to the nobles and courtiers standing round: 'I am determined to marry the Princess Helena, but how shall I do it?'

The nobles, courtiers and counsellors said nothing, but tried to hide behind each other. Then the third Simon said:

'Pardon me, your Majesty, if I offer my advice. You wish to go to the Island of Busan? What can be easier? In my ship you will get there in a week instead of in ten years. But ask your council to advise you what to do when you arrive—in one word, whether you will win the princess peacefully or by war?'

But the wise men were as silent as ever.

The king frowned, and was about to say something sharp, when the Court Fool pushed his way to the front and said: 'Dear me, what are all you clever people so puzzled about? The matter is quite clear. As it seems it will not take long to reach the island why not send the seventh Simon? He will steal the fair maiden fast enough, and then the king, her father, may consider how he is going to bring his army over here—it will take him ten years to do it!—no less! What do you think of my plan?'

'What do I think? Why, that your idea is capital, and you shall be rewarded for it. Come, guards, hurry as fast as you can and bring the seventh Simon before me.'

Not many minutes later, Simon the seventh stood before the king, who explained to him what he wished done, and also that to steal for the benefit of his king and country was by no means a wrong thing, though it was very wrong to steal for his own advantage.

The youngest Simon, who looked very pale and hungry, only nodded his head.

'Come,' said the king, 'tell me truly. Do you think you could steal the Princess Helena?'

'Why should I not steal her sire? The thing is easy enough. Let my brother's ship be laden with rich stuffs, brocades, Persian carpets, pearls and jewels. Send me in the ship. Give me my four middle brothers as companions, and keep the two others as hostages.'

When the king heard these words his heart became filled with longing, and he ordered all to be done as Simon wished. Every one ran about to do his bidding; and in next to no time the wonder-ship was laden and ready to start.

The five Simons took leave of the king, went on board, and had no sooner set sail than they were almost out of sight. The ship cut through the waters like a falcon through the air, and just a week after starting sighted the Island of Busan. The coast appeared to be strongly guarded, and from afar the watchman on a high tower called out: 'Halt and anchor! Who are you? Where do you come from, and what do you want?'

The seventh Simon answered from the ship: 'We are peaceful people. We come from the country of the great and good King Archidej, and we bring foreign wares—rich brocades, carpets, and costly jewels, which we wish to show to your king and the princess. We desire to trade—to sell, to buy, and to exchange.'

The brothers launched a small boat, took some of their

valuable goods with them, rowed to shore and went up to the palace. The princess sat in a rose-red room, and when she saw the brothers coming near she called her nurse and other women, and told them to inquire who and what these people were, and what they wanted.

The seventh Simon answered the nurse: 'We come from the country of the wise and good King Archidej,' said he, 'and we have brought all sorts of goods for sale. We trust the king of this country may condescend to welcome us, and to let his servants take charge of our wares. If he considers them worthy to adorn his followers we shall be content.'

This speech was repeated to the princess, who ordered the brothers to be brought to the red-room at once. They bowed respectfully to her and displayed some splendid velvets and brocades, and opened cases of pearls and precious stones. Such beautiful things had never been seen in the island, and the nurse and waiting women stood bewildered by all the magnificence. They whispered together that they had never beheld anything like it. The princess too saw and wondered, and her eyes could not weary of looking at the lovely things, or her fingers of stroking the rich soft stuffs, and of holding up the sparkling jewels to the light.

'Fairest of princesses,' said Simon. 'Be pleased to order your waiting-maids to accept the silks and velvets, and let your women trim their head-dresses with the jewels; these are no special treasures. But permit me to say that they are as nothing to the many coloured tapestries, the gorgeous stones and ropes of pearls in our ship. We did not like to bring more with us, not knowing what your royal taste might be; but if it seems good to you to honour our ship with a visit, you might condescend to choose such things as were pleasing in your eyes.'

This polite speech pleased the princess very much. She went to the king and said: 'Dear father, some merchants have arrived with the most splendid wares. Pray allow me to go to their ship and choose out what I like.'

The king thought and thought, frowned hard and rubbed his ear. At last he gave consent, and ordered out his royal yacht, with 100 cross-bows, 100 knights, and 1,000 soldiers, to escort the Princess Helena.

Off sailed the yacht with the princess and her escort. The brothers Simon came on board to conduct the princess to their ship, and, led by the brothers and followed by her nurse and other women, she crossed the crystal plank from one vessel to another.

The seventh Simon spread out his goods, and had so many curious and interesting tales to tell about them, that the princess forgot everything else in looking and listening, so that she did not know that the fourth Simon had seized the prow of the ship, and that all of a sudden it had vanished from sight, and was racing along in the depths of the sea.

The crew of the royal yacht shouted aloud, the knights stood still with terror, the soldiers were struck dumb and hung their heads. There was nothing to be done but to sail back and tell the king of his loss.

How he wept and stormed! 'Oh, light of my eyes,' he sobbed; 'I am indeed punished for my pride. I thought no one good enough to be your husband, and now you are lost in the depths of the sea, and have left me alone! As for all of you who saw this thing—away with you! Let them be put in irons and lock them up in prison, whilst I think how I can best put them to death!'

Whilst the King of Busan was raging and lamenting in this fashion, Simon's ship was swimming like any fish under the sea, and when the island was well out of sight he brought it up to the surface again. At that moment the princess recollected herself. 'Nurse,' said she, 'we have been gazing at these wonders only too long. I hope my father won't be vexed at our delay.'

She tore herself away and stepped on deck. Neither the yacht nor the island was in sight! Helena wrung her hands and beat her breast. Then she changed herself into a white swan and flew off. But the fifth Simon seized his bow and shot the swan, and the sixth Simon did not let it fall into the water but caught it in the ship, and the swan turned into a silver fish, but Simon lost no time and caught the fish, when, quick as thought, the fish turned into a black mouse and ran about the ship. It darted towards a hole, but before it could reach it Simon sprang upon it more swiftly than any cat, and then the little mouse turned once more into the beautiful Princess Helena.

Early one morning King Archidej sat thoughtfully at his window gazing out to sea. His heart was sad and he would neither eat nor drink. His thoughts were full of the Princess Helena, who was as lovely as a dream. Is that a white gull he sees flying towards the shore, or is it a sail? No, it is no gull, it is the wonder-ship flying along with billowing sails. Its flags wave, the fiddlers play on the wire rigging, the anchor is thrown out and the crystal plank laid from the ship to the pier. The lovely Helena steps across the plank. She shines like the sun, and the stars of heaven seem to sparkle in her eyes.

Up sprang King Archidej in haste: 'Hurry, hurry,' he cried. 'Let us hasten to meet her! Let the bugles sound and the joy bells be rung!'

And the whole Court swarmed with courtiers and servants. Golden carpets were laid down and the great gates thrown open to welcome the princess.

King Archidej went out himself, took her by the hand and led her into the royal apartments.

'Madam,' said he, 'the fame of your beauty had reached me, but I had not dared to expect such loveliness. Still I will not keep you here against your will. If you wish it, the wonder-ship shall take you back to your father and your own country; but if you will consent to

The lovely Helena comes ashore!

stay here, then reign over me and my country as our queen.'

What more is there to tell? It is not hard to guess that the princess listened to the king's wooing, and their betrothal took place with great pomp and rejoicings.

The brothers Simon were sent again to the Island of Busan with a letter to the king from his daughter to invite him to their wedding. And the wonder-ship arrived at the Island of Busan just as all the knights and soldiers who had escorted the princess were being led out to execution.

Then the seventh Simon cried out from the ship: 'Stop! stop! I bring a letter from the Princess Helena!'

The King of Busan read the letter over and over again, and ordered the knights and soldiers to be set free. He entertained King Archidej's ambassadors hospitably, and sent his blessing to his daughter, but he could not be brought to attend the wedding.

When the wonder-ship got home King Archidej and Princess Helena were enchanted with the news it brought.

The king sent for the seven Simons. 'A thousand thanks to you, my brave fellows,' he cried. 'Take what gold, silver, and precious stones you will out of my treasury. Tell me if there is anything else you wish for and I will give it you, my good friends. Do you wish to be made nobles, or to govern towns? Only speak.'

Then the eldest Simon bowed and said: 'We are plain folk, your Majesty, and understand simple things best. What figures should we cut as nobles or governors? Nor do we desire gold. We have our fields which give us food, and as much money as we need. If you wish to reward us then grant that our land may be free of taxes, and of your goodness pardon the seventh Simon. He is not the first who has been a thief by trade and he will certainly not be the last.'

'So be it,' said the king; 'your land shall be free of all taxes, and Simon the seventh is pardoned.'

Then the king gave each brother a goblet of wine and invited them to the wedding feast. And *what* a feast that was!

[From *Ungarischen Mährchen.*]

THE LANGUAGE OF BEASTS

Once upon a time a man had a shepherd who served him many years faithfully and honestly. One day, whilst herding his flock, this shepherd heard a hissing sound, coming out of the forest near by, which he could not account for. So he went into the wood in the direction of the noise to try to discover the cause. When he approached the place he found that the dry grass and leaves were on fire, and on a tree, surrounded by flames, a snake was coiled, hissing with terror.

The shepherd stood wondering how the poor snake could escape, for the wind was blowing the flames that way, and soon that tree would be burning like the rest. Suddenly the snake cried: 'O shepherd! for the love of heaven save me from this fire!'

Then the shepherd stretched his staff out over the flames and the snake wound itself round the staff and up to his hand, and from his hand it crept up his arm, and twined itself about his neck. The shepherd trembled with fright, expecting every instant to be stung to death, and said: 'What an unlucky man I am! Did I rescue you only to be destroyed myself?' But the snake answered: 'Have no fear; only carry me home to my father who is the King of the Snakes.' The shepherd, however, was much too frightened to listen, and said that he could not go away and leave his flock alone; but the snake said: 'You need not be afraid to leave your flock, no evil shall befall them; but make all the haste you can.'

So he set off through the wood carrying the snake, and after a time he came to a great gateway, made entirely of snakes intertwined one with another. The shepherd stood still with surprise, but the snake round his neck whistled, and immediately all the arch unwound itself.

'When we are come to my father's house,' said his own snake to him, 'he will reward you with anything you like to ask—silver, gold, jewels, or whatever on this earth is most precious; but take none of all these things, ask rather to understand the language of beasts. He will refuse it to you a long time, but in the end he will grant it to you.'

Soon after that they arrived at the house of the King of the Snakes, who burst into tears of joy at the sight of his daughter, as he had given her up for dead. 'Where have you been all this time?' he asked, directly he could speak, and she told him that she had been caught in a forest fire, and had been rescued from the flames by the shepherd. The King of the Snakes, then turning to the shepherd, said to him: 'What reward will you choose for saving my child?'

'Make me to know the language of beasts,' answered the shepherd, 'that is all I desire.'

The king replied: 'Such knowledge would be of no benefit to you, for if I granted it to you and you told any one of it, you would immediately die; ask me rather for whatever else you would most like to possess, and it shall be yours.'

But the shepherd answered him: 'Sir, if you wish to reward me for saving your daughter, grant me, I pray you, to know the language of beasts. I desire nothing else'; and he turned as if to depart.

Then the king called him back, saying: 'If nothing else will satisfy you, open your mouth.' The man obeyed, and the king spat into it, and said: 'Now spit into my mouth.' The shepherd did as he was told, then the King of the Snakes spat again into the shepherd's mouth. When they had spat into each other's mouths three times, the king said:

THE SHEPHERD COMES TO THE ARCH OF SNAKES

'Now you know the language of beasts, go in peace; but, if you value your life, beware lest you tell any one of it, else you will immediately die.'

So the shepherd set out for home, and on his way through the wood he heard and understood all that was said by the birds, and by every living creature. When he got back to his sheep he found the flock grazing peacefully, and as he was very tired he laid himself down by them to rest a little. Hardly had he done so when two ravens flew down and perched on a tree near by, and began to talk to each other in their own language: 'If that shepherd only knew that there is a vault full of gold and silver beneath where that lamb is lying, what would he not do?' When the shepherd heard these words he went straight to his master and told him, and the master at once took a waggon, and broke open the door of the vault, and they carried off the treasure. But instead of keeping it for himself, the master, who was an honourable man, gave it all up to the shepherd, saying: 'Take it, it is yours. The gods have given it to you.' So the shepherd took the treasure and built himself a house. He married a wife, and they lived in great peace and happiness, and he was acknowledged to be the richest man, not only of his native village, but of all the country-side. He had flocks of sheep, and cattle, and horses without end, as well as beautiful clothes and jewels.

One day, just before Christmas, he said to his wife: 'Prepare everything for a great feast, to-morrow we will take things with us to the farm that the shepherds there may make merry.' The wife obeyed, and all was prepared as he desired. Next day they both went to the farm, and in the evening the master said to the shepherds: 'Now come, all of you, eat, drink, and make merry. I will watch the flocks myself to-night in your stead.' Then he went out to spend the night with the flocks.

When midnight struck the wolves howled and the

dogs barked, and the wolves spoke in their own tongue, saying :

'Shall we come in and work havoc, and you too shall eat flesh?' And the dogs answered in their tongue : 'Come in, and for once we shall have enough to eat.'

Now amongst the dogs there was one so old that he had only two teeth left in his head, and he spoke to the wolves, saying : 'So long as I have my two teeth still in my head, I will let no harm be done to my master.'

All this the master heard and understood, and as soon as morning dawned he ordered all the dogs to be killed excepting the old dog. The farm servants wondered at this order, and exclaimed : 'But surely, sir, that would be a pity?'

The master answered : 'Do as I bid you'; and made ready to return home with his wife, and they mounted their horses, her steed being a mare. As they went on their way, it happened that the husband rode on ahead, while the wife was a little way behind. The husband's horse, seeing this, neighed, and said to the mare : 'Come along, make haste; why are you so slow?' And the mare answered : 'It is very easy for you, you carry only your master, who is a thin man, but I carry my mistress, who is so fat that she weighs as much as three.' When the husband heard that he looked back and laughed, which the wife perceiving, she urged on the mare till she caught up with her husband, and asked him why he laughed. 'For nothing at all,' he answered; 'just because it came into my head.' She would not be satisfied with this answer, and urged him more and more to tell her why he had laughed. But he controlled himself and said : 'Let me be, wife; what ails you? I do not know myself why I laughed.' But the more he put her off, the more she tormented him to tell her the cause of his laughter. At length he said to her : 'Know, then, that if I tell it you I shall immediately and surely die.' But even this did not quiet her; she only besought him the more to tell her.

Meanwhile they had reached home, and before getting down from his horse the man called for a coffin to be brought; and when it was there he placed it in front of the house, and said to his wife:

'See, I will lay myself down in this coffin, and will then tell you why I laughed, for as soon as I have told you I shall surely die.' So he lay down in the coffin, and while he took a last look around him, his old dog came out from the farm and sat down by him, and whined. When the master saw this, he called to his wife: 'Bring a piece of bread to give to the dog.' The wife brought some bread and threw it to the dog, but he would not look at it. Then the farm cock came and pecked at the bread; but the dog said to it: 'Wretched glutton, you can eat like that when you see that your master is dying?' The cock answered: 'Let him die, if he is so stupid. I have a hundred wives, which I call together when I find a grain of corn, and as soon as they are there I swallow it myself; should one of them dare to be angry, I would give her a lesson with my beak. He has only one wife, and he cannot keep her in order.'

As soon as the man understood this, he got up out of the coffin, seized a stick, and called his wife into the room, saying: 'Come, and I will tell you what you so much want to know'; and then he began to beat her with the stick, saying with each blow: 'It is that, wife, it is that!' And in this way he taught her never again to ask why he had laughed.

THE BOY WHO COULD KEEP A SECRET

ONCE upon a time there lived a poor widow who had one little boy. At first sight you would not have thought that he was different from a thousand other little boys; but then you noticed that by his side hung the scabbard of a sword, and as the boy grew bigger the scabbard grew bigger too. The sword which belonged to the scabbard was found by the little boy sticking out of the ground in the garden, and every day he pulled it up to see if it would go into the scabbard. But though it was plainly becoming longer and longer, it was some time before the two would fit.

However, there came a day at last when it slipped in quite easily. The child was so delighted that he could hardly believe his eyes, so he tried it seven times, and each time it slipped in more easily than before. But pleased though the boy was, he determined not to tell anyone about it, particularly not his mother, who never could keep anything from her neighbours.

Still, in spite of his resolutions, he could not hide altogether that something had happened, and when he went in to breakfast his mother asked him what was the matter.

'Oh, mother, I had such a nice dream last night,' said he; 'but I can't tell it to anybody.'

'You can tell it to me,' she answered. 'It must have been a nice dream, or you wouldn't look so happy.'

'No, mother; I can't tell it to anybody,' returned the boy, 'till it comes true.'

'I want to know what it was, and know it I will,' cried she, 'and I will beat you till you tell me.'

But it was no use, neither words nor blows would get the secret out of the boy; and when her arm was quite tired and she had to leave off, the child, sore and aching, ran into the garden and knelt weeping beside his little sword. It was working round and round in its hole all by itself, and if anyone except the boy had tried to catch hold of it, he would have been badly cut. But the moment he stretched out his hand it stopped and slid quietly into the scabbard.

For a long time the child sat sobbing, and the noise was heard by the king as he was driving by. 'Go and see who it is that is crying so,' said he to one of his servants, and the man went. In a few minutes he returned saying: 'Your Majesty, it is a little boy who is kneeling there sobbing because his mother has beaten him.'

'Bring him to me at once,' commanded the monarch, 'and tell him that it is the king who sends for him, and that he has never cried in all his life and cannot bear anyone else to do so.' On receiving this message the boy dried his tears and went with the servant to the royal carriage. 'Will you be my son?' asked the king.

'Yes, if my mother will let me,' answered the boy. And the king bade the servant go back to the mother and say that if she would give her boy to him, he should live in the palace and marry his prettiest daughter as soon as he was a man.

The widow's anger now turned into joy, and she came running to the splendid coach and kissed the king's hand. 'I hope you will be more obedient to his Majesty than you were to me,' she said; and the boy shrank away half-frightened. But when she had gone back to her cottage, he asked the king if he might fetch something that he had left in the garden, and when he was given permission, he pulled up his little sword, which he slid into the scabbard.

Then he climbed into the coach and was driven away.

After they had gone some distance the king said: 'Why were you crying so bitterly in the garden just now?'

'Because my mother had been beating me,' replied the boy.

'And what did she do that for?' asked the king again.

'Because I would not tell her my dream.'

'And why wouldn't you tell it to her?'

'Because I will never tell it to anyone till it comes true,' answered the boy.

'And won't you tell it to me either?' asked the king in surprise.

'No, not even to you, your Majesty,' replied he.

'Oh, I am sure you will when we get home,' said the king smiling, and he talked to him about other things till they came to the palace.

'I have brought you such a nice present,' he said to his daughters, and as the boy was very pretty they were delighted to have him and gave him all their best toys.

'You must not spoil him,' observed the king one day, when he had been watching them playing together. He has a secret which he won't tell to anyone.'

'He will tell me,' answered the eldest princess; but the boy only shook his head.

'He will tell me,' said the second girl.

'Not I,' replied the boy.

'He will tell me,' cried the youngest, who was the prettiest too.

'I will tell nobody till it comes true,' said the boy, as he had said before; 'and I will beat anybody who asks me.'

The king was very sorry when he heard this, for he loved the boy dearly; but he thought it would never do to keep anyone near him who would not do as he was bid. So he commanded his servants to take him away, and not to let him enter the palace again until he had come to his right senses.

The sword clanked loudly as the boy was led away, but the child said nothing, though he was very unhappy at being treated so badly when he had done nothing. However, the servants were very kind to him, and their children brought him fruit and all sorts of nice things, and he soon grew merry again, and lived amongst them for many years till his seventeenth birthday.

Meanwhile the two eldest princesses had become women, and had married two powerful kings who ruled over great countries across the sea. The youngest one was old enough to be married too, but she was very particular, and turned up her nose at all the young princes who had sought her hand.

One day she was sitting in the palace feeling rather dull and lonely, and suddenly she began to wonder what the servants were doing, and whether it was not more amusing down in their quarters. The king was at his council and the queen was ill in bed, so there was no one to stop the princess, and she hastily ran across the gardens to the houses where the servants lived. Outside she noticed a youth who was handsomer than any prince she had ever seen, and in a moment she knew him to be the little boy she had once played with.

'Tell me your secret and I will marry you,' she said to him; but the boy only gave her the beating he had promised her long ago, when she asked him the same question. The girl was very angry, besides being hurt, and ran home to complain to her father.

'If he had a thousand souls, I would kill them all,' swore the king.

That very day a gallows was built outside the town, and all the people crowded round to see the execution of the young man who had dared to beat the king's daughter. The prisoner, with his hands tied behind his back, was brought out by the hangman, and amidst dead silence his sentence was being read by the judge when suddenly the sword clanked against his side. Instantly a great noise was heard and a golden coach rumbled over the stones, with a white flag waving out of the window. It stopped underneath the gallows, and from it stepped the king of the Magyars, who begged that the life of the boy might be spared.

'Sir, he has beaten my daughter, who only asked him to tell her his secret. I cannot pardon that,' answered the princess's father.

'Give him to me, I'm sure he will tell me the secret; or, if not, I have a daughter who is like the Morning Star, and he is sure to tell it to her.'

The sword clanked for the third time, and the king said angrily: 'Well, if you want him so much you can have him; only never let me see his face again.' And he made a sign to the hangman. The bandage was removed from the young man's eyes, and the cords from his wrists, and he took his seat in the golden coach beside the king of the Magyars. Then the coachman whipped up his horses, and they set out for Buda.

The king talked very pleasantly for a few miles, and when he thought that his new companion was quite at ease with him, he asked him what was the secret which had brought him into such trouble. 'That I cannot tell you,' answered the youth, 'until it comes true.'

'You will tell my daughter,' said the king, smiling.

'I will tell nobody,' replied the youth, and as he spoke the sword clanked loudly. The king said no more, but trusted to his daughter's beauty to get the secret from him.

The journey to Buda was long, and it was several days before they arrived there. The beautiful princess happened to be picking roses in the garden, when her father's coach drove up.

'Oh, what a handsome youth! Have you brought him from fairyland?' cried she, when they all stood upon the marble steps in front of the castle.

THE BOY WHO COULD KEEP A SECRET

'I have brought him from the gallows,' answered the king; rather vexed at his daughter's words, as never before had she consented to speak to any man.

'I don't care where you brought him from,' said the spoilt girl. 'I will marry him and nobody else, and we will live together till we die.'

'You will tell another tale,' replied the king, 'when you ask him his secret. After all he is no better than a servant.'

'That is nothing to me,' said the princess, 'for I love him. He will tell his secret to me, and will find a place in the middle of my heart.'

But the king shook his head, and gave orders that the lad was to be lodged in the summer-house.

One day, about a week later, the princess put on her finest dress, and went to pay him a visit. She looked so beautiful that, at the sight of her, the book dropped from his hand, and he stood up speechless. 'Tell me,' she said, coaxingly, 'what is this wonderful secret? Just whisper it in my ear, and I will give you a kiss.'

'My angel,' he answered, 'be wise, and ask no questions, if you wish to get safely back to your father's palace; I have kept my secret all these years, and do not mean to tell it now.'

However, the girl would not listen, and went on pressing him, till at last he slapped her face so hard that her nose bled. She shrieked with pain and rage, and ran screaming back to the palace, where her father was waiting to hear if she had succeeded. 'I will starve you to death, you son of a dragon,' cried he, when he saw her dress streaming with blood; and he ordered all the masons and bricklayers in the town to come before him.

'Build me a tower as fast as you can,' he said, 'and see that there is room for a stool and a small table, and for nothing else. The men set to work, and in two hours the tower was built, and they proceeded to the palace to inform the king that his commands were fulfilled. On the way they met the princess, who began to talk to one of the masons, and when the rest were out of hearing she asked if he could manage to make a hole in the tower, which nobody could see, large enough for a bottle of wine and some food to pass through.

'To be sure I can,' said the mason, turning back, and in a few minutes the hole was bored.

At sunset a large crowd assembled to watch the youth being led to the tower, and after his misdeeds had been proclaimed he was solemnly walled up. But every morning the princess passed him in food through the hole, and every third day the king sent his secretary to climb up a ladder and look down through a little window to see if he was dead. But the secretary always brought back the report that he was fat and rosy.

'There is some magic about this,' said the king.

This state of affairs lasted some time, till one day a messenger arrived from the Sultan bearing a letter for the king, and also three canes. 'My master bids me say,' said the messenger, bowing low, 'that if you cannot tell him which of these three canes grows nearest the root, which in the middle, and which at the top, he will declare war against you.'

The king was very much frightened when he heard this, and though he took the canes and examined them closely, he could see no difference between them. He looked so sad that his daughter noticed it, and inquired the reason.

'Alas! my daughter,' he answered, 'how can I help being sad? The Sultan has sent me three canes, and says that if I cannot tell him which of them grows near the root, which in the middle, and which at the top, he will make war upon me. And you know that his army is far greater than mine.'

'Oh, do not despair, my father,' said she. 'We shall be sure to find out the answer'; and she ran away to the tower, and told the young man what had occurred.

THE PRINCESS FEEDS THE BOY

'Go to bed as usual,' replied he, 'and when you wake, tell your father that you have dreamed that the canes must be placed in warm water. After a little while one will sink to the bottom; that is the one that grows nearest the root. The one which neither sinks nor comes to the surface is the cane that is cut from the middle; and the one that floats is from the top.'

So, the next morning, the princess told her father of her dream, and by her advice he cut notches in each of the canes when he took them out of the water, so that he might make no mistake when he handed them back to the messenger. The Sultan could not imagine how he had found out, but he did not declare war.

The following year the Sultan again wanted to pick a quarrel with the king of the Magyars, so he sent another messenger to him with three foals, begging him to say which of the animals was born in the morning, which at noon, and which in the evening. If an answer was not ready in three days, war would be declared at once. The king's heart sank when he read the letter. He could not expect his daughter to be lucky enough to dream rightly a second time, and as a plague had been raging through the country, and had carried off many of his soldiers, his army was even weaker than before. At this thought his face became so gloomy that his daughter noticed it, and inquired what was the matter.

'I have had another letter from the Sultan,' replied the king, 'and he says that if I cannot tell him which of three foals was born in the morning, which at noon, and which in the evening, he will declare war at once.'

'Oh, don't be cast down,' said she, 'something is sure to happen'; and she ran down to the tower to consult the youth.

'Go home, idol of my heart, and when night comes, pretend to scream out in your sleep, so that your father hears you. Then tell him that you have dreamt that he was just being carried off by the Turks because he could not answer the question about the foals, when the lad whom he had shut up in the tower ran up and told them which was foaled in the morning, which at noon, and which in the evening.'

So the princess did exactly as the youth had bidden her ; and no sooner had she spoken than the king ordered the tower to be pulled down, and the prisoner brought before him.

'I did not think that you could have lived so long without food,' said he, 'and as you have had plenty of time to repent your wicked conduct, I will grant you pardon, on condition that you help me in a sore strait. Read this letter from the Sultan ; you will see that if I fail to answer his question about the foals, a dreadful war will be the result.'

The youth took the letter and read it through. 'Yes, I can help you,' replied he ; 'but first you must bring me three troughs, all exactly alike. Into one you must put oats, into another wheat, and into the third barley. The foal which eats the oats is that which was foaled in the morning ; the foal which eats the wheat is that which was foaled at noon ; and the foal which eats the barley is that which was foaled at night.' The king followed the youth's directions, and, marking the foals, sent them back to Turkey, and there was no war that year.

Now the Sultan was very angry that both his plots to get possession of Hungary had been such total failures, and he sent for his aunt, who was a witch, to consult her as to what he should do next.

'It is not the king who has answered your questions,' observed the aunt, when he had told his story. 'He is far too stupid ever to have done that! The person who has found out the puzzle is the son of a poor woman, who, if he lives, will become King of Hungary. Therefore, if you want the crown yourself, you must get him here and kill him.'

After this conversation another letter was written to

the Court of Hungary, saying that if the youth, now in the palace, was not sent to Turkey within three days, a large army would cross the border. The king's heart was sorrowful as he read, for he was grateful to the lad for what he had done to help him ; but the boy only laughed, and bade the king fear nothing, but to search the town instantly for two youths just like each other, and he would paint himself a mask that was just like them. And the sword at his side clanked loudly.

After a long search twin brothers were found, so exactly resembling each other that even their own mother could not tell the difference. The youth painted a mask that was the precise copy of them, and when he had put it on, no one would have known one boy from the other. They set out at once for the Sultan's palace, and when they reached it, they were taken straight into his presence. He made a sign for them to come near ; they all bowed low in greeting. He asked them about their journey ; they answered his questions all together, and in the same words. If one sat down to supper, the others sat down at the same instant. When one got up, the others got up too, as if there had been only one body between them. The Sultan could not detect any difference between them, and he told his aunt that he would not be so cruel as to kill all three.

'Well, you will see a difference to-morrow,' replied the witch, 'for one will have a cut on his sleeve. That is the youth you must kill.' And one hour before midnight, when witches are invisible, she glided into the room where all three lads were sleeping in the same bed. She took out a pair of scissors and cut a small piece out of the boy's coat-sleeve which was hanging on the wall, and then crept silently from the room. But in the morning the youth saw the slit, and he marked the sleeves of his two companions in the same way, and all three went down to breakfast with the Sultan. The old witch was standing in the window and pretended not to see them ; but all witches have eyes in the backs of their heads, and she knew at once that not one sleeve but three were cut, and they were all as alike as before. After breakfast, the Sultan, who was getting tired of the whole affair and wanted to be alone to invent some other plan, told them they might return home. So, bowing low with one accord, they went.

The princess welcomed the boy back joyfully, but the poor youth was not allowed to rest long in peace, for one day a fresh letter arrived from the Sultan, saying that he had discovered that the young man was a very dangerous person, and that he must be sent to Turkey at once, and alone. The girl burst into tears when the boy told her what was in the letter which her father had bade her to carry to him. 'Do not weep, love of my heart,' said the boy, 'all will be well. I will start at sunrise to-morrow.'

So next morning at sunrise the youth set forth, and in a few days he reached the Sultan's palace. The old witch was waiting for him at the gate, and whispered as he passed : 'This is the last time you will ever enter it.' But the sword clanked, and the lad did not even look at her. As he crossed the threshold fifteen armed Turks barred his way, with the Sultan at their head. Instantly the sword darted forth and cut off the heads of everyone but the Sultan, and then went quietly back to its scabbard. The witch, who was looking on, saw that as long as the youth had possession of the sword, all her schemes would be in vain, and tried to steal the sword in the night, but it only jumped out of its scabbard and sliced off her nose, which was of iron. And in the morning, when the Sultan brought a great army to capture the lad and deprive him of his sword, they were all cut to pieces, while he remained without a scratch.

Meanwhile the princess was in despair because the days slipped by, and the young man did not return, and she never rested until her father let her lead some troops against the Sultan. She rode proudly before them, dressed

The Witch loses her Iron Nose

in uniform ; but they had not left the town more than a mile behind them, when they met the lad and his little sword. When he told them what he had done they shouted for joy, and carried him back in triumph to the palace ; and the king declared that as the youth had shown himself worthy to become his son-in-law, he should marry the princess and succeed to the throne at once, as he himself was getting old, and the cares of government were too much for him. But the young man said he must first go and see his mother, and the king sent him in state, with a troop of soldiers as his bodyguard.

The old woman was quite frightened at seeing such an array draw up before her little house, and still more surprised when a handsome young man, whom she did not know, dismounted and kissed her hand, saying : 'Now, dear mother, you shall hear my secret at last ! I dreamed that I should become King of Hungary, and my dream has come true. When I was a child, and you begged me to tell you, I had to keep silence, or the Magyar king would have killed me. And if you had not beaten me nothing would have happened that has happened, and I should not now be King of Hungary.'

[From the *Folk Tales of the Magyars.*]

THE PRINCE AND THE DRAGON

Once upon a time there lived an emperor who had three sons. They were all fine young men, and fond of hunting, and scarcely a day passed without one or other of them going out to look for game.

One morning the eldest of the three princes mounted his horse and set out for a neighbouring forest, where wild animals of all sorts were to be found. He had not long left the castle, when a hare sprang out of a thicket and dashed across the road in front. The young man gave chase at once, and pursued it over hill and dale, till at last the hare took refuge in a mill which was standing by the side of a river. The prince followed and entered the mill, but stopped in terror by the door, for, instead of a hare, before him stood a dragon, breathing fire and flame. At this fearful sight the prince turned to fly, but a fiery tongue coiled round his waist, and drew him into the dragon's mouth, and he was seen no more.

A week passed away, and when the prince never came back everyone in the town began to grow uneasy. At last his next brother told the emperor that he likewise would go out to hunt, and that perhaps he would find some clue as to his brother's disappearance. But hardly had the castle gates closed on the prince than the hare sprang out of the bushes as before, and led the huntsman up hill and down dale, till they reached the mill. Into this the hare flew with the prince at his heels, when, lo ! instead of the hare, there stood a dragon breathing fire and flame ; and out shot a fiery tongue which coiled round the prince's

HOW THE DRAGON CAUGHT THE PRINCE

waist, and lifted him straight into the dragon's mouth, and he was seen no more.

Days went by, and the emperor waited and waited for the sons who never came, and could not sleep at night for wondering where they were and what had become of them. His youngest son wished to go in search of his brothers, but for long the emperor refused to listen to him, lest he should lose him also. But the prince prayed so hard for leave to make the search, and promised so often that he would be very cautious and careful, that at length the emperor gave him permission, and ordered the best horse in the stables to be saddled for him.

Full of hope the young prince started on his way, but no sooner was he outside the city walls than a hare sprang out of the bushes and ran before him, till they reached the mill. As before, the animal dashed in through the open door, but this time he was not followed by the prince. Wiser than his brothers, the young man turned away, saying to himself: 'There are as good hares in the forest as any that have come out of it, and when I have caught them, I can come back and look for you.'

For many hours he rode up and down the mountain, but saw nothing, and at last, tired of waiting, he went back to the mill. Here he found an old woman sitting, whom he greeted pleasantly.

'Good morning to you, little mother,' he said; and the old woman answered: 'Good morning, my son.'

'Tell me, little mother,' went on the prince, 'where shall I find my hare?'

'My son,' replied the old woman, 'that was no hare, but a dragon who has led many men hither, and then has eaten them all.' At these words the prince's heart grew heavy, and he cried, 'Then my brothers must have come here, and have been eaten by the dragon!'

'You have guessed right,' answered the old woman; 'and I can give you no better counsel than to go home at once, before the same fate overtakes you.'

'Will you not come with me out of this dreadful place?' said the young man.

'He took me prisoner, too,' answered she, 'and I cannot shake off his chains.'

'Then listen to me,' cried the prince. 'When the dragon comes back, ask him where he always goes when he leaves here, and what makes him so strong; and when you have coaxed the secret from him, tell me the next time I come.'

So the prince went home, and the old woman remained in the mill, and as soon as the dragon returned she said to him:

'Where have you been all this time—you must have travelled far?'

'Yes, little mother, I have indeed travelled far,' answered he. Then the old woman began to flatter him, and to praise his cleverness; and when she thought she had got him into a good temper, she said: 'I have wondered so often where you get your strength from; I do wish you would tell me. I would stoop and kiss the place out of pure love!' The dragon laughed at this, and answered:

'In the hearthstone yonder lies the secret of my strength.'

Then the old woman jumped up and kissed the hearth; whereat the dragon laughed the more, and said:

'You foolish creature! I was only jesting. It is not in the hearthstone, but in that tall tree that lies the secret of my strength.' Then the old woman jumped up again and put her arms round the tree, and kissed it heartily. Loudly laughed the dragon when he saw what she was doing.

'Old fool,' he cried, as soon as he could speak, 'did you really believe that my strength came from that tree?'

'Where is it then?' asked the old woman, rather crossly, for she did not like being made fun of.

'My strength,' replied the dragon, 'lies far away;

so far that you could never reach it. Far, far from here is a kingdom, and by its capital city is a lake, and in the lake is a dragon, and inside the dragon is a wild boar, and inside the wild boar is a pigeon, and inside the pigeon a sparrow, and inside the sparrow is my strength.' And when the old woman heard this, she thought it was no use flattering him any longer, for never, never, could she take his strength from him.

The following morning, when the dragon had left the mill, the prince came back, and the old woman told him all that the creature had said. He listened in silence, and then returned to the castle, where he put on a suit of shepherd's clothes, and taking a staff in his hand, he went forth to seek a place as tender of sheep.

For some time he wandered from village to village and from town to town, till he came at length to a large city in a distant kingdom, surrounded on three sides by a great lake, which happened to be the very lake in which the dragon lived. As was his custom, he stopped everybody whom he met in the streets that looked likely to want a shepherd and begged them to engage him, but they all seemed to have shepherds of their own, or else not to need any. The prince was beginning to lose heart, when a man who had overheard his question turned round and said that he had better go and ask the emperor, as he was in search of some one to see after his flocks.

'Will you take care of my sheep?' said the emperor, when the young man knelt before him.

'Most willingly, your Majesty,' answered the young man, and he listened obediently while the emperor told him what he was to do.

'Outside the city walls,' went on the emperor, 'you will find a large lake, and by its banks lie the richest meadows in my kingdom. When you are leading out your flocks to pasture, they will all run straight to these meadows, and none that have gone there have ever been known to come back. Take heed, therefore, my son, not to suffer your sheep to go where they will, but drive them to any spot that you think best.'

With a low bow the prince thanked the emperor for his warning, and promised to do his best to keep the sheep safe. Then he left the palace and went to the market-place, where he bought two greyhounds, a hawk, and a set of pipes; after that he took the sheep out to pasture. The instant the animals caught sight of the lake lying before them, they trotted off as fast as their legs would go to the green meadows lying round it. The prince did not try to stop them; he only placed his hawk on the branch of a tree, laid his pipes on the grass, and bade the greyhounds sit still; then, rolling up his sleeves and trousers, he waded into the water crying as he did so: 'Dragon! dragon! if you are not a coward, come out and fight with me!' And a voice answered from the depths of the lake:

'I am waiting for you, O prince'; and the next minute the dragon reared himself out of the water, huge and horrible to see. The prince sprang upon him and they grappled with each other and fought together till the sun was high, and it was noonday. Then the dragon gasped:

'O prince, let me dip my burning head once into the lake, and I will hurl you up to the top of the sky.' But the prince answered, 'Oh, ho! my good dragon, do not crow too soon! If the emperor's daughter were only here, and would kiss me on the forehead, I would throw you up higher still!' And suddenly the dragon's hold loosened, and he fell back into the lake.

As soon as it was evening, the prince washed away all signs of the fight, took his hawk upon his shoulder, and his pipes under his arm, and with his greyhounds in front and his flock following after him he set out for the city. As they all passed through the streets the people stared in wonder, for never before had any flock returned from the lake.

The next morning he rose early, and led his sheep down the road to the lake. This time, however, the emperor sent two men on horseback to ride behind him, with orders to watch the prince all day long. The horsemen kept the prince and his sheep in sight, without being seen themselves. As soon as they beheld the sheep running towards the meadows, they turned aside up a steep hill, which overhung the lake. When the shepherd reached the place he laid, as before, his pipes on the grass and bade the greyhounds sit beside them, while the hawk he perched on the branch of the tree. Then he rolled up his trousers and his sleeves, and waded into the water crying:

'Dragon! dragon! if you are not a coward, come out and fight with me!' And the dragon answered:

'I am waiting for you, O prince,' and the next minute he reared himself out of the water, huge and horrible to see. Again they clasped each other tight round the body and fought till it was noon, and when the sun was at its hottest, the dragon gasped:

'O prince, let me dip my burning head once in the lake, and I will hurl you up to the top of the sky.' But the prince answered:

'Oh, ho! my good dragon, do not crow too soon! If the emperor's daughter were only here, and would kiss me on the forehead, I would throw you up higher still!' And suddenly the dragon's hold loosened, and he fell back into the lake.

As soon as it was evening the prince again collected his sheep, and playing on his pipes he marched before them into the city. When he passed through the gates all the people came out of their houses to stare in wonder, for never before had any flock returned from the lake.

Meanwhile the two horsemen had ridden quickly back, and told the emperor all that they had seen and heard. The emperor listened eagerly to their tale, then called his daughter to him and repeated it to her.

'To-morrow,' he said, when he had finished, 'you shall go with the shepherd to the lake, and then you shall kiss him on the forehead as he wishes.'

But when the princess heard these words, she burst into tears, and sobbed out:

'Will you really send me, your only child, to that dreadful place, from which most likely I shall never come back?'

'Fear nothing, my little daughter, all will be well. Many shepherds have gone to that lake and none have ever returned; but this one has in these two days fought twice with the dragon and has escaped without a wound. So I hope to-morrow he will kill the dragon altogether, and deliver this land from the monster who has slain so many of our bravest men.'

Scarcely had the sun begun to peep over the hills next morning, when the princess stood by the shepherd's side, ready to go to the lake. The shepherd was brimming over with joy, but the princess only wept bitterly. 'Dry your tears, I implore you,' said he. 'If you will just do what I ask you, and when the time comes, run and kiss my forehead, you have nothing to fear.'

Merrily the shepherd blew on his pipes as he marched at the head of his flock, only stopping every now and then to say to the weeping girl at his side:

'Do not cry so, Heart of Gold; trust me and fear nothing.' And so they reached the lake.

In an instant the sheep were scattered all over the meadows, and the prince placed his hawk on the tree, and his pipes on the grass, while he bade his greyhounds lie beside them. Then he rolled up his trousers and his sleeves, and waded into the water, calling:

'Dragon! dragon! if you are not a coward, come forth, and let us have one more fight together.' And the dragon answered: 'I am waiting for you, O prince'; and the next minute he reared himself out of the water, huge and horrible to see. Swiftly he drew near to the

THE KISS THAT GAVE THE VICTORY

bank, and the prince sprang to meet him, and they grasped each other round the body and fought till it was noon. And when the sun was at its hottest, the dragon cried:

'O prince, let me dip my burning head in the lake, and I will hurl you to the top of the sky.' But the prince answered:

'Oh, ho! my good dragon, do not crow too soon! If the emperor's daughter were only here, and she would kiss my forehead, I would throw you higher still.'

Hardly had he spoken, when the princess, who had been listening, ran up and kissed him on the forehead. Then the prince swung the dragon straight up into the clouds, and when he touched the earth again, he broke into a thousand pieces. Out of the pieces there sprang a wild boar and galloped away, but the prince called his hounds to give chase, and they caught the boar and tore it to bits. Out of the pieces there sprang a hare, and in a moment the greyhounds were after it, and they caught it and killed it; and out of the hare there came a pigeon. Quickly the prince let loose his hawk, which soared straight into the air, then swooped upon the bird and brought it to his master. The prince cut open its body and found the sparrow inside, as the old woman had said.

'Now,' cried the prince, holding the sparrow in his hand, 'now you shall tell me where I can find my brothers.'

'Do not hurt me,' answered the sparrow, 'and I will tell you with all my heart.' Behind your father's castle stands a mill, and in the mill are three slender twigs. Cut off these twigs and strike their roots with them, and the iron door of a cellar will open. In the cellar you will find as many people, young and old, women and children, as would fill a kingdom, and among them are your brothers.'

By this time twilight had fallen, so the prince washed himself in the lake, took the hawk on his shoulder and the pipes under his arm, and with his greyhounds before him and his flock behind him, marched gaily into the town, the princess following them all, still trembling with fright. And so they passed through the streets, thronged with a wondering crowd, till they reached the castle.

Unknown to anyone, the emperor had stolen out on horseback, and had hidden himself on the hill, where he could see all that happened. When all was over, and the power of the dragon was broken for ever, he rode quickly back to the castle, and was ready to receive the prince with open arms, and to promise him his daughter to wife. The wedding took place with great splendour, and for a whole week the town was hung with coloured lamps, and tables were spread in the hall of the castle for all who chose to come and eat. And when the feast was over, the prince told the emperor and the people who he really was, and at this everyone rejoiced still more, and preparations were made for the prince and princess to return to their own kingdom, for the prince was impatient to set free his brothers.

The first thing he did when he reached his native country was to hasten to the mill, where he found the three twigs as the sparrow had told him. The moment that he struck the root the iron door flew open, and from the cellar a countless multitude of men and women streamed forth. He bade them go one by one wheresoever they would, while he himself waited by the door till his brothers passed through. How delighted they were to meet again, and to hear all that the prince had done to deliver them from their enchantment. And they went home with him and served him all the days of their lives, for they said that he only who had proved himself brave and faithful was fit to be king

[From *Volksmärchen der Serben.*]

LITTLE WILDROSE

ONCE upon a time the things in this story happened, and if they had not happened then the story would never have been told. But that was the time when wolves and lambs lay peacefully together in one stall, and shepherds dined on grassy banks with kings and queens.

Once upon a time, then, my dear good children, there lived a man. Now this man was really a hundred years old, if not fully twenty years more. And his wife was very old too—how old I do not know; but some said she was as old as the goddess Venus herself. They had been very happy all these years, but they would have been happier still if they had had any children; but old though they were they had never made up their minds to do without them, and often they would sit over the fire and talk of how they would have brought up their children if only some had come to their house.

One day the old man seemed sadder and more thoughtful than was common with him, and at last he said to his wife: 'Listen to me, old woman!'

'What do you want?' asked she.

'Get me some money out of the chest, for I am going a long journey—all through the world—to see if I cannot find a child, for my heart aches to think that after I am dead my house will fall into the hands of a stranger. And this let me tell you: that if I never find a child I shall not come home again.'

Then the old man took a bag and filled it with food and money, and throwing it over his shoulders, bade his wife farewell.

For long he wandered, and wandered, and wandered, but no child did he see; and one morning his wanderings led him to a forest which was so thick with trees that no light could pass through the branches. The old man stopped when he saw this dreadful place, and at first was afraid to go in; but he remembered that, after all, as the proverb says: 'It is the unexpected that happens,' and perhaps in the midst of this black spot he might find the child he was seeking. So summoning up all his courage he plunged boldly in.

How long he might have been walking there he never could have told you, when at last he reached the mouth of a cave where the darkness seemed a hundred times darker than the wood itself. Again he paused, but he felt as if something was driving him to enter, and with a beating heart he stepped in.

For some minutes the silence and darkness so appalled him that he stood where he was, not daring to advance one step. Then he made a great effort and went on a few paces, and suddenly, far before him, he saw the glimmer of a light. This put new heart into him, and he directed his steps straight towards the faint rays, till he could see, sitting by it, an old hermit, with a long white beard.

The hermit either did not hear the approach of his visitor, or pretended not to do so, for he took no notice, and continued to read his book. After waiting patiently for a little while, the old man fell on his knees, and said: 'Good morning, holy father!' But he might as well have spoken to the rock. 'Good morning, holy father,' he said again, a little louder than before, and this time the hermit made a sign to him to come nearer. 'My son,' whispered he, in a voice that echoed through the cavern, 'what brings you to this dark and dismal place? Hundreds of years have passed since my eyes have rested on the face of a man, and I did not think to look on one again.'

'My misery has brought me here,' replied the old man; 'I have no child, and all our lives my wife and I have longed for one. So I left my home, and went out into the world, hoping that somewhere I might find what I was seeking.'

Then the hermit picked up an apple from the ground, and gave it to him, saying: 'Eat half of this apple, and give the rest to your wife, and cease wandering through the world.'

The old man stooped and kissed the feet of the hermit for sheer joy, and left the cave. He made his way through the forest as fast as the darkness would let him, and at length arrived in flowery fields, which dazzled him with their brightness. Suddenly he was seized with a desperate thirst, and a burning in his throat. He looked for a stream but none was to be seen, and his tongue grew more parched every moment. At length his eyes fell on the apple, which all this while he had been holding in his hand, and in his thirst he forgot what the hermit had told him, and instead of eating merely his own half, he ate up the old woman's also; after that he went to sleep.

When he woke up he saw something strange lying on a bank a little way off, amidst long trails of pink roses. The old man got up, rubbed his eyes, and went to see what it was, when, to his surprise and joy, it proved to be a little girl about two years old, with a skin as pink and white as the roses above her. He took her gently in his arms, but she did not seem at all frightened, and only jumped and crowed with delight; and the old man wrapped his cloak round her, and set off for home as fast as his legs would carry him.

When they were close to the cottage where they lived he laid the child in a pail that was standing near the door, and ran into the house, crying: Come quickly, wife, quickly, for I have brought you a daughter, with hair of gold and eyes like stars!'

At this wonderful news the old woman flew downstairs,

almost tumbling down in her eagerness to see the treasure; but when her husband led her to the pail it was perfectly empty! The old man was nearly beside himself with horror, while his wife sat down and sobbed with grief and disappointment. There was not a spot round about which they did not search, thinking that somehow the child might have got out of the pail and hidden itself for fun; but the little girl was not there, and there was no sign of her.

'Where *can* she be?' moaned the old man, in despair. 'Oh, why did I ever leave her, even for a moment? Have the fairies taken her, or has some wild beast carried her off?' And they began their search all over again; but neither fairies nor wild beasts did they meet with, and with sore hearts they gave it up at last and turned sadly into the hut.

And what had become of the baby? Well, finding herself left alone in a strange place she began to cry with fright, and an eagle hovering near, heard her, and went to see what the sound came from. When he beheld the fat pink and white creature he thought of his hungry little ones at home, and swooping down he caught her up in his claws and was soon flying with her over the tops of the trees. In a few minutes he reached the one in which he had built his nest, and laying little Wildrose (for so the old man had called her) among his downy young eaglets, he flew away. The eaglets naturally were rather surprised at this strange animal, so suddenly popped down in their midst, but instead of beginning to eat her, as their father expected, they nestled up close to her and spread out their tiny wings to shield her from the sun.

Now, in the depths of the forest where the eagle had built his nest, there ran a stream whose waters were poisonous, and on the banks of this stream dwelt a horrible lindworm with seven heads. The lindworm had often watched the eagle flying about the top of the tree, carrying food to his young ones and, accordingly, he watched

The Eagle carries off little Wildrose

carefully for the moment when the eaglets began to try their wings and to fly away from the nest. Of course, if the eagle himself was there to protect them even the lindworm, big and strong as he was, knew that he could do nothing; but when he was absent, any little eaglets who ventured too near the ground would be sure to disappear down the monster's throat. Their brothers, who had been left behind as too young and weak to see the world, knew nothing of all this, but supposed their turn would soon come to see the world also. And in a few days their eyes, too, opened and their wings flapped impatiently, and they longed to fly away above the waving tree-tops to mountain and the bright sun beyond. But that very midnight the lindworm, who was hungry and could not wait for his supper, came out of the brook with a rushing noise, and made straight for the tree. Two eyes of flame came creeping nearer, nearer, and two fiery tongues were stretching themselves out closer, closer, to the little birds who were trembling and shuddering in the farthest corner of the nest. But just as the tongues had almost reached them, the lindworm gave a fearful cry, and turned and fell backwards. Then came the sound of battle from the ground below, and the tree shook, though there was no wind, and roars and snarls mixed together, till the eaglets felt more frightened than ever, and thought their last hour had come. Only Wildrose was undisturbed, and slept sweetly through it all.

In the morning the eagle returned and saw traces of a fight below the tree, and here and there a handful of yellow mane lying about, and here and there a hard scaly substance; when he saw that he rejoiced greatly, and hastened to the nest.

'Who has slain the lindworm?' he asked of his children; there were so many that he did not at first miss the two which the lindworm had eaten. But the eaglets answered that they could not tell, only that they had been in danger of their lives, and at the last moment they had been delivered. Then the sunbeam had struggled through the thick branches and caught Wildrose's golden hair as she lay curled up in the corner, and the eagle wondered, as he looked, whether the little girl had brought him luck, and it was her magic which had killed his enemy.

'Children,' he said, 'I brought her here for your dinner, and you have not touched her ; what is the meaning of this ?' But the eaglets did not answer, and Wildrose opened her eyes, and seemed seven times lovelier than before.

From that day Wildrose lived like a little princess. The eagle flew about the wood and collected the softest, greenest moss he could find to make her a bed, and then he picked with his beak all the brightest and prettiest flowers in the fields or on the mountains to decorate it. So cleverly did he manage it that there was not a fairy in the whole of the forest who would not have been pleased to sleep there, rocked to and fro by the breeze on the treetops. And when the little ones were able to fly from their nest he taught them where to look for the fruits and berries which she loved.

So the time passed by, and with each year Wildrose grew taller and more beautiful, and she lived happily in her nest and never wanted to go out of it, only standing at the edge in the sunset, and looking upon the beautiful world. For company she had all the birds in the forest, who came and talked to her, and for playthings the strange flowers which they brought her from far, and the butterflies which danced with her. And so the days slipped away, and she was fourteen years old.

One morning the emperor's son went out to hunt, and he had not ridden far, before a deer started from under a grove of trees, and ran before him. The prince instantly gave chase, and where the stag led he followed, till at length he found himself in the depths of the forest, where no man before had trod.

THE RAY OF LIGHT

The trees were so thick and the wood so dark, that he paused for a moment and listened, straining his ears to catch some sound to break a silence which almost frightened him. But nothing came, not even the baying

LITTLE WILDROSE PEEPS DOWN FROM THE EAGLE'S NEST

of a hound or the note of a horn. He stood still, and wondered if he should go on, when, on looking up, a stream of light seemed to flow from the top of a tall tree. In its rays he could see the nest with the young eaglets, who were watching him over the side. The prince fitted an arrow into his bow and took his aim, but, before he could let fly, another ray of light dazzled him ; so brilliant was it, that his bow dropped, and he covered his face with his hands. When at last he ventured to peep, Wildrose, with her golden hair flowing round her, was looking at him. This was the first time she had seen a man.

'Tell me how I can reach you ?' cried he ; but Wildrose smiled and shook her head, and sat down quietly.

The prince saw that it was no use, and turned and made his way out of the forest. But he might as well have stayed there, for any good he was to his father, so full was his heart of longing for Wildrose. Twice he returned to the forest in the hopes of finding her, but this time fortune failed him, and he went home as sad as ever.

At length the emperor, who could not think what had caused this change, sent for his son and asked him what was the matter. Then the prince confessed that the image of Wildrose filled his soul, and that he would never be happy without her. At first the emperor felt rather distressed. He doubted whether a girl from a tree top would make a good empress ; but he loved his son so much that he promised to do all he could to find her. So the next morning heralds were sent forth throughout the whole land to inquire if anyone knew where a maiden could be found who lived in a forest on the top of a tree, and to promise great riches and a place at court to any person who should find her. But nobody knew. All the girls in the kingdom had their homes on the ground, and laughed at the notion of being brought up in a tree. 'A nice kind of empress she would make,' they said, as the emperor had done, tossing their heads with disdain ; for, having read many books, they guessed what she was wanted for.

The heralds were almost in despair, when an old woman stepped out of the crowd and came and spoke to them. She was not only very old, but she was very ugly, with a hump on her back and a bald head, and when the heralds saw her they broke into rude laughter. 'I can show you the maiden who lives in the tree-top,' she said, but they only laughed the more loudly.

'Get away, old witch!' they cried, 'you will bring us bad luck'; but the old woman stood firm, and declared that she alone knew where to find the maiden.

'Go with her,' said the eldest of the heralds at last. 'The emperor's orders are clear, that whoever knew anything of the maiden was to come at once to court. Put her in the coach and take her with us.'

So in this fashion the old woman was brought to court.

'You have declared that you can bring hither the maiden from the wood?' said the emperor, who was seated on his throne.

'Yes, your Majesty, and I will keep my word,' said she.

'Then bring her at once,' said the emperor.

'Give me first a kettle and a tripod,' asked the old woman, and the emperor ordered them to be brought instantly. The old woman picked them up, and tucking them under her arm went on her way, keeping at a little distance behind the royal huntsmen, who in their turn followed the prince.

Oh, what a noise that old woman made as she walked along! She chattered to herself so fast and clattered her kettle so loudly that you would have thought that a whole campful of gipsies must be coming round the next corner. But when they reached the forest, she bade them all wait outside, and entered the dark wood by herself.

She stopped underneath the tree where the maiden dwelt and, gathering some dry sticks, kindled a fire. Next, she placed the tripod over it, and the kettle on top. But something was the matter with the kettle. As fast as the old woman put it where it was to stand, that kettle was sure to roll off, falling to the ground with a crash.

It really seemed bewitched, and no one knows what might have happened if Wildrose, who had been all the time peeping out of her nest, had not lost patience at the old

THE WITCH RUNS AWAY WITH WILDROSE

woman's stupidity, and cried out: 'The tripod won't stand on that hill, you must move it!'

'But where am I to move it to, my child?' asked the

old woman, looking up to the nest, and at the same moment trying to steady the kettle with one hand and the tripod with the other.

'Didn't I tell you that it was no good doing that,' said Wildrose, more impatiently than before. 'Make a fire near a tree and hang the kettle from one of the branches.'

The old woman took the kettle and hung it on a little twig, which broke at once, and the kettle fell to the ground.

'If you would only show me how to do it, perhaps I should understand,' said she.

Quick as thought, the maiden slid down the smooth trunk of the tree, and stood beside the stupid old woman, to teach her how things ought to be done. But in an instant the old woman had caught up the girl and swung her over her shoulders, and was running as fast as she could go to the edge of the forest, where she had left the prince. When he saw them coming he rushed eagerly to meet them, and he took the maiden in his arms and kissed her tenderly before them all. Then a golden dress was put on her, and pearls were twined in her hair, and she took her seat in the emperor's carriage which was drawn by six of the whitest horses in the world, and they carried her, without stopping to draw breath, to the gates of the palace. And in three days the wedding was celebrated, and the wedding feast was held, and everyone who saw the bride declared that if anybody wanted a perfect wife they must go to seek her on top of a tree.

[Adapted from the Roumanian.]

TIIDU THE PIPER

Once upon a time there lived a poor man who had more children than bread to feed them with. However, they were strong and willing, and soon learned to make themselves of use to their father and mother, and when they were old enough they went out to service, and everyone was very glad to get them for servants, for they worked hard and were always cheerful. Out of all the ten or eleven, there was only one who gave his parents any trouble, and this was a big lazy boy whose name was Tiidu. Neither scoldings nor beatings nor kind words had any effect on him, and the older he grew the idler he got. He spent his winters crouching close to a warm stove, and his summers asleep under a shady tree; and if he was not doing either of these things he was playing tunes on his flute.

One day he was sitting under a bush playing so sweetly that you might easily have mistaken the notes for those of a bird, when an old man passed by. 'What trade do you wish to follow, my son?' he asked in a friendly voice, stopping as he did so in front of the youth.

'If I were only a rich man, and had no need to work,' replied the boy, 'I should not follow any. I could not bear to be anybody's servant, as all my brothers and sisters are.'

The old man laughed as he heard this answer, and said: 'But I do not exactly see where your riches are to come from if you do not work for them. Sleeping cats catch no mice. He who wishes to become rich must use either his hands or his head, and be ready to toil night and day, or else——'

But here the youth broke in rudely:

'Be silent, old man! I have been told all that a hundred times over; and it runs off me like water off a duck's back. No one will ever make a worker out of me.'

'You have one gift,' replied the old man, taking no notice of this speech, 'and if you would only go about and play the pipes, you would easily earn, not only your daily bread, but a little money into the bargain. Listen to me; get yourself a set of pipes, and learn to play on them as well as you do on your flute, and wherever there are men to hear you, I promise you will never lack money.'

'But where am I to get the pipes from?' asked the youth.

'Blow on your flute for a few days,' replied the old man, 'and you will soon be able to buy your pipes. By-and-by I will come back again and see if you have taken my advice, and whether you are likely to grow rich.' And so saying he went his way.

Tiidu stayed where he was a little longer, thinking of all the old man had told him, and the more he thought the surer he felt that the old man was right. He determined to try whether his plan would really bring luck; but as he did not like being laughed at he resolved not to tell anyone a word about it. So next morning he left home—and never came back! His parents did not take his loss much to heart, but were rather glad that their useless son had for once shown a little spirit, and they hoped that time and hardship might cure Tiidu of his idle folly.

For some weeks Tiidu wandered from one village to another, and proved for himself the truth of the old man's promise. The people he met were all friendly and kind, and enjoyed his flute-playing, giving him his food in return, and even a few pence. These pence the youth hoarded carefully till he had collected enough to buy a beautiful pair of pipes. Then he felt himself indeed on the high road to riches. Nowhere could pipes be found as fine as his, or played in so masterly a manner. Tiidu's pipes set everybody's legs dancing. Wherever there was a marriage, a christening, or a feast of any kind, Tiidu must be there, or the evening would be a failure. In a few years he had become so noted a piper that people would travel far and wide to hear him.

One day he was invited to a christening where many rich men from the neighbouring town were present, and all agreed that never in all their lives had they heard such playing as his. They crowded round him, and praised him, and pressed him to come to their homes, declaring that it was a shame not to give their friends the chance of hearing such music. Of course all this delighted Tiidu, who accepted gladly, and left their houses laden with money and presents of every kind; one great lord clothed him in a magnificent dress, a second hung a chain of pearls round his neck, while a third handed him a set of new pipes encrusted in silver. As for the ladies, the girls twisted silken scarves round his plumed hat, and their mothers knitted him gloves of all colours, to keep out the cold. Any other man in Tiidu's place would have been contented and happy in this life; but his craving for riches gave him no rest, and only goaded him day by day to fresh exertions, so that even his own mother would not have known him for the lazy boy who was always lying asleep in one place or the other.

Now Tiidu saw quite clearly that he could only hope to become rich by means of his pipes, and set about thinking if there was nothing he could do to make the money flow in faster. At length he remembered having heard some stories of a kingdom in the Kungla country, where musicians of all sorts were welcomed and highly paid; but where it was, or how it was reached, he could not recollect, however hard he thought. In despair, he wandered along the coast, hoping to see some ship or sailing boat that would take him where he wished to go, and at length he reached the town of Narva, where several merchantmen were lying at anchor. To his great joy, he found that one of them was sailing for Kungla in a few days, and he hastily went on board, and asked for the captain. But the cost of the passage was more than the prudent Tiidu cared to pay, and though he played his best on his pipes, the captain refused to lower his price, and Tiidu was just thinking of returning on shore when his usual luck flew to his aid. A young sailor, who had heard him play, came secretly to him, and offered to hide him on board, in the absence of the captain. So the next night, as soon as it was dark, Tiidu stepped softly on deck, and was hidden by his friend down in the hold in a corner between two casks. Unseen by the rest of the crew the sailor managed to bring him food and drink, and when they were well out of sight of land he proceeded to carry out a plan he had invented to deliver Tiidu from his cramped quarters. At midnight, while he was keeping watch and everyone else was sleeping, the man bade his friend Tiidu follow him on deck, where he tied a rope round Tiidu's body, fastening the other end carefully to one of the ship's ropes. 'Now,' he said, 'I will throw you into the sea, and you must shout for help; and when you see the sailors coming untie the rope from your waist, and tell them that you have swum after the ship all the way from shore.'

At first Tiidu did not much like this scheme, for the sea ran high, but he was a good swimmer, and the sailor assured him that there was no danger. As soon as he was in the water, his friend hastened to rouse his mates, declaring that he was sure that there was a man in the sea, following the ship. They all came on deck, and what was their surprise when they recognised the person who had bargained about a passage the previous day with the captain.

'Are you a ghost, or a dying man?' they asked him trembling, as they stooped over the side of the ship.

'I shall soon indeed be a dead man if you do not help me,' answered Tiidu, 'for my strength is going fast.'

Then the captain seized a rope and flung it out to him, and Tiidu held it between his teeth, while, unseen by the sailors, he loosed the one tied round his waist.

'Where have you come from?' said the captain, when Tiidu was brought up on board the ship.

'I have followed you from the harbour,' answered he, 'and have been often in sore dread lest my strength should fail me. I hoped that by swimming after the ship I might at last reach Kungla, as I had no money to pay my passage.' The captain's heart melted at these words, and he said kindly: 'You may be thankful that you were not drowned. I will land you at Kungla free of payment, as you are so anxious to get there. So he gave him dry clothes to wear, and a berth to sleep in, and Tiidu and his friend secretly made merry over their cunning trick.

For the rest of the voyage the ship's crew treated Tiidu as something higher than themselves, seeing that in all their lives they had never met with any man that could swim for as many hours as he had done. This pleased Tiidu very much, though he knew that he had really done nothing to deserve it, and in return he delighted them by tunes on his pipes. When, after some days, they cast anchor at Kungla, the story of his wonderful swim brought him many friends, for everybody wished to hear him tell the tale himself. This might have been all very well, had not Tiidu lived in dread that some day he would be asked to give proof of his marvellous swimming powers, and then everything would be found out. Meanwhile he was dazzled with the splendour around him, and more than ever he longed for part of the riches, about which the owners seemed to care so little.

He wandered through the streets for many days, seeking some one who wanted a servant; but though more than one person would have been glad to engage him, they seemed to Tiidu not the sort of people to help him to get rich quickly. At last, when he had almost made up his mind that he must accept the next place offered him, he happened to knock at the door of a rich merchant who was in need of a scullion, and gladly agreed to do the cook's bidding, and it was in this merchant's house that he first learned how great were the riches of the land of Kungla. All the vessels which in other countries are made of iron, copper, brass, or tin, in Kungla were made of silver, or even of gold. The food was cooked in silver saucepans, the bread baked in a silver oven, while the dishes and their covers were all of gold. Even the very pigs' troughs were of silver too. But the sight of these things only made Tiidu more covetous than before. 'What is the use of all this wealth that I have constantly before my eyes,' thought he, 'if none of it is mine? I shall never grow rich by what I earn as a scullion, even though I am paid as much in a month as I should get elsewhere in a year.'

By this time he had been in his place for two years, and had put by quite a large sum of money. His passion of saving had increased to such a pitch that it was only by his master's orders that he ever bought any new clothes, 'For,' said the merchant, 'I will not have dirty people in my house.' So with a heavy heart Tiidu spent some of his next month's wages on a cheap coat.

One day the merchant held a great feast in honour of the christening of his youngest child, and he gave each of his servants a handsome garment for the occasion. The following Sunday, Tiidu, who liked fine clothes when he did not have to pay for them, put on his new coat, and went for a walk to some beautiful pleasure gardens, which were always full of people on a sunny day. He sat down under a shady tree, and watched the passers-by, but after a little he began to feel rather lonely, for he knew nobody and nobody knew him. Suddenly his eyes fell on the figure of an old man, which seemed familiar to him, though he could not tell when or where he had seen it. He watched the figure for some time, till at length the old man left the crowded paths, and threw himself on the soft grass under a lime tree, which stood at some distance from where Tiidu was sitting. Then the young man walked slowly past, in order that he might look at him more closely, and as he did so the old man smiled, and held out his hand.

'What have you done with your pipes?' asked he; and then in a moment Tiidu knew him. Taking his arm he drew him into a quiet place and told him all that had happened since they had last met. The old man shook his head as he listened, and when Tiidu had finished his tale, he said: 'A fool you are, and a fool you will always be! Was there ever such a piece of folly as to exchange your pipes for a scullion's ladle? You could have made as much by the pipes in a day as your wages would have come to in half a year. Go home and fetch your pipes, and play them here, and you will soon see if I have spoken the truth.'

Tiidu did not like this advice—he was afraid that the people would laugh at him; and, besides, it was long since he had touched his pipes—but the old man persisted, and at last Tiidu did as he was told.

'Sit down on the bank by me,' said the old man, when he came back, 'and begin to play, and in a little while the people will flock round you.' Tiidu obeyed, at first without much heart; but somehow the tone of the pipes was sweeter than he had remembered, and as he played, the crowd ceased to walk and chatter, and stood still and silent round him. When he had played for some time he took off his hat and passed it round, and dollars, and small silver coins, and even gold pieces, came tumbling in. Tiidu played a couple more tunes by way of thanks, then turned to go home, hearing on all sides murmurs of

'What a wonderful piper! Come back, we pray you, next Sunday to give us another treat.'

'What did I tell you?' said the old man, as they passed through the garden gate. 'Was it not pleasanter to play for a couple of hours on the pipes than to be stirring sauces all day long? For the second time I have shown you the path to follow; try to learn wisdom, and take the bull by the horns, lest your luck should slip from you! I can be your guide no longer, therefore listen to what I say, and obey me. Go every Sunday afternoon to those gardens; and sit under the lime tree and play to the people, and bring a felt hat with a deep crown, and lay it on the ground at your feet, so that everyone can throw some money into it. If you are invited to play at a feast, accept willingly, but beware of asking a fixed price; say you will take whatever they may feel inclined to give. You will get far more money in the end. Perhaps, some day, our paths may cross, and then I shall see how far you have followed my advice. Till then, farewell'; and the old man went his way.

As before, his words came true, though Tiidu could not at once do his bidding, as he had first to fulfil his appointed time of service. Meanwhile he ordered some fine clothes, in which he played every Sunday in the gardens, and when he counted his gains in the evening they were always more than on the Sunday before. At length he was free to do as he liked, and he had more invitations to play than he could manage to accept, and at night, when the citizens used to go and drink in the inn, the landlord always begged Tiidu to come and play to them. Thus he grew so rich that very soon he had his silver pipes covered with gold, so that they glistened in the light of the sun or the fire. In all Kungla there was no prouder man than Tiidu.

In a few years he had saved such a large sum of money that he was considered a rich man even in Kungla, where everybody was rich. And then he had leisure to remember that he had once had a home, and a family, and that he should like to see them both again, and show them how well he could play. This time he would not need to hide in the ship's hold, but could hire the best cabin if he wished to, or even have a vessel all to himself. So he packed all his treasures in large chests, and sent them on board the first ship that was sailing to his native land, and followed them with a light heart. The wind at starting was fair, but it soon freshened, and in the night rose to a gale. For two days they ran before it, and hoped that by keeping well out to sea they might be able to weather the storm, when, suddenly, the ship struck on a rock, and began to fill. Orders were given to lower the boats, and Tiidu with three sailors got into one of them, but before they could push away from the ship a huge wave overturned it, and all four were flung into the water. Luckily for Tiidu an oar was floating near him, and with its help he was able to keep on the surface of the water; and when the sun rose, and the mist cleared away, he saw that he was not far from shore. By hard swimming, for the sea still ran high, he managed to reach it, and pulled himself out of the water, more dead than alive. Then he flung himself down on the ground and fell fast asleep.

When he awoke he got up to explore the island, and see if there were any men upon it; but though he found streams and fruit trees in abundance, there was no trace either of man or beast. Then, tired with his wanderings he sat down and began to think.

For perhaps the first time in his life his thoughts did not instantly turn to money. It was not on his lost treasures that his mind dwelt, but on his conduct to his parents: his laziness and disobedience as a boy; his forgetfulness of them as a man. 'If wild animals were to come and tear me to pieces,' he said to himself bitterly, 'it would be only what I deserve! My gains are all at the bottom of the sea—well! lightly won, lightly lost—

but it is odd that I feel I should not care for that if only my pipes were left me.' Then he rose and walked a little further, till he saw a tree with great red apples shining amidst the leaves, and he pulled some down, and ate them greedily. After that he stretched himself out on the soft moss and went to sleep.

In the morning he ran to the nearest stream to wash himself, but to his horror, when he caught sight of his face, he saw his nose had grown the colour of an apple, and reached nearly to his waist. He started back thinking he was dreaming, and put up his hand; but, alas! the dreadful thing was true. 'Oh, why does not some wild beast devour me?' he cried to himself; 'never, never, can I go again amongst my fellow-men! If only the sea had swallowed me up, how much happier it had been for me!' And he hid his head in his hands and wept. His grief was so violent, that it exhausted him, and growing hungry he looked about for something to eat. Just above him was a bough of ripe, brown nuts, and he picked them and ate a handful. To his surprise, as he was eating them, he felt his nose grow shorter and shorter, and after a while he ventured to feel it with his hand, and even to look in the stream again! Yes, there was no mistake, it was as short as before, or perhaps a little shorter. In his joy at this discovery Tiidu did a very bold thing. He took one of the apples out of his pocket, and cautiously bit a piece out of it. In an instant his nose was as long as his chin, and in a deadly fear lest it should stretch further, he hastily swallowed a nut, and awaited the result with terror. Supposing that the shrinking of his nose had only been an accident before! Supposing that that nut and no other was able to cause its shrinking! In that case he had, by his own folly, in not letting well alone, ruined his life completely. But, no! he had guessed rightly, for in no more time than his nose had taken to grow long did it take to return to its proper size. 'This may make my fortune,' he said joyfully to himself ; and he gathered some of the apples, which he put into one pocket, and a good supply of nuts which he put into the other. Next day he wove a basket out of some rushes, so that if he ever left the island he might be able to carry his treasures about.

That night he dreamed that his friend the old man appeared to him and said : 'Because you did not mourn for your lost treasure, but only for your pipes, I will give you a new set to replace them.' And, behold ! in the morning when he got up a set of pipes was lying in the basket. With what joy did he seize them and begin one of his favourite tunes ; and as he played hope sprang up in his heart, and he looked out to sea, to try to detect the sign of a sail. Yes ! there it was, making straight for the island ; and Tiidu, holding his pipes in his hand, dashed down to the shore.

The sailors knew the island to be uninhabited, and were much surprised to see a man standing on the beach, waving his arms in welcome to them. A boat was put off, and two sailors rowed to the shore to discover how he came there, and if he wished to be taken away. Tiidu told them the story of his shipwreck, and the captain promised that he should come on board, and sail with them back to Kungla ; and thankful indeed was Tiidu to accept the offer, and to show his gratitude by playing on his pipes whenever he was asked to do so.

They had a quick voyage, and it was not long before Tiidu found himself again in the streets of the capital of Kungla, playing as he went along. The people had heard no music like his since he went away, and they crowded round him, and in their joy gave him whatever money they had in their pockets. His first care was to buy himself some new clothes, which he sadly needed, taking care, however, that they should be made after a foreign fashion. When they were ready, he set out one day with a small basket of his famous apples, and went up to the palace. He did not have to wait long before one of the royal servants passed by and bought all the apples, begging as he did

THE LONG NOSES

so that the merchant should return and bring some more. This Tiidu promised, and hastened away as if he had a mad bull behind him, so afraid was he that the man should begin to eat an apple at once.

It is needless to say that for some days he took no more apples back to the palace, but kept well away on the other side of the town, wearing other clothes, and disguised by a long black beard, so that even his own mother would not have known him.

The morning after his visit to the castle the whole city was in an uproar about the dreadful misfortune that had happened to the Royal Family, for not only the king but his wife and children, had eaten of the stranger's apples, and all, so said the rumour, were very ill. The most famous doctors and the greatest magicians were hastily summoned to the palace, but they shook their heads and came away again ; never had they met with such a disease in all the course of their experience. By-and-bye a story went round the town, started no one knew how, that the malady was in some way connected with the nose ; and men rubbed their own anxiously, to be sure that nothing catching was in the air.

Matters had been in this state for more than a week when it reached the ears of the king that a man was living in an inn on the other side of the town who declared himself able to cure all manner of diseases. Instantly the royal carriage was commanded to drive with all speed and bring back this magician, offering him riches untold if he could restore their noses to their former length. Tiidu had expected this summons, and had sat up all night changing his appearance, and so well had he succeeded that not a trace remained either of the piper or of the apple seller. He stepped into the carriage, and was driven post haste to the king, who was feverishly counting every moment, for both his nose and the queen's were by this time more than a yard long, and they did not know where they would stop.

Now Tiidu thought it would not look well to cure the royal family by giving them the raw nuts ; he felt that it might arouse suspicion. So he had carefully pounded them into a powder, and divided the powder up into small doses, which were to be put on the tongue and swallowed at once. He gave one of these to the king and another to the queen, and told them that before taking them they were to get into bed in a dark room and not to move for some hours, after which they might be sure that they would come out cured.

The king's joy was so great at this news that he would gladly have given Tiidu half of his kingdom; but the piper was no longer so greedy of money as he once was, before he had been shipwrecked on the island. If he could get enough to buy a small estate and live comfortably on it for the rest of his life, that was all he now cared for. However, the king ordered his treasurer to pay him three times as much as he asked, and with this Tiidu went down to the harbour and engaged a small ship to carry him back to his native country. The wind was fair, and in ten days the coast, which he had almost forgotten, stood clear before him. In a few hours he was standing in his old home, where his father, three sisters, and two brothers gave him a hearty welcome. His mother and his other brothers had died some years before.

When the meeting was over, he began to make inquiries about a small estate that was for sale near the town, and after he had bought it the next thing was to find a wife to share it with him. This did not take long either; and people who were at the wedding feast declared that the best part of the whole day was the hour when Tiidu played to them on the pipes before they bade each other farewell and returned to their homes.

[From *Esthnische Mährchen*.]

PAPERARELLO

ONCE upon a time there lived a king and a queen who had one son. The king loved the boy very much, but the queen, who was a wicked woman, hated the sight of him; and this was the more unlucky for, when he was twelve years old, his father died, and he was left alone in the world.

Now the queen was very angry because the people, who knew how bad she was, seated her son on the throne instead of herself, and she never rested till she had formed a plan to get him out of the way. Fortunately, however, the young king was wise and prudent, and knew her too well to trust her.

One day, when his mourning was over, he gave orders that everything should be made ready for a grand hunt. The queen pretended to be greatly delighted that he was going to amuse himself once more, and declared that she would accompany him. 'No, mother, I cannot let you come,' he answered; 'the ground is rough, and you are not strong.' But he might as well have spoken to the winds: when the horn was sounded at daybreak the queen was there with the rest.

All that day they rode, for game was plentiful, but towards evening the mother and son found themselves alone in a part of the country that was strange to them. They wandered on for some time, without knowing where they were going, till they met with a man whom they begged to give them shelter. 'Come with me,' said the man gladly, for he was an ogre, and fed on human flesh;

The Horse brings the boy to the Fairies' House

and the king and his mother went with him, and he led them to his house. When they got there they found to what a dreadful place they had come, and, falling on their knees, they offered him great sums of money, if he would only spare their lives. The ogre's heart was moved at the sight of the queen's beauty, and he promised that he would do her no harm ; but he stabbed the boy at once, and binding his body on a horse, turned him loose in the forest.

The ogre had happened to choose a horse which he had bought only the day before, and he did not know it was a magician, or he would not have been so foolish as to fix upon it on this occasion. The horse no sooner had been driven off with the prince's body on its back than it galloped straight to the home of the fairies, and knocked at the door with its hoof. The fairies heard the knock, but were afraid to open till they had peeped from an upper window to see that it was no giant or ogre who could do them harm. 'Oh, look, sister!' cried the first to reach the window, 'it is a horse that has knocked, and on its back there is bound a dead boy, the most beautiful boy in all the world!' Then the fairies ran to open the door, and let in the horse and unbound the ropes which fastened the young king on its back. And they gathered round to admire his beauty, and whispered one to the other: 'We will make him alive again, and will keep him for our brother.' And so they did, and for many years they all lived together as brothers and sisters.

By-and-by the boy grew into a man, as boys will, and then the oldest of the fairies said to her sisters: 'Now I will marry him, and he shall be really your brother.' So the young king married the fairy, and they lived happily together in the castle ; but though he loved his wife he still longed to see the world.

At length this longing grew so strong on him that he could bear it no more ; and, calling the fairies together, he said to them: 'Dear wife and sisters, I must leave you for a time, and go out and see the world. But I shall think of you often, and one day I shall come back to you.'

The fairies wept and begged him to stay, but he would not listen, and at last the eldest, who was his wife, said to him: 'If you really will abandon us, take this lock of my hair with you; you will find it useful in time of need.' So she cut off a long curl, and handed it to him.

The prince mounted his horse, and rode on all day without stopping once. Towards evening he found himself in a desert, and, look where he would, there was no such thing as a house or a man to be seen. 'What am I to do now?' he thought. 'If I go to sleep here wild beasts will come and eat me! Yet both I and my horse are worn out, and can go no further.' Then suddenly he remembered the fairy's gift, and taking out the curl he said to it: 'I want a castle here, and servants, and dinner, and everything to make me comfortable to-night; and besides that, I must have a stable and fodder for my horse.' And in a moment the castle was before him just as he had wished.

In this way he travelled through many countries, till at last he came to a land that was ruled over by a great king. Leaving his horse outside the walls, he clad himself in the dress of a poor man, and went up to the palace. The queen, who was looking out of the window, saw him approaching, and filled with pity sent a servant to ask who he was and what he wanted. 'I am a stranger here,' answered the young king, 'and very poor. I have come to beg for some work.' 'We have everybody we want,' said the queen, when the servant told her the young man's reply. 'We have a gate-keeper, and a hall porter, and servants of all sorts in the palace; the only person we have not got is a goose-boy. Tell him that he can be our goose-boy if he likes.' The youth answered that he was quite content to be goose-boy; and that was how he got his nickname of Paperarello. And in order that no one should guess that he was any better than a

THE KING GIVES THE PRINCESS TO PAPERARELLO IN THE BAKEHOUSE

goose-boy should be, he rubbed his face and his rags over with mud, and made himself altogether such a disgusting object that every one crossed over to the other side of the road when he was seen coming.

'Do go and wash yourself, Paperarello!' said the queen sometimes, for he did his work so well that she took an interest in him. 'Oh, I should not feel comfortable if I was clean, your Majesty,' answered he, and went whistling after his geese.

It happened one day that, owing to some accident to the great flour mills which supplied the city, there was no bread to be had, and the king's army had to do without. When the king heard of it, he sent for the cook, and told him that by the next morning he must have all the bread that the oven, heated seven times over, could bake. 'But, your Majesty, it is not possible,' cried the poor man in despair. 'The mills have only just begun working, and the flour will not be ground till evening, and how can I heat the oven seven times in one night?' 'That is your affair,' answered the King, who, when he took anything into his head, would listen to nothing. 'If you succeed in baking the bread you shall have my daughter to wife, but if you fail your head will pay for it.'

Now Paperarello, who was passing through the hall where the king was giving his orders, heard these words, and said: 'Your Majesty, have no fears; I will bake your bread.' 'Very well,' answered the king; 'but if you fail, you will pay for it with your head!' and signed that both should leave his presence.

The cook was still trembling with the thought of what he had escaped, but to his surprise Paperarello did not seem disturbed at all, and when night came he went to sleep as usual. 'Paperarello,' cried the other servants, when they saw him quietly taking off his clothes, 'you cannot go to bed; you will need every moment of the night for your work. Remember, the king is not to be played with!'

'I really must have some sleep first,' replied Paperarello, stretching himself and yawning; and he flung himself on his bed, and was fast asleep in a moment. In an hour's time, the servants came and shook him by the shoulder. 'Paperarello, are you mad?' said they. 'Get up, or you will lose your head.' 'Oh, do let me sleep a little more,' answered he. And this was all he would say, though the servants returned to wake him many times in the night.

At last the dawn broke, and the servants rushed to his room, crying: 'Paperarello! Paperarello! get up, the king is coming. You have baked no bread, and of a surety he will have your head.'

'Oh, don't scream so,' replied Paperarello, jumping out of bed as he spoke; and taking the lock of hair in his hand, he went into the kitchen. And, behold! there stood the bread piled high—four, five, six ovens full, and the seventh still waiting to be taken out of the oven. The servants stood and stared in surprise, and the king said: 'Well done, Paperarello, you have won my daughter.' And he thought to himself: 'This fellow must really be a magician.'

But when the princess heard what was in store for her she wept bitterly, and declared that never, never would she marry that dirty Paperarello! However, the king paid no heed to her tears and prayers, and before many days were over the wedding was celebrated with great splendour, though the bridegroom had not taken the trouble to wash himself, and was as dirty as before.

When night came he went as usual to sleep among his geese, and the princess went to the king and said: 'Father, I entreat you to have that horrible Paperarello put to death.' 'No, no!' replied her father, 'he is a great magician, and before I put him to death, I must first find out the secret of his power, and then—we shall see.'

Soon after this a war broke out, and everybody about

the palace was very busy polishing up armour and sharpening swords, for the king and his sons were to ride at the head of the army. Then Paperarello left his geese, and came and told the king that he wished to go to fight also. The king gave him leave, and told him that he might go to the stable and take any horse he liked from the stables. So Paperarello examined the horses carefully, but instead of picking out one of the splendid well-groomed creatures, whose skin shone like satin, he chose a poor lame thing, put a saddle on it, and rode after the other men-at-arms who were attending the king. In a short time he stopped, and said to them: 'My horse can go no further; you must go on to the war without me, and I will stay here, and make some little clay soldiers, and will play at a battle.' The men laughed at him for being so childish, and rode on after their master.

Scarcely were they out of sight than Paperarello took out his curl, and wished himself the best armour, the sharpest sword, and the swiftest horse in the world, and the next minute was riding as fast as he could to the field of battle. The fight had already begun, and the enemy was getting the best of it, when Paperarello rode up, and in a moment the fortunes of the day had changed. Right and left this strange knight laid about him, and his sword pierced the stoutest breast-plate, and the strongest shield. He was indeed 'a host in himself,' and his foes fled before him thinking he was only the first of a troop of such warriors, whom no one could withstand. When the battle was over, the king sent for him to thank him for his timely help, and to ask what reward he should give him. 'Nothing but your little finger, your Majesty,' was his answer; and the king cut off his little finger and gave it to Paperarello, who bowed and hid it in his surcoat. Then he left the field, and when the soldiers rode back they found him still sitting in the road making whole rows of little clay dolls.

The next day the king went out to fight another

battle, and again Paperarello appeared, mounted on his lame horse. As on the day before, he halted on the road, and sat down to make his clay soldiers; then a second time he wished himself armour, sword, and a horse, all sharper and better than those he had previously had, and galloped after the rest. He was only just in time: the enemy had almost beaten the king's army back, and men whispered to each other that if the strange knight did not soon come to their aid, they would be all dead men. Suddenly someone cried: 'Hold on a little longer, I see him in the distance; and his armour shines brighter, and his horse runs swifter, than yesterday.' Then they took fresh heart and fought desperately on till the knight came up, and threw himself into the thick of the battle. As before, the enemy gave way before him, and in a few minutes the victory remained with the king.

The first thing that the victor did was to send for the knight to thank him for his timely help, and to ask what gift he could bestow on him in token of gratitude. 'Your Majesty's ear,' answered the knight; and as the king could not go back from his word, he cut it off and gave it to him. Paperarello bowed, fastened the ear inside his surcoat and rode away. In the evening, when they all returned from the battle, there he was, sitting in the road, making clay dolls.

On the third day the same thing happened, and this time he asked for the king's nose as the reward of his aid. Now, to lose one's nose, is worse even than losing one's ear or one's finger, and the king hesitated as to whether he should comply. However, he had always prided himself on being an honourable man, so he cut off his nose, and handed it to Paperarello. Paperarello bowed, put the nose in his surcoat, and rode away. In the evening, when the king returned from the battle, he found Paperarello sitting in the road making clay dolls. And Paperarello got up and said to him: 'Do you know who

I am? I am your dirty goose-boy, yet you have given me your finger, and your ear, and your nose.'

That night, when the king sat at dinner, Paperarello came in, and laying down the ear, and the nose, and the finger on the table, turned and said to the nobles and courtiers who were waiting on the king: 'I am the invincible knight, who rode three times to your help, and I also am a king's son, and no goose-boy as you all think.' And he went away and washed himself, and dressed himself in fine clothes and entered the hall again, looking so handsome that the proud princess fell in love with him on the spot. But Paperarello took no notice of her, and said to the king: 'It was kind of you to offer me your daughter in marriage, and for that I thank you; but I have a wife at home whom I love better, and it is to her that I am going. But as a token of farewell, I wish that your ear, and nose, and finger may be restored to their proper places.' So saying, he bade them all good-bye, and went back to his home and his fairy bride, with whom he lived happily till the end of his life.

[From *Siciliänischen Mährchen.*]

THE GIFTS OF THE MAGICIAN

ONCE upon a time there was an old man who lived in a little hut in the middle of a forest. His wife was dead, and he had only one son, whom he loved dearly. Near their hut was a group of birch trees, in which some black-game had made their nests, and the youth had often begged his father's permission to shoot the birds, but the old man always strictly forbade him to do anything of the kind.

One day, however, when the father had gone to a little distance to collect some sticks for the fire, the boy fetched his bow, and shot at a bird that was just flying towards its nest. But he had not taken proper aim, and the bird was only wounded, and fluttered along the ground. The boy ran to catch it, but though he ran very fast, and the bird seemed to flutter along very slowly, he never could quite come up with it; it was always just a little in advance. But so absorbed was he in the chase that he did not notice for some time that he was now deep in the forest, in a place where he had never been before. Then he felt it would be foolish to go any further, and he turned to find his way home.

He thought it would be easy enough to follow the path along which he had come, but somehow it was always branching off in unexpected directions. He looked about for a house where he might stop and ask his way, but there was not a sign of one anywhere, and he was afraid to stand still, for it was cold, and there were many stories of wolves being seen in that part of the

·THE·MAGICIAN·SAVED·FROM·THE·WOLVES·

forest. Night fell, and he was beginning to start at every sound, when suddenly a magician came running towards him, with a pack of wolves snapping at his heels. Then all the boy's courage returned to him. He took his bow, and aiming an arrow at the largest wolf, shot him through the heart, and a few more arrows soon put the rest to flight. The magician was full of gratitude to his deliverer, and promised him a reward for his help if the youth would go back with him to his house.

'Indeed there is nothing that would be more welcome to me than a night's lodging,' answered the boy; 'I have been wandering all day in the forest, and did not know how to get home again.

'Come with me, you must be hungry as well as tired,' said the magician, and led the way to his house, where the guest flung himself on a bed, and went fast asleep. But his host returned to the forest to get some food, for the larder was empty.

While he was absent the housekeeper went to the boy's room and tried to wake him. She stamped on the floor, and shook him and called to him, telling him that he was in great danger, and must take flight at once. But nothing would rouse him, and if he did ever open his eyes he shut them again directly.

Soon after, the magician came back from the forest, and told the housekeeper to bring them something to eat. The meal was quickly ready, and the magician called to the boy to come down and eat it, but he could not be wakened, and they had to sit down to supper without him. By-and-by the magician went out into the wood again for some more hunting, and on his return he tried afresh to waken the youth. But finding it quite impossible, he went back for the third time to the forest.

While he was absent the boy woke up and dressed himself. Then he came downstairs and began to talk to the housekeeper. The girl had heard how he had saved her master's life, so she said nothing more about his running away, but instead told him that if the magician offered him the choice of a reward, he was to ask for the horse which stood in the third stall of the stable.

By-and-by the old man came back and they all sat down to dinner. When they had finished the magician said: 'Now, my son, tell me what you will have as the reward of your courage?'

'Give me the horse that stands in the third stall of your stable,' answered the youth. 'For I have a long way to go before I get home, and my feet will not carry me so far.'

'Ah! my son,' replied the magician, 'it is the best horse in my stable that you want! Will not anything else please you as well?'

But the youth declared that it was the horse, and the horse only, that he desired, and in the end the old man gave way. And besides the horse, the magician gave him a zither, a fiddle, and a flute, saying: 'If you are in danger, touch the zither; and if no one comes to your aid, then play on the fiddle; but if that brings no help, blow on the flute.'

The youth thanked the magician, and fastening his treasures about him mounted the horse and rode off. He had already gone some miles when, to his great surprise, the horse spoke, and said: 'It is no use your returning home just now, your father will only beat you. Let us visit a few towns first, and something lucky will be sure to happen to us.'

This advice pleased the boy, for he felt himself almost a man by this time, and thought it was high time he saw the world. When they entered the capital of the country everyone stopped to admire the beauty of the horse. Even the king heard of it, and came to see the splendid creature with his own eyes. Indeed, he wanted directly to buy it, and told the youth he would give any price he liked. The young man hesitated for a moment, but before he could speak, the horse contrived to whisper to him:

'Do not sell me, but ask the king to take me to his stable, and feed me there; then his other horses will become just as beautiful as I.'

The king was delighted when he was told what the horse had said, and took the animal at once to the stables, and placed it in his own particular stall. Sure enough, the horse had scarcely eaten a mouthful of corn out of the manger, when the rest of the horses seemed to have undergone a transformation. Some of them were old favourites which the king had ridden in many wars, and they bore the signs of age and of service. But now they arched their heads, and pawed the ground with their slender legs as they had been wont to do in days long gone by. The king's heart beat with delight, but the old groom who had had the care of them stood crossly by, and eyed the owner of this wonderful creature with hate and envy. Not a day passed without his bringing some story against the youth to his master, but the king understood all about the matter and paid no attention. At last the groom declared that the young man had boasted that he could find the king's war horse which had strayed into the forest several years ago, and had not been heard of since. Now the king had never ceased to mourn for his horse, so this time he listened to the tale which the groom had invented, and sent for the youth. 'Find me my horse in three days,' said he, 'or it will be the worse for you.'

The youth was thunderstruck at this command, but he only bowed, and went off at once to the stable.

'Do not worry yourself,' answered his own horse. 'Ask the king to give you a hundred oxen, and to let them be killed and cut into small pieces. Then we will start on our journey, and ride till we reach a certain river. There a horse will come up to you, but take no notice of him. Soon another will appear, and this also you must leave alone, but when the third horse shows itself, throw my bridle over it.'

Everything happened just as the horse had said, and the third horse was safely bridled. Then the other horse spoke again: 'The magician's raven will try to eat us as we ride away, but throw it some of the oxen's flesh, and then I will gallop like the wind, and carry you safe out of the dragon's clutches.'

So the young man did as he was told, and brought the horse back to the king.

The old stableman was very jealous, when he heard of it, and wondered what he could do to injure the youth in the eyes of his royal master. At last he hit upon a plan, and told the king that the young man had boasted that he could bring home the king's wife, who had vanished many months before, without leaving a trace behind her. Then the king bade the young man come into his presence, and desired him to fetch the queen home again, as he had boasted he could do. And if he failed, his head would pay the penalty.

The poor youth's heart stood still as he listened. Find the queen? But how was he to do that, when nobody in the palace had been able to do so! Slowly he walked to the stable, and laying his head on his horse's shoulder, he said: 'The king has ordered me to bring his wife home again, and how can I do that when she disappeared so long ago, and no one can tell me anything about her?'

'Cheer up!' answered the horse, 'we will manage to find her. You have only got to ride me back to the same river that we went to yesterday, and I will plunge into it and take my proper shape again. For I am the king's wife, who was turned into a horse by the magician from whom you saved me.'

Joyfully the young man sprang into the saddle and rode away to the banks of the river. Then he threw himself off, and waited while the horse plunged in. The moment it dipped its head into the water its black skin vanished, and the most beautiful woman in the world was

THE MAGICIAN THROWS THE TREE AND THE KING UP INTO THE AIR

floating on the water. She came smiling towards the youth, and held out her hand, and he took it and led her back to the palace. Great was the king's surprise and happiness when he beheld his lost wife stand before him, and in gratitude to her rescuer he loaded him with gifts.

You would have thought that after this the poor youth would have been left in peace; but no, his enemy the stableman hated him as much as ever, and laid a new plot for his undoing. This time he presented himself before the king and told him that the youth was so puffed up with what he had done that he had declared he would seize the king's throne for himself.

At this news the king waxed so furious that he ordered a gallows to be erected at once, and the young man to be hanged without a trial. He was not even allowed to speak in his own defence, but on the very steps of the gallows he sent a message to the king and begged, as a last favour, that he might play a tune on his zither. Leave was given him, and taking the instrument from under his cloak he touched the strings. Scarcely had the first notes sounded than the hangman and his helper began to dance, and the louder grew the music the higher they capered, till at last they cried for mercy. But the youth paid no heed, and the tunes rang out more merrily than before, and by the time the sun set they both sank on the ground exhausted, and declared that the hanging must be put off till to-morrow.

The story of the zither soon spread through the town, and on the following morning the king and his whole court and a large crowd of people were gathered at the foot of the gallows to see the youth hanged. Once more he asked a favour—permission to play on his fiddle, and this the king was graciously pleased to grant. But with the first notes, the leg of every man in the crowd was lifted high, and they danced to the sound of the music the whole day till darkness fell, and there was no light to hang the musician by.

The third day came, and the youth asked leave to play on his flute. 'No, no,' said the king, 'you made me dance all day yesterday, and if I do it again it will certainly be my death. You shall play no more tunes. Quick! the rope round his neck.'

At these words the young man looked so sorrowful that the courtiers said to the king: 'He is very young to die. Let him play a tune if it will make him happy.' So, very unwillingly, the king gave him leave; but first he had himself bound to a big fir tree, for fear that he should be made to dance.

When he was made fast, the young man began to blow softly on his flute, and bound though he was, the king's body moved to the sound, up and down the fir tree till his clothes were in tatters, and the skin nearly rubbed off his back. But the youth had no pity, and went on blowing, till suddenly the old magician appeared and asked: 'What danger are you in, my son, that you have sent for me?'

'They want to hang me,' answered the young man; 'the gallows are all ready and the hangman is only waiting for me to stop playing.'

'Oh, I will put that right,' said the magician; and taking the gallows, he tore it up and flung it into the air, and no one knows where it came down. 'Who has ordered you to be hanged?' asked he.

The young man pointed to the king, who was still bound to the fir; and without wasting words the magician took hold of the tree also, and with a mighty heave both fir and man went spinning through the air, and vanished in the clouds after the gallows.

Then the youth was declared to be free, and the people elected him for their king; and the stable helper drowned himself from envy, for, after all, if it had not been for him the young man would have remained poor all the days of his life.

[From *Finnische Mährchen.*]

THE STRONG PRINCE

Once upon a time there lived a king who was so fond of wine that he could not go to sleep unless he knew he had a great flaskful tied to his bed-post. All day long he drank till he was too stupid to attend to his business, and everything in the kingdom went to rack and ruin. But one day an accident happened to him, and he was struck on the head by a falling bough, so that he fell from his horse and lay dead upon the ground.

His wife and son mourned his loss bitterly, for, in spite of his faults, he had always been kind to them. So they abandoned the crown and forsook their country, not knowing or caring where they went.

At length they wandered into a forest, and being very tired, sat down under a tree to eat some bread that they had brought with them. When they had finished the queen said: 'My son, I am thirsty; fetch me some water.'

The prince got up at once and went to a brook which he heard gurgling near at hand. He stooped and filled his hat with the water, which he brought to his mother; then he turned and followed the stream up to its source in a rock, where it bubbled out clear and fresh and cold. He knelt down to take a draught from the deep pool below the rock, when he saw the reflection of a sword hanging from the branch of a tree over his head. The young man drew back with a start; but in a moment he climbed the tree, cutting the rope which held the sword, and carried the weapon to his mother.

The queen was greatly surprised at the sight of anything so splendid in such a lonely place, and took it in her hands to examine it closely. It was of curious workmanship, wrought with gold, and on its handle was written: 'The man who can buckle on this sword will become stronger than other men.' The queen's heart swelled with joy as she read these words, and she bade her son lose no time in testing their truth. So he fastened it round his waist, and instantly a glow of strength seemed to run through his veins. He took hold of a thick oak tree and rooted it up as easily as if it had been a weed.

This discovery put new life into the queen and her son, and they continued their walk through the forest. But night was drawing on, and the darkness grew so thick that it seemed as if it could be cut with a knife. They did not want to sleep in the wood, for they were afraid of wolves and other wild beasts, so they groped their way along, hand in hand, till the prince tripped over something which lay across the path. He could not see what it was, but stooped down and tried to lift it. The thing was very heavy, and he thought his back would break under the strain. At last with a great heave he moved it out of the road, and as it fell he knew it was a huge rock. Behind the rock was a cave which it was quite clear was the home of some robbers, though not one of the band was there.

Hastily putting out the fire which burned brightly at the back, and bidding his mother come in and keep very still, the prince began to pace up and down, listening for the return of the robbers. But he was very sleepy, and in spite of all his efforts he felt he could not keep awake much longer, when he heard the sound of the robbers returning, shouting and singing as they marched along. Soon the singing ceased, and straining his ears he heard them discussing anxiously what had become of their cave, and why they could not see the fire as usual. 'This *must*

THE PRINCE WINS THE SWORD

be the place,' said a voice, which the prince took to be that of the captain. 'Yes, I feel the ditch before the entrance. Someone forgot to pile up the fire before we left and it has burnt itself out! But it is all right. Let every man jump across, and as he does so cry out "Hop! I am here." I will go last. Now begin.'

The man who stood nearest jumped across, but he had no time to give the call which the captain had ordered, for with one swift, silent stroke of the prince's sword, his head rolled into a corner. Then the young man cried instead, 'Hop! I am here.'

The second man, hearing the signal, leapt the ditch in confidence, and was met by the same fate, and in a few minutes eleven of the robbers lay dead, and there remained only the captain.

Now the captain had wound round his neck the shawl of his lost wife, and the stroke of the prince's sword fell harmless. Being very cunning, however, he made no resistance, and rolled over as if he were as dead as the other men. Still, the prince was no fool, and wondered if indeed he was as dead as he seemed to be; but the captain lay so stiff and stark, that at last he was taken in.

The prince next dragged the headless bodies into a chamber in the cave, and locked the door. Then he and his mother ransacked the place for some food, and when they had eaten it they lay down and slept in peace.

With the dawn they were both awake again, and found that, instead of the cave which they had come to the night before, they now were in a splendid castle, full of beautiful rooms. The prince went round all these and carefully locked them up, bidding his mother take care of the keys while he was hunting.

Unfortunately, the queen, like all women, could not bear to think that there was anything which she did not know. So the moment that her son had turned his back, she opened the doors of all the rooms, and peeped in, till she came to the one where the robbers lay. But if the sight of the blood on the ground turned her faint, the sight of the robber captain walking up and down was a greater shock still. She quickly turned the key in the lock, and ran back to the chamber she had slept in.

Soon after her son came in, bringing with him a large bear, which he had killed for supper. As there was enough food to last them for many days, the prince did not hunt the next morning, but, instead, began to explore the castle. He found that a secret way led from it into the forest; and following the path, he reached another castle larger and more splendid than the one belonging to the robbers. He knocked at the door with his fist, and said that he wanted to enter; but the giant, to whom the castle belonged, only answered: 'I know who you are. I have nothing to do with robbers.'

'I am no robber,' answered the prince. 'I am the son of a king, and I have killed all the band. If you do not open to me at once I will break in the door, and your head shall go to join the others.'

He waited a little, but the door remained shut as tightly as before. Then he just put his shoulder to it, and immediately the wood began to crack. When the giant found that it was no use keeping it shut, he opened it, saying: 'I see you are a brave youth. Let there be peace between us.'

And the prince was glad to make peace, for he had caught a glimpse of the giant's beautiful daughter, and from that day he often sought the giant's house.

Now the queen led a dull life all alone in the castle, and to amuse herself she paid visits to the robber captain, who flattered her till at last she agreed to marry him. But as she was much afraid of her son, she told the robber that the next time the prince went to bathe in the river, he was to steal the sword from its place above the bed, for without it the young man would have no power to punish him for his boldness.

The robber captain thought this good counsel, and the

The Strong Prince enters the Giant's Castle by H.J. FORD. 1903

next morning, when the young man went to bathe, he unhooked the sword from its nail and buckled it round his waist. On his return to the castle, the prince found the robber waiting for him on the steps, waving the sword above his head, and knowing that some horrible fate was in store, fell on his knees and begged for mercy. But he might as well have tried to squeeze blood out of a stone. The robber, indeed, granted him his life, but took out both his eyes, which he thrust into the prince's hand, saying brutally :

'Here, you had better keep them! You may find them useful!'

Weeping, the blind youth felt his way to the giant's house, and told him all the story.

The giant was full of pity for the poor young man, but inquired anxiously what he had done with the eyes. The prince drew them out of his pocket, and silently handed them to the giant, who washed them well, and then put them back in the prince's head. For three days he lay in utter darkness ; then the light began to come back, till soon he saw as well as ever.

But though he could not rejoice enough over the recovery of his eyes, he bewailed bitterly the loss of his sword, and that it should have fallen to the lot of his bitter enemy.

'Never mind, my friend,' said the giant, 'I will get it back for you.' And he sent for the monkey who was his head servant.

'Tell the fox and the squirrel that they are to go with you, and fetch me back the prince's sword,' ordered he.

The three servants set out at once, one seated on the back of the others, the ape, who disliked walking, being generally on top. Directly they came to the window of the robber captain's room, the monkey sprang from the backs of the fox and the squirrel, and climbed in. The room was empty, and the sword hanging from a nail. He took it down, and buckling it round his waist, as he had seen the prince do, swung himself down again, and mounting on the backs of his two companions, hastened to his master. The giant bade him give the sword to the prince, who girded himself with it, and returned with all speed to the castle.

'Come out, you rascal! come out, you villain!' cried he, 'and answer to me for the wrong you have done. I will show you who is the master in this house!'

The noise he made brought the robber into the room. He glanced up to where the sword usually hung, but it was gone; and instinctively he looked at the prince's hand, where he saw it gleaming brightly. In his turn he fell on his knees to beg for mercy, but it was too late. As he had done to the prince, so the prince did to him, and, blinded, he was thrust forth, and fell down a deep hole, where he is to this day. His mother the prince sent back to her father, and never would see her again. After this he returned to the giant, and said to him:

'My friend, add one more kindness to those you have already heaped on me. Give me your daughter as my wife.'

So they were married, and the wedding feast was so splendid that there was not a kingdom in the world that did not hear of it. And the prince never went back to his father's throne, but lived peacefully with his wife in the forest, where, if they are not dead, they are living still.

[From *Ungarische Volksmärchen.*]

THE TREASURE SEEKER

ONCE, long ago, in a little town that lay in the midst of high hills and wild forests, a party of shepherds sat one night in the kitchen of the inn talking over old times, and telling of the strange things that had befallen them in their youth.

Presently up spoke the silver-haired Father Martin.

'Comrades,' said he, 'you have had wonderful adventures; but I will tell you something still more astonishing that happened to myself. When I was a young lad I had no home and no one to care for me, and I wandered from village to village all over the country with my knapsack on my back; but as soon as I was old enough I took service with a shepherd in the mountains, and helped him for three years. One autumn evening as we drove the flock homeward ten sheep were missing, and the master bade me go and seek them in the forest. I took my dog with me, but he could find no trace of them, though we searched among the bushes till night fell; and then, as I did not know the country and could not find my way home in the dark, I decided to sleep under a tree. At midnight my dog became uneasy, and began to whine and creep close to me with his tail between his legs; by this I knew that something was wrong, and, looking about, I saw in the bright moonlight a figure standing beside me. It seemed to be a man with shaggy hair, and a long beard which hung down to his knees. He had a garland upon his head, and a girdle of oak-leaves about his body, and carried an uprooted fir-tree in his right hand. I shook like an aspen leaf at the sight, and my spirit quaked for fear. The strange being beckoned with his hand that I should follow him; but as I did not stir from the spot he spoke in a hoarse, grating voice: "Take courage, faint-hearted shepherd. I am the Treasure Seeker of the mountain. If you will come with me you shall dig up much gold."

'Though I was still deadly cold with terror I plucked up my courage and said: "Get away from me, evil spirit; I do not desire your treasures."

'At this the spectre grinned in my face and cried mockingly:

'"Simpleton! Do you scorn your good fortune? Well, then, remain a ragamuffin all your days."

'He turned as if to go away from me, then came back again and said: "Bethink yourself, bethink yourself, rogue. I will fill your knapsack—I will fill your pouch."

'"Away from me, monster," I answered, "I will have nothing to do with you."

'When the apparition saw that I gave no heed to him he ceased to urge me, saying only: "Some day you will rue this," and looked at me sadly. Then he cried: "Listen to what I say, and lay it well to heart, it may be of use to you when you come to your senses. A vast treasure of gold and precious stones lies in safety deep under the earth. At twilight and at high noon it is hidden, but at midnight it may be dug up. For seven hundred years have I watched over it, but now my time has come; it is common property, let him find it who can. So I thought to give it into your hand, having a kindness for you because you feed your flock upon my mountain."

'Thereupon the spectre told me exactly where the treasure lay, and how to find it. It might be only yesterday so well do I remember every word he spoke.

'"Go towards the little mountains," said he, "and ask there for the Black King's Valley, and when you come to a tiny brook follow the stream till you reach the stone

SHEPHERD AND TREASURE SEEKER

bridge beside the saw-mill. Do not cross the bridge, but keep to your right along the bank till a high rock stands before you. A bow-shot from that you will discover a little hollow like a grave. When you find this hollow dig it out; but it will be hard work, for the earth has been pressed down into it with care. Still, work away till you find solid rock on all sides of you, and soon you will come to a square slab of stone; force it out of the wall, and you will stand at the entrance of the treasure house. Into this opening you must crawl, holding a lamp in your mouth. Keep your hands free lest you knock your nose against a stone, for the way is steep and the stones sharp. If it bruises your knees never mind; you are on the road to fortune. Do not rest till you reach a wide stairway, down which you will go till you come out into a spacious hall, in which there are three doors; two of them stand open, the third is fastened with locks and bolts of iron. Do not go through the door to the right lest you disturb the bones of the lords of the treasure. Neither must you go through the door to the left, it leads to the snake's chamber, where adders and serpents lodge; but open the fast-closed door by means of the well-known spring-root, which you must on no account forget to take with you, or all your trouble will be for naught, for no crowbar or mortal tools will help you. If you want to procure the root ask a wood-seller; it is a common thing for hunters to need, and it is not hard to find. If the door bursts open suddenly with great crackings and groanings do not be afraid, the noise is caused by the power of the magic root, and you will not be hurt. Now trim your lamp that it may not fail you, for you will be nearly blinded by the flash and glitter of the gold and precious stones on the walls and pillars of the vault; but beware how you stretch out a hand towards the jewels! In the midst of the cavern stands a copper chest, in that you will find gold and silver, enough and to spare, and you may help yourself to your heart's content. If you take as much as you can carry you will have sufficient to last your lifetime, and you may return three times; but woe betide you if you venture to come a fourth time. You would have your trouble for your pains, and would be punished for your greediness by falling down the stone steps and breaking your leg. Do not neglect each time to heap back the loose earth which concealed the entrance of the king's treasure chamber."

'As the apparition left off speaking my dog pricked up his ears and began to bark. I heard the crack of a carter's whip and the noise of wheels in the distance, and when I looked again the spectre had disappeared.'

So ended the shepherd's tale; and the landlord who was listening with the rest, said shrewdly:

'Tell us now, Father Martin, did you go to the mountain and find what the spirit promised you; or is it a fable?'

'Nay, nay,' answered the greybeard. 'I cannot tell if the spectre lied, for never a step did I go towards finding the hollow, for two reasons:—one was that my neck was too precious for me to risk it in such a snare as that; the other, that no one could ever tell me where the spring-root was to be found.'

Then Blaize, another aged shepherd, lifted up his voice.

''Tis a pity, Father Martin, that your secret has grown old with you. If you had told it forty years ago truly you would not long have been lacking the spring-root. Even though you will never climb the mountain now, I will tell you, for a joke, how it is to be found. The easiest way to get it is by the help of a black woodpecker. Look, in the spring, where she builds her nest in a hole in a tree, and when the time comes for her brood to fly off block up the entrance to the nest with a hard sod, and lurk in ambush behind the tree till the bird returns to feed her nestlings. When she perceives that she cannot get into her nest she will fly round the tree uttering cries of distress, and then dart off towards the sun-setting. When you see her do this, take a scarlet cloak, or if that be lacking to you, buy a few yards of scarlet cloth, and hurry back to the tree before the woodpecker returns with the spring-root in her beak. So soon as she touches with the root the sod that blocks the nest, it will fly violently out of the hole. Then spread the red cloth quickly under the tree, so that the woodpecker may think it is a fire, and in her terror drop the root. Some people really light a fire and strew spikenard blossoms in it; but that is a clumsy method, for if the flames do not shoot up at the right moment away will fly the woodpecker, carrying the root with her.'

The party had listened with interest to this speech, but by the time it was ended the hour was late, and they went their ways homeward, leaving only one man who had sat unheeded in a corner the whole evening through.

Master Peter Bloch had once been a prosperous inn-keeper, and a master-cook; but he had gone steadily down in the world for some time, and was now quite poor.

Formerly he had been a merry fellow, fond of a joke, and in the art of cooking had no equal in the town. He could make fish-jelly, and quince fritters, and even wafer-cakes; and he gilded the ears of all his boars' heads. Peter had looked about him for a wife early in life, but unluckily his choice fell upon a woman whose evil tongue was well known in the town. Ilse was hated by every-body, and the young folks would go miles out of their way rather than meet her, for she had some ill-word for every-one. Therefore, when Master Peter came along, and let himself be taken in by her boasted skill as a housewife, she jumped at his offer, and they were married the next day. But they had not got home before they began to quarrel. In the joy of his heart Peter had tasted freely of his own good wine, and as the bride hung upon his arm he stumbled and fell, dragging her down with him; whereupon she beat him soundly, and the neighbours said truly that things did not promise well for Master Peter's comfort. Even when the ill-matched couple were presently blessed with children, his happiness was but short-lived, the savage temper of his quarrelsome wife seemed to blight them from the first, and they died like little kids in a cold winter.

Though Master Peter had no great wealth to leave behind him, still it was sad to him to be childless; and he would bemoan himself to his friends, when he laid one baby after another in the grave, saying: 'The lightning has been among the cherry-blossoms again, so there will be no fruit to grow ripe.'

But, by-and-by, he had a little daughter so strong and healthy that neither her mother's temper nor her father's spoiling could keep her from growing up tall and beautiful. Meanwhile the fortunes of the family had changed. From his youth up, Master Peter had hated trouble; when he had money he spent it freely, and fed all the hungry folk who asked him for bread. If his pockets were empty he borrowed of his neighbours, but he always took good care to prevent his scolding wife from finding out that he had done so. His motto was: 'It will all come right in the end'; but what it did come to was ruin for Master Peter. He was at his wits' end to know how to earn an honest living, for try as he might ill-luck seemed to pursue him, and he lost one post after another, till at last all he could do was to carry sacks of corn to the mill for his wife, who scolded him well if he was slow about it, and grudged him his portion of food.

This grieved the tender heart of his pretty daughter, who loved him dearly, and was the comfort of his life.

Peter was thinking of her as he sat in the inn kitchen and heard the shepherds talking about the buried treasure, and for her sake he resolved to go and seek for it. Before he rose from the landlord's arm-chair his plan was made, and Master Peter went home more joyful and full of hope than he had been for many a long day; but on the way he suddenly remembered that he was not yet possessed of the magic spring-root, and he stole into the house with a heavy heart, and threw himself down upon his hard straw bed. He could neither sleep nor rest; but as soon as it was light he got up and wrote down exactly all that was to be done to find the treasure, that he might not forget anything, and when it lay clear and plain before his eyes he comforted himself with the thought that, though he must do the rough work for his wife during one more winter at least, he would not have to tread the path to the mill for the rest of his life. Soon he heard his wife's harsh voice singing its morning song as she went about her household affairs, scolding her daughter the while. She burst open his door while he was still dressing: 'Well, Toper!' was her greeting, 'have you been drinking all night, wasting money that you steal from my housekeeping? For shame, drunkard!'

Master Peter, who was well used to this sort of talk, did not disturb himself, but waited till the storm blew over, then he said calmly:

'Do not be annoyed, dear wife. I have a good piece of business in hand which may turn out well for us.'

'*You* with a good business?' cried she, 'you are good for nothing but talk!'

'I am making my will,' said he, 'that when my hour comes my house may be in order.'

These unexpected words cut his daughter to the heart; she remembered that all night long she had dreamed of a newly dug grave, and at this thought she broke out into loud lamentations. But her mother only cried: 'Wretch! have you not wasted goods and possessions, and now do you talk of making a will?'

And she seized him like a fury, and tried to scratch out his eyes. But by-and-by the quarrel was patched up, and everything went on as before. From that day Peter saved up every penny that his daughter Lucia gave him on the sly, and bribed the boys of his acquaintance to spy out a black woodpecker's nest for him. He sent them into the woods and fields, but instead of looking for a nest they only played pranks on him. They led him miles over hill and vale, stock and stone, to find a raven's brood, or a nest of squirrels in a hollow tree, and when he was angry with them they laughed in his face and ran away. This went on for some time, but at last one of the boys spied out a woodpecker in the meadow-lands among the wood-pigeons, and when he had found her nest in a half-dead alder tree, came running to Peter with the news of his discovery. Peter could hardly believe his good fortune, and went quickly to see for himself if it was really true; and when he reached the tree there certainly was a bird flying in and out as if she had a nest in it. Peter was overjoyed at this fortunate discovery, and instantly set himself to obtain a red cloak. Now in the whole town there was only one red cloak, and that belonged to a man of whom nobody ever willingly asked a favour—Master Hammerling the hangman. It cost Master Peter many struggles before he could bring himself to visit such a person, but there was no help for it, and, little as he liked it, he ended by making his request to the hangman, who was flattered that so respectable a man as Peter should borrow his robe of office, and willingly lent it to him.

Peter now had all that was necessary to secure the magic root; he stopped up the entrance to the nest, and everything fell out exactly as Blaize had foretold. As soon as the woodpecker came back with the root in her beak out rushed Master Peter from behind the tree and displayed the fiery red cloak so adroitly that the terrified bird dropped the root just where it could be easily seen. All Peter's plans had succeeded, and he actually held in his hand the magic root—that master-key which would unlock all doors, and bring its possessor unheard-of luck. His thoughts now turned to the mountain, and he secretly made preparations for his journey. He took with him only a staff, a strong sack, and a little box which his daughter Lucia had given him.

It happened that on the very day Peter had chosen for setting out, Lucia and her mother went off early to the town, leaving him to guard the house; but in spite of that he was on the point of taking his departure when it occurred to him that it might be as well first to test the much-vaunted powers of the magic root for himself. Dame Ilse had a strong cupboard with seven locks built into the wall of her room, in which she kept all the money she had saved, and she wore the key of it always hung about her neck. Master Peter had no control at all of the money affairs of the household, so the contents of this secret hoard were quite unknown to him, and this seemed to be a good opportunity for finding out what they were. He held the magic root to the key-hole, and to his astonishment heard all the seven locks creaking and turning, the door flew suddenly wide open, and his greedy wife's store of gold pieces lay before his eyes. He stood still in sheer amazement, not knowing which to rejoice over most—this unexpected find, or the proof of the magic root's real power; but at last he remembered that it was quite time to be starting on his journey. So, filling his pockets with the gold, he carefully locked the empty cupboard again and left the house without further delay. When Dame Ilse and her daughter returned they wondered to find the house door shut, and Master Peter nowhere to be seen. They knocked and called, but nothing stirred within but the house cat, and at last the blacksmith had to be fetched to open the door. Then the house was searched from garret to cellar, but no Master Peter was to be found.

'Who knows?' cried Dame Ilse at last, 'the wretch may have been idling in some tavern since early morning.'

Then a sudden thought startled her, and she felt for

her keys. Suppose they had fallen into her good-for-nothing husband's hands and he had helped himself to her treasure! But no, the keys were safe in their usual place, and the cupboard looked quite untouched. Mid-day came, then evening, then midnight, and still no Master Peter appeared, and the matter became really serious. Dame Ilse knew right well what a torment she had been to her husband, and remorse caused her the gloomiest forebodings.

'Ah! Lucia,' she cried, 'I greatly fear that your father has done himself a mischief.' And they sat till morning weeping over their own fancies.

As soon as it was light they searched every corner of the house again, and examined every nail in the wall and every beam; but, luckily, Master Peter was not hanging from any of them. After that the neighbours went out with long poles to fish in every ditch and pond, but they found nothing, and then Dame Ilse gave up the idea of ever seeing her husband again and very soon consoled herself, only wondering how the sacks of corn were to be carried to the mill in future. She decided to buy a strong ass to do the work, and having chosen one, and after some bargaining with the owner as to its price, she went to the cupboard in the wall to fetch the money. But what were her feelings when she perceived that every shelf lay empty and bare before her! For a moment she stood bewildered, then broke into such frightful ravings that Lucia ran to her in alarm; but as soon as she heard of the disappearance of the money she was heartily glad, and no longer feared that her father had come to any harm, but understood that he must have gone out into the world to seek his fortune in some new way.

About a month after this, someone knocked at Dame Ilse's door one day, and she went to see if it was a customer for meal; but in stepped a handsome young man, dressed like a duke's son, who greeted her respectfully, and asked after her pretty daughter as if he were an old friend, though she could not remember having ever set eyes upon him before.

However, she invited him to step into the house and be seated while he unfolded his business. With a great air of mystery he begged permission to speak to the fair Lucia, of whose skill in needlework he had heard so much, as he had a commission to give her. Dame Ilse had her own opinion as to what kind of commission it was likely to be—brought by a young stranger to a pretty maiden; however, as the meeting would be under her own eye, she made no objection, but called to her industrious daughter, who left off working and came obediently; but when she saw the stranger she stopped short, blushing, and casting down her eyes. He looked at her fondly, and took her hand, which she tried to draw away, crying:

'Ah! Friedlin, why are you here? I thought you were a hundred miles away. Are you come to grieve me again?'

'No, dearest girl,' answered he; 'I am come to complete your happiness and my own. Since we last met my fortune has utterly changed; I am no longer the poor vagabond that I was then. My rich uncle has died, leaving me money and goods in plenty, so that I dare to present myself to your mother as a suitor for your hand. That I love you I know well; if you can love me I am indeed a happy man.'

Lucia's pretty blue eyes had looked up shyly as he spoke, and now a smile parted her rosy lips; and she stole a glance at her mother to see what she thought about it all; but the dame stood lost in amazement to find that her daughter, whom she could have declared had never been out of her sight, was already well acquainted with the handsome stranger, and quite willing to be his bride. Before she had done staring, this hasty wooer had smoothed his way by covering the shining table with gold pieces as a wedding gift to the bride's mother, and had filled Lucia's apron into the bargain; after which the dame made no difficulties, and the matter was speedily settled.

While Ilse gathered up the gold and hid it away safely, the lovers whispered together, and what Friedlin told her seemed to make Lucia every moment more happy and contented.

Now a great hurly-burly began in the house, and preparations for the wedding went on apace. A few days later a heavily laden waggon drove up, and out of it came so many boxes and bales that Dame Ilse was lost in wonder at the wealth of her future son-in-law. The day for the wedding was chosen, and all their friends and neighbours were bidden to the feast. As Lucia was trying on her bridal wreath she said to her mother: 'This wedding-garland would please me indeed if father Peter could lead me to the church. If only he could come back again! Here we are rolling in riches while he may be nibbling at hunger's table.' And the very idea of such a thing made her weep, while even Dame Ilse said:

'I should not be sorry myself to see him come back—there is always something lacking in a house when the good man is away.'

But the fact was that she was growing quite tired of having no one to scold. And what do you think happened?

On the very eve of the wedding a man pushing a wheelbarrow arrived at the city gate, and paid toll upon a barrel of nails which it contained, and then made the best of his way to the bride's dwelling and knocked at the door.

The bride herself peeped out of the window to see who it could be, and there stood father Peter! Then there was great rejoicing in the house; Lucia ran to embrace him, and even Dame Ilse held out her hand in welcome, and only said: 'Rogue, mend your ways,' when she remembered the empty treasure cupboard. Father Peter greeted the bridegroom, looking at him shrewdly, while the mother and daughter hastened to say all they knew in his favour, and appeared to be satisfied with him as a son-in-law. When Dame Ilse had set something to eat before her husband, she was curious to hear his adventures, and questioned him eagerly as to why he had gone away.

'God bless my native place,' said he. 'I have been marching through the country, and have tried every kind of work, but now I have found a job in the iron trade; only, so far, I have put more into it than I have earned by it. This barrel of nails is my whole fortune, which I wish to give as my contribution towards the bride's house furnishing.'

This speech roused Dame Ilse to anger, and she broke out into such shrill reproaches that the bystanders were fairly deafened, and Friedlin hastily offered Master Peter a home with Lucia and himself, promising that he should live in comfort, and be always welcome. So Lucia had her heart's desire, and father Peter led her to the church next day, and the marriage took place very happily. Soon afterwards the young people settled in a fine house which Friedlin had bought, and had a garden and meadows, a fishpond, and a hill covered with vines, and were as happy as the day was long. Father Peter also stayed quietly with them, living, as everybody believed, upon the generosity of his rich son-in law. No one suspected that his barrel of nails was the real 'Horn of Plenty,' from which all this prosperity overflowed.

Peter had made the journey to the treasure mountain successfully, without being found out by anybody. He had enjoyed himself by the way, and taken his own time, until he actually reached the little brook in the valley which it had cost him some trouble to find. Then he pressed on eagerly, and soon came to the little hollow in the wood; down he went, burrowing like a mole into the earth; the magic root did its work, and at last the treasure lay before his eyes. You may imagine how gaily Peter filled his sack with as much gold as he could carry, and how he staggered up the seventy-seven steps with a heart full of hope and delight. He did not quite trust the gnome's promises of safety, and was in such haste to find himself once more in the light of day that he looked neither to the right nor the left, and could not afterwards remember whether the walls and pillars had sparkled with jewels or not.

However, all went well—he neither saw nor heard anything alarming; the only thing that happened was that the great iron-barred door shut with a crash as soon as he was fairly outside it, and then he remembered that he had left the magic root behind him, so he could not go back for another load of treasure. But even that did not trouble Peter much; he was quite satisfied with what he had already. After he had faithfully done everything according to Father Martin's instructions, and pressed the earth well back into the hollow, he sat down to consider how he could bring his treasure back to his native place, and enjoy it there, without being forced to share it with his scolding wife, who would give him no peace if she once found out about it. At last, after much thinking, he hit upon a plan. He carried his sack to the nearest village, and there bought a wheelbarrow, a strong barrel, and a quantity of nails. Then he packed his gold into the barrel, covered it well with a layer of nails, hoisted it on to the wheelbarrow with some difficulty, and set off with it upon his homeward way. At one place upon the road he met a handsome young man who seemed by his downcast air to be in some great trouble. Father Peter, who wished everybody to be as happy as he was himself, greeted him cheerfully, and asked where he was going, to which he answered sadly:

'Into the wide world, good father, or out of it, wherever my feet may chance to carry me.'

'Why out of it?' said Peter. 'What has the world been doing to you?'

'It has done nothing to me, nor I to it,' he replied. 'Nevertheless there is not anything left in it for me.'

Father Peter did his best to cheer the young man up, and invited him to sup with him at the first inn they came to, thinking that perhaps hunger and poverty were causing the stranger's trouble. But when good food was set before him he seemed to forget to eat. So Peter perceived that what ailed his guest was sorrow of heart, and asked him kindly to tell him his story.

'Where is the good, father?' said he. 'You can give me neither help nor comfort.'

'Who knows?' answered Master Peter. 'I might be able to do something for you. Often enough in life help comes to us from the most unexpected quarter.'

The young man, thus encouraged, began his tale.

'I am,' said he, 'a crossbow-man in the service of a noble count, in whose castle I was brought up. Not long ago my master went on a journey, and brought back with him, amongst other treasures, the portrait of a fair maiden so sweet and lovely that I lost my heart at first sight of it, and could think of nothing but how I might seek her out and marry her. The count had told me her name, and where she lived, but laughed at my love, and absolutely refused to give me leave to go in search of her, so I was forced to run away from the castle by night. I soon reached the little town where the maiden dwelt; but there fresh difficulties awaited me. She lived under the care of her mother, who was so severe that she was never allowed to look out of the window, or set her foot outside the door alone, and how to make friends with her I did not know. But at last I dressed myself as an old woman, and knocked boldly at her door. The lovely maiden herself opened it, and so charmed me that I came near forgetting my disguise; but I soon recovered my wits, and begged her to work a fine table-cloth for me, for she is reported to be the best needlewoman in all the country round. Now I was free to go and see her often under the pretence of seeing how the work was going on, and one day, when her mother had gone to the town, I ventured to throw off my disguise, and tell her of my love. She was startled at first; but I persuaded her to listen to me, and I soon saw that I was not displeasing to her, though she scolded me gently for my disobedience to my master, and my deceit in disguising myself. But when I begged her to marry me, she told me sadly that her mother would scorn a penniless wooer, and implored me to go away at once, lest trouble should fall upon her.

'Bitter as it was to me, I was forced to go when she bade me, and I have wandered about ever since, with grief gnawing at my heart; for how can a masterless man, without money or goods, ever hope to win the lovely Lucia?'

Master Peter, who had been listening attentively, pricked up his ears at the sound of his daughter's name, and very soon found out that it was indeed with her that this young man was so deeply in love.

'Your story is strange indeed,' said he. 'But where is the father of this maiden—why do you not ask him for her hand? He might well take your part, and be glad to have you for his son-in-law.'

'Alas!' said the young man, 'her father is a wandering good-for-naught, who has forsaken wife and child, and gone off—who knows where? The wife complains of him bitterly enough, and scolds my dear maiden when she takes her father's part.'

Father Peter was somewhat amused by this speech; but he liked the young man well, and saw that he was the very person he needed to enable him to enjoy his wealth in peace, without being separated from his dear daughter.

'If you will take my advice,' said he, 'I promise you that you shall marry this maiden whom you love so much, and that before you are many days older.'

'Comrade,' cried Friedlin indignantly, for he thought

Peter did but jest with him, 'it is ill done to mock at an unhappy man; you had better find someone else who will let himself be taken in with your fine promises.' And up he sprang, and was going off hastily, when Master Peter caught him by the arm.

'Stay, hothead!' he cried; 'it is no jest, and I am prepared to make good my words.'

Thereupon he showed him the treasure hidden under the nails, and unfolded to him his plan, which was that Friedlin should play the part of the rich son-in-law, and keep a still tongue, that they might enjoy their wealth together in peace.

The young man was overjoyed at this sudden change in his fortunes, and did not know how to thank father Peter for his generosity. They took the road again at dawn the next morning, and soon reached a town, where Friedlin equipped himself as a gallant wooer should. Father Peter filled his pockets with gold for the wedding dowry, and agreed with him that when all was settled he should secretly send him word that Peter might send off the waggon load of house plenishings with which the rich bridegroom was to make such a stir in the little town where the bride lived. As they parted, father Peter's last commands to Friedlin were to guard well their secret, and not even to tell it to Lucia till she was his wife.

Master Peter long enjoyed the profits of his journey to the mountain, and no rumour of it ever got abroad. In his old age his prosperity was so great that he himself did not know how rich he was; but it was always supposed that the money was Friedlin's. He and his beloved wife lived in the greatest happiness and peace, and rose to great honour in the town. And to this day, when the citizens wish to describe a wealthy man, they say: 'As rich as Peter Bloch's son-in-law!'

THE COTTAGER AND HIS CAT

ONCE upon a time there lived an old man and his wife in a dirty, tumble-down cottage, not very far from the splendid palace where the king and queen dwelt. In spite of the wretched state of the hut, which many people declared was too bad even for a pig to live in, the old man was very rich, for he was a great miser, and lucky besides, and would often go without food all day sooner than change one of his beloved gold pieces.

But after a while he found that he had starved himself once too often. He fell ill, and had no strength to get well again, and in a few days he died, leaving his wife and one son behind him.

The night following his death, the son dreamed that an unknown man appeared to him and said: 'Listen to me; your father is dead and your mother will soon die, and all their riches will belong to you. Half of his wealth is ill-gotten, and this you must give back to the poor from whom he squeezed it. The other half you must throw into the sea. Watch, however, as the money sinks into the water, and if anything should swim, catch it and keep it, even if it is nothing more than a bit of paper.'

Then the man vanished, and the youth awoke.

The remembrance of his dream troubled him greatly. He did not want to part with the riches that his father had left him, for he had known all his life what it was to be cold and hungry, and now he had hoped for a little comfort and pleasure. Still, he was honest and good-hearted, and if his father had come wrongfully by his wealth he felt he could never enjoy it, and at last he made up his mind to do as he had been bidden. He found out who were the people who were poorest in the village, and spent half of his money in helping them, and the other half he put in his pocket. From a rock that jutted right out into the sea he flung it in. In a moment it was out of sight, and no man could have told the spot where it had sunk, except for a tiny scrap of paper floating on the water. He stretched down carefully and managed to reach it, and on opening it found six shillings wrapped inside. This was now all the money he had in the world.

The young man stood and looked at it thoughtfully. 'Well, I can't do much with this,' he said to himself; but, after all, six shillings were better than nothing, and he wrapped them up again and slipped them into his coat.

He worked in his garden for the next few weeks, and he and his mother contrived to live on the fruit and vegetables he got out of it, and then she too died suddenly. The poor fellow felt very sad when he had laid her in her grave, and with a heavy heart he wandered into the forest, not knowing where he was going. By-and-by he began to get hungry, and seeing a small hut in front of him, he knocked at the door and asked if they could give him some milk. The old woman who opened it begged him to come in, adding kindly, that if he wanted a night's lodging he might have it without its costing him anything.

Two women and three men were at supper when he entered, and silently made room for him to sit down by them. When he had eaten he began to look about him, and was surprised to see an animal sitting by the fire different from anything he had ever noticed before. It was grey in colour, and not very big; but its eyes were large and very bright, and it seemed to be singing in an odd way, quite unlike any animal in the forest. 'What is the name of that strange little creature?' asked he. And they answered, 'We call it a cat.'

'I should like to buy it—if it is not too dear,' said the young man; 'it would be company for me.' And they told him that he might have it for six shillings, if he cared to give so much. The young man took out his precious bit of paper, handed them the six shillings, and the next morning bade them farewell, with the cat lying snugly in his cloak.

For the whole day they wandered through meadows and forests, till in the evening they reached a house. The young fellow knocked at the door and asked the old man who opened it if he could rest there that night, adding that he had no money to pay for it. 'Then I must give it to you,' answered the man, and led him into a room where two women and two men were sitting at supper. One of the women was the old man's wife, the other his daughter. He placed the cat on the mantel-shelf, and they all crowded round to examine this strange beast, and the cat rubbed itself against them, and held out its paw, and sang to them; and the women were delighted, and gave it everything that a cat could eat, and a great deal more besides.

After hearing the youth's story, and how he had nothing in the world left him except his cat, the old man advised him to go to the palace, which was only a few miles distant, and take counsel of the king, who was kind to everyone, and would certainly be his friend. The young man thanked him, and said he would gladly take his advice; and early next morning he set out for the royal palace.

He sent a message to the king to beg for an audience, and received a reply that he was to go into the great hall, where he would find his Majesty.

The king was at dinner with his court when the young man entered, and he signed to him to come near. The youth bowed low, and then gazed in surprise at the crowd of little black creatures who were running about the floor, and even on the table itself. Indeed, they were so bold that they snatched pieces of food from the King's own plate, and if he drove them away, tried to bite his hands, so that he could not eat his food, and his courtiers fared no better.

'What sort of animals are these?' asked the youth of one of the ladies sitting near him.

'They are called rats,' answered the king, who had overheard the question, 'and for years we have tried some way of putting an end to them, but it is impossible. They come into our very beds.'

At this moment something was seen flying through the air. The cat was on the table, and with two or three shakes a number of rats were lying dead round him. Then a great scuffling of feet was heard, and in a few minutes the hall was clear.

For some minutes the King and his courtiers only looked at each other in astonishment. 'What kind of animal is that which can work magic of this sort?' asked he. And the young man told him that it was called a cat, and that he had bought it for six shillings.

And the King answered: 'Because of the luck you have brought me, in freeing my palace from the plague which has tormented me for many years, I will give you the choice of two things. Either you shall be my Prime Minister, or else you shall marry my daughter and reign after me. Say, which shall it be?'

'The princess and the kingdom,' said the young man.

And so it was.

[From *Isländische Märchen.*]

THE PRINCE WHO WOULD SEEK IMMORTALITY

Once upon a time, in the very middle of the middle of a large kingdom, there was a town, and in the town a palace, and in the palace a king. This king had one son whom his father thought was wiser and cleverer than any son ever was before, and indeed his father had spared no pains to make him so. He had been very careful in choosing his tutors and governors when he was a boy, and when he became a youth he sent him to travel, so that he might see the ways of other people, and find that they were often as good as his own.

It was now a year since the prince had returned home, for his father felt that it was time that his son should learn how to rule the kingdom which would one day be his. But during his long absence the prince seemed to have changed his character altogether. From being a merry and light-hearted boy, he had grown into a gloomy and thoughtful man. The king knew of nothing that could have produced such an alteration. He vexed himself about it from morning till night, till at length an explanation occurred to him—the young man was in love!

Now the prince never talked about his feelings—for the matter of that he scarcely talked at all; and the father knew that if he was to come to the bottom of the prince's dismal face, he would have to begin. So one day, after dinner, he took his son by the arm and led him into another room, hung entirely with the pictures of beautiful maidens, each one more lovely than the other.

'My dear boy,' he said, 'you are very sad; perhaps after all your wanderings it is dull for you here all alone with me. It would be much better if you would marry, and I have collected here the portraits of the most beautiful women in the world of a rank equal to your own. Choose which among them you would like for a wife, and I will send an embassy to her father to ask for her hand.'

'Alas! your Majesty,' answered the prince, 'it is not love or marriage that makes me so gloomy; but the thought, which haunts me day and night, that all men, even kings, must die. Never shall I be happy again till I have found a kingdom where death is unknown. And I have determined to give myself no rest till I have discovered the Land of Immortality.

The old king heard him with dismay; things were worse than he thought. He tried to reason with his son, and told him that during all these years he had been looking forward to his return, in order to resign his throne and its cares, which pressed so heavily upon him. But it was in vain that he talked; the prince would listen to nothing, and the following morning buckled on his sword and set forth on his journey.

He had been travelling for many days, and had left his fatherland behind him, when close to the road he came upon a huge tree, and on its topmost bough an eagle was sitting shaking the branches with all his might. This seemed so strange and so unlike an eagle, that the prince stood still with surprise, and the bird saw him and flew to the ground. The moment its feet touched the ground he changed into a king.

'Why do you look so astonished?' he asked.

'I was wondering why you shook the boughs so fiercely,' answered the prince.

'I am condemned to do this, for neither I nor any of

my kindred can die till I have rooted up this great tree,' replied the king of the eagles. 'But it is now evening, and I need work no more to-day. Come to my house with me, and be my guest for the night.'

The prince accepted gratefully the eagle's invitation, for he was tired and hungry. They were received at the palace by the king's beautiful daughter, who gave orders that dinner should be laid for them at once. While they were eating, the eagle questioned his guest about his travels, and if he was wandering for pleasure's sake, or with any special aim. Then the prince told him everything, and how he could never turn back till he had discovered the Land of Immortality.

'Dear brother,' said the eagle, 'you have discovered it already, and it rejoices my heart to think that you will stay with us. Have you not just heard me say that death has no power either over myself or any of my kindred till that great tree is rooted up? It will take me six hundred years' hard work to do that; so marry my daughter and let us all live happily together here. After all, six hundred years is an eternity!'

'Ah, dear king,' replied the young man, 'your offer is very tempting! But at the end of six hundred years we should have to die, so we should be no better off! No, I must go on till I find the country where there is no death at all.'

Then the princess spoke, and tried to persuade the guest to change his mind, but he sorrowfully shook his head. At length, seeing that his resolution was firmly fixed, she took from a cabinet a little box which contained her picture, and gave it to him saying:

'As you will not stay with us, prince, accept this box, which will sometimes recall us to your memory. If you are tired of travelling before you come to the Land of Immortality, open this box and look at my picture, and you will be borne along either on earth or in the air, quick as thought, or swift as the whirlwind.'

The prince thanked her for her gift, which he placed in his tunic, and sorrowfully bade the eagle and his daughter farewell.

Never was any present in the world as useful as that

The Baldheaded Man on The Mountain

little box, and many times did he bless the kind thought of the princess. One evening it had carried him to the top of a high mountain, where he saw a man with a bald head, busily engaged in digging up spadefuls of earth and throwing them in a basket. When the basket was full he took it away and returned with an empty one, which he likewise filled. The prince stood and watched him for a little, till the bald-headed man looked up and said to him: 'Dear brother, what surprises you so much?'

'I was wondering why you were filling the basket,' replied the prince.

'Oh!' replied the man, 'I am condemned to do this, for neither I nor any of my family can die till I have dug away the whole of this mountain and made it level with the plain. But, come, it is almost dark, and I shall work no longer.' And he plucked a leaf from a tree close by, and from a rough digger he was changed into a stately bald-headed king. 'Come home with me,' he added; 'you must be tired and hungry, and my daughter will have supper ready for us.' The prince accepted gladly, and they went back to the palace, where the bald-headed king's daughter, who was still more beautiful than the other princess, welcomed them at the door and led the way into a large hall and to a table covered with silver dishes. While they were eating, the bald-headed king asked the prince how he had happened to wander so far, and the young man told him all about it, and how he was seeking the Land of Immortality. 'You have found it already,' answered the king, 'for, as I said, neither I nor my family can die till I have levelled this great mountain; and that will take full eight hundred years longer. Stay here with us and marry my daughter. Eight hundred years is surely long enough to live.'

'Oh, certainly,' answered the prince; 'but, all the same, I would rather go and seek the land where there is no death at all.'

So next morning he bade them farewell, though the

princess begged him to stay with all her might; and when she found that she could not persuade him she gave him as a remembrance a gold ring. This ring was still more useful than the box, because when one wished oneself at any place one was there directly, without even the trouble of flying to it through the air. The prince put it on his finger, and thanking her heartily, went his way.

He walked on for some distance, and then he recollected the ring and thought he would try if the princess had spoken truly as to its powers. 'I wish I was at the end of the world,' he said, shutting his eyes, and when he opened them he was standing in a street full of marble palaces. The men who passed him were tall and strong, and their clothes were magnificent. He stopped some of them and asked in all the twenty-seven languages he knew what was the name of the city, but no one answered him. Then his heart sank within him; what should he do in this strange place if nobody could understand anything? he said. Suddenly his eyes fell upon a man dressed after the fashion of his native country, and he ran up to him and spoke to him in his own tongue. 'What city is this, my friend?' he inquired.

'It is the capital city of the Blue Kingdom,' replied the man, 'but the king himself is dead, and his daughter is now the ruler.'

With this news the prince was satisfied, and begged his countryman to show him the way to the young queen's palace. The man led him through several streets into a large square, one side of which was occupied by a splendid building that seemed borne up on slender pillars of soft green marble. In front was a flight of steps, and on these the queen was sitting wrapped in a veil of shining silver mist, listening to the complaints of her people and dealing out justice. When the prince came up she saw directly that he was no ordinary man, and telling her chamberlain to dismiss the rest of her petitioners for that day, she signed to the prince to follow her into the palace. Luckily she had been taught his language as a child, so they had no difficulty in talking together.

The prince told all his story and how he was journeying in search of the Land of Immortality. When he had finished, the princess, who had listened attentively, rose, and taking his arm, led him to the door of another room, the floor of which was made entirely of needles, stuck so close together that there was not room for a single needle more.

'Prince,' she said, turning to him, 'you see these needles? Well, know that neither I nor any of my family can die till I have worn out these needles in sewing. It will take at least a thousand years for that. Stay here, and share my throne; a thousand years is long enough to live!'

'Certainly,' answered he; 'still, at the end of the thousand years I should have to die! No, I must find the land where there is no death.'

The queen did all she could to persuade him to stay, but as her words proved useless, at length she gave it up. Then she said to him: 'As you will not stay, take this little golden rod as a remembrance of me. It has the power to become anything you wish it to be, when you are in need.'

So the prince thanked her, and putting the rod in his pocket, went his way.

Scarcely had he left the town behind him when he came to a broad river which no man might pass, for he was standing at the end of the world, and this was the river which flowed round it. Not knowing what to do next, he walked a little distance up the bank, and there, over his head, a beautiful city was floating in the air. He longed to get to it, but how? neither road nor bridge was anywhere to be seen, yet the city drew him upwards, and he felt that here at last was the country which he sought. Suddenly he remembered the golden rod which

HOW THE PRINCE ARRIVED AT THE CITY OF IMMORTALITY

the mist-veiled queen had given him. With a beating heart he flung it to the ground, wishing with all his might that it should turn into a bridge, and fearing that, after all, this might prove beyond its power. But no, instead of the rod, there stood a golden ladder, leading straight up to the city of the air. He was about to enter the golden gates, when there sprang at him a wondrous beast, whose like he had never seen. 'Out sword from the sheath,' cried the prince, springing back with a cry. And the sword leapt from the scabbard and cut off some of the monster's heads, but others grew again directly, so that the prince, pale with terror, stood where he was, calling for help, and put his sword back in the sheath again.

The queen of the city heard the noise and looked from her window to see what was happening. Summoning one of her servants, she bade him go and rescue the stranger, and bring him to her. The prince thankfully obeyed her orders, and entered her presence.

The moment she looked at him, the queen also felt that he was no ordinary man, and she welcomed him graciously, and asked him what had brought him to the city. In answer the prince told all his story, and how he had travelled long and far in search of the Land of Immortality.

'You have found it,' said she, 'for I am queen over life and over death. Here you can dwell among the immortals.'

A thousand years had passed since the prince first entered the city, but they had flown so fast that the time seemed no more than six months. There had not been one instant of the thousand years that the prince was not happy till one night when he dreamed of his father and mother. Then the longing for his home came upon him with a rush, and in the morning he told the Queen of the Immortals that he must go and see his father and mother once more. The queen stared at him with amazement, and cried: 'Why, prince, are you out of your senses? It is more than eight hundred years since your father and mother died! There will not even be their dust remaining.'

'I must go all the same,' said he.

'Well, do not be in a hurry,' continued the queen, understanding that he would not be prevented. 'Wait till I make some preparations for your journey.' So she unlocked her great treasure chest, and took out two beautiful flasks, one of gold and one of silver, which she hung round his neck. Then she showed him a little trap-door in one corner of the room, and said: 'Fill the silver flask with this water, which is below the trap-door. It is enchanted, and whoever you sprinkle with the water will become a dead man at once, even if he had lived a thousand years. The golden flask you must fill with the water here,' she added, pointing to a well in another corner. 'It springs from the rock of eternity; you have only to sprinkle a few drops on a body and it will come to life again, if it had been a thousand years dead.'

The prince thanked the queen for her gifts, and, bidding her farewell, went on his journey.

He soon arrived in the town where the mist-veiled queen reigned in her palace, but the whole city had changed, and he could scarcely find his way through the streets. In the palace itself all was still, and he wandered through the rooms without meeting anyone to stop him. At last he entered the queen's own chamber, and there she lay, with her embroidery still in her hands, fast asleep. He pulled at her dress, but she did not waken. Then a dreadful idea came over him, and he ran to the chamber where the needles had been kept, but it was quite empty. The queen had broken the last over the work she held in her hand, and with it the spell was broken too, and she lay dead.

Quick as thought the prince pulled out the golden flask, and sprinkled some drops of the water over the queen. In a moment she moved gently, and raising her head, opened her eyes.

'Oh, my dear friend, I am so glad you wakened me; I must have slept a long while!'

'You would have slept till eternity,' answered the prince, 'if I had not been here to waken you.'

At these words the queen remembered about the needles. She knew now that she had been dead, and that the prince had restored her to life. She gave him thanks from her heart for what he had done, and vowed she would repay him if she ever got a chance.

The prince took his leave, and set out for the country of the bald-headed king. As he drew near the place he saw that the whole mountain had been dug away, and that the king was lying dead on the ground, his spade and bucket beside him. But as soon as the water from the golden flask touched him he yawned and stretched himself, and slowly rose to his feet. 'Oh, my dear friend, I am so glad to see you,' cried he, 'I must have slept a long while!'

'You would have slept till eternity if I had not been here to waken you,' answered the prince. And the king remembered the mountain, and the spell, and vowed to repay the service if he ever had a chance.

Further along the road which led to his old home the prince found the great tree torn up by its roots, and the king of the eagles sitting dead on the ground, with his wings outspread as if for flight. A flutter ran through the feathers as the drops of water fell on them, and the eagle lifted his beak from the ground and said: 'Oh, how long I must have slept! How can I thank you for having awakened me, my dear, good friend!'

'You would have slept till eternity if I had not been here to waken you'; answered the prince. Then the king remembered about the tree, and knew that he had been dead, and promised, if ever he had the chance, to repay what the prince had done for him.

At last he reached the capital of his father's kingdom, but on reaching the place where the royal palace had stood, instead of the marble galleries where he used to play, there lay a great sulphur lake, its blue flames darting into the air. How was he to find his father and mother, and bring them back to life, if they were lying at the bottom of that horrible water? He turned away sadly and wandered back into the streets, hardly knowing where he was going; when a voice behind him cried: 'Stop, prince, I have caught you at last! It is a thousand years since I first began to seek you.' And there beside him stood the old, white-bearded, figure of Death. Swiftly he drew the ring from his finger, and the king of the eagles, the bald-headed king, and the mist-veiled queen, hastened to his rescue. In an instant they had seized upon Death and held him tight, till the prince should have time to reach the Land of Immortality. But they did not know how quickly Death could fly, and the prince had only one foot across the border, when he felt the other grasped from behind, and the voice of Death calling: 'Halt! now you are mine.'

The Queen of the Immortals was watching from her window, and cried to Death that he had no power in her kingdom, and that he must seek his prey elsewhere.

'Quite true,' answered Death; 'but his foot is in *my* kingdom, and that belongs to me!'

'At any rate half of him is mine,' replied the Queen, 'and what good can the other half do you? Half a man is no use, either to you or to me! But this once I will allow you to cross into my kingdom, and we will decide by a wager whose he is.'

And so it was settled. Death stepped across the narrow line that surrounds the Land of Immortality, and the queen proposed the wager which was to decide the prince's fate. 'I will throw him up into the sky,' she said, 'right to the back of the morning star, and if he falls down into this city, then he is mine. But if he should fall outside the walls, he shall belong to you.'

In the middle of the city was a great open square, and here the queen wished the wager to take place. When all was ready, she put her foot under the foot of the prince and swung him into the air. Up, up, he went, high amongst the stars, and no man's eyes could follow him. Had she thrown him up straight? the queen wondered anxiously, for, if not, he would fall outside the walls, and she would lose him for ever. The moments seemed long while she and Death stood gazing up into the air, waiting to know whose prize the prince would be. Suddenly they both caught sight of a tiny speck no bigger than a wasp, right up in the blue. Was he coming straight? No! Yes! But as he was nearing the city, a light wind sprang up, and swayed him in the direction of the wall. Another second and he would have fallen half over it, when the queen sprang forward, seized him in her arms, and flung him into the castle. Then she commanded her servants to cast Death out of the city, which they did, with such hard blows that he never dared to show his face again in the Land of Immortality.

[From *Ungarischen Völksmärchen.*]

THE STONE-CUTTER

Once upon a time there lived a stone-cutter, who went every day to a great rock in the side of a big mountain and cut out slabs for gravestones or for houses. He understood very well the kinds of stones wanted for the different purposes, and as he was a careful workman he had plenty of customers. For a long time he was quite happy and contented, and asked for nothing better than what he had.

Now in the mountain dwelt a spirit which now and then appeared to men, and helped them in many ways to become rich and prosperous. The stone-cutter, however, had never seen this spirit, and only shook his head, with an unbelieving air, when anyone spoke of it. But a time was coming when he learned to change his opinion.

One day the stone-cutter carried a gravestone to the house of a rich man, and saw there all sorts of beautiful things, of which he had never even dreamed. Suddenly his daily work seemed to grow harder and heavier, and he said to himself: 'Oh, if only I were a rich man, and could sleep in a bed with silken curtains and golden tassels, how happy I should be!'

And a voice answered him: 'Your wish is heard; a rich man you shall be!'

At the sound of the voice the stone-cutter looked round, but could see nobody. He thought it was all his fancy, and picked up his tools and went home, for he did not feel inclined to do any more work that day. But when he reached the little house where he lived, he stood still with amazement, for instead of his wooden hut was a stately palace filled with splendid furniture, and most splendid of all was the bed, in every respect like the one he had envied. He was nearly beside himself with joy, and in his new life the old one was soon forgotten.

It was now the beginning of summer, and each day the sun blazed more fiercely. One morning the heat was so great that the stone-cutter could scarcely breathe, and he determined he would stop at home till the evening. He was rather dull, for he had never learned how to amuse himself, and was peeping through the closed blinds to see what was going on in the street, when a little carriage passed by, drawn by servants dressed in blue and silver. In the carriage sat a prince, and over his head a golden umbrella was held, to protect him from the sun's rays.

'Oh, if I were only a prince!' said the stone-cutter to himself, as the carriage vanished round the corner. 'Oh, if I were only a prince, and could go in such a carriage and have a golden umbrella held over me, how happy I should be!'

And the voice of the mountain spirit answered: 'Your wish is heard; a prince you shall be.'

And a prince he was. Before his carriage rode one company of men and another behind it; servants dressed in scarlet and gold bore him along, the coveted umbrella was held over his head, everything heart could desire was his. But yet it was not enough. He looked round still for something to wish for, and when he saw that in spite of the water he poured on his grass the rays of the sun scorched it, and that in spite of the umbrella held over his head each day his face grew browner and browner, he cried in his anger: 'The sun is mightier than I; oh, if I were only the sun!'

And the mountain spirit answered: 'Your wish is heard; the sun you shall be.'

And the sun he was, and felt himself proud in his

power. He shot his beams above and below, on earth and in heaven; he burnt up the grass in the fields and scorched the faces of princes as well as of poorer folk. But in a short time he began to grow tired of his might, for there seemed nothing left for him to do. Discontent once more filled his soul, and when a cloud covered his face, and hid the earth from him, he cried in his anger: 'Does the cloud hold captive my rays, and is it mightier than I? Oh, that I were a cloud, and mightier than any!'

And the mountain spirit answered: 'Your wish is heard; a cloud you shall be!'

And a cloud he was, and lay between the sun and the earth. He caught the sun's beams and held them, and to his joy the earth grew green again and flowers blossomed. But that was not enough for him, and for days and weeks he poured forth rain till the rivers overflowed their banks, and the crops of rice stood in water. Towns and villages were destroyed by the power of the rain, only the great rock on the mountain side remained unmoved. The cloud was amazed at the sight, and cried in wonder: 'Is the rock, then, mightier than I? Oh, if I were only the rock!'

And the mountain spirit answered: 'Your wish is heard; the rock you shall be!'

And the rock he was, and gloried in his power. Proudly he stood, and neither the heat of the sun nor the force of the rain could move him. 'This is better than all!' he said to himself. But one day he heard a strange noise at his feet, and when he looked down to see what it could be, he saw a stone-cutter driving tools into his surface. Even while he looked a trembling feeling ran all through him, and a great block broke off and fell upon the ground. Then he cried in his wrath: 'Is a mere child of earth mightier than a rock? Oh, if I were only a man!'

And the mountain spirit answered: 'Your wish is heard. A man once more you shall be!'

THE STONE-CUTTER BECOMES HIMSELF AGAIN

And a man he was, and in the sweat of his brow he toiled again at his trade of stone-cutting. His bed was hard and his food scanty, but he had learned to be satisfied with it, and did not long to be something or somebody else. And as he never asked for things he had not got, or desired to be greater and mightier than other people, he was happy at last, and heard the voice of the mountain spirit no longer.

[From *Japanische Mährchen.*]

THE GOLD-BEARDED MAN

Once upon a time there lived a great king who had a wife and one son whom he loved very much. The boy was still young when, one day, the king said to his wife: 'I feel that the hour of my death draws near, and I want you to promise that you will never take another husband but will give up your life to the care of our son.'

The queen burst into tears at these words, and sobbed out that she would never, never marry again, and that her son's welfare should be her first thought as long as she lived. Her promise comforted the troubled heart of the king, and a few days after he died, at peace with himself and with the world.

But no sooner was the breath out of his body, than the queen said to herself, 'To promise is one thing, and to keep is quite another.' And hardly was the last spadeful of earth flung over the coffin than she married a noble from a neighbouring country, and got him made king instead of the young prince. Her new husband was a cruel, wicked man, who treated his stepson very badly, and gave him scarcely anything to eat, and only rags to wear; and he would certainly have killed the boy but for fear of the people.

Now by the palace grounds there ran a brook, but instead of being a water-brook it was a milk-brook, and both rich and poor flocked to it daily and drew as much milk as they chose. The first thing the new king did when he was seated on the throne, was to forbid anyone to go near the brook, on pain of being seized by the watchmen. And this was purely spite, for there was plenty of milk for everybody.

For some days no one dared venture near the banks of the stream, but at length some of the watchmen noticed that early in the mornings, just at dawn, a man with a gold beard came down to the brook with a pail, which he filled up to the brim with milk, and then vanished like smoke before they could get near enough to see who he was. So they went and told the king what they had seen.

At first the king would not believe their story, but as they persisted it was quite true, he said that he would go and watch the stream that night himself. With the earliest streaks of dawn the gold-bearded man appeared, and filled his pail as before. Then in an instant he had vanished, as if the earth had swallowed him up.

The king stood staring with eyes and mouth open at the place where the man had disappeared. He had never seen him before, that was certain; but what mattered much more was how to catch him, and what should be done with him when he was caught? He would have a cage built as a prison for him, and everyone would talk of it, for in other countries thieves were put in prison, and it was long indeed since any king had used a cage. It was all very well to plan, and even to station a watchman behind every bush, but it was of no use, for the man was never caught. They would creep up to him softly on the grass, as he was stooping to fill his pail, and just as they stretched out their hands to seize him, he vanished before their eyes. Time after time this happened, till the king grew mad with rage, and offered a large reward to anyone who could tell him how to capture his enemy.

The first person that came with a scheme was an old soldier who promised the king that if he would only put some bread and bacon and a flask of wine on the bank of the stream, the gold-bearded man would be sure to eat and drink, and they could shake some powder into the wine, which would send him to sleep at once. After that there was nothing to do but to shut him in the cage.

This idea pleased the king, and he ordered bread and bacon and a flask of drugged wine to be placed on the bank of the stream, and the watchers to be redoubled. Then, full of hope, he awaited the result.

Everything turned out just as the soldier had said. Early next morning the gold-bearded man came down to the brook, ate, drank, and fell sound asleep, so that the watchers easily bound him, and carried him off to the palace. In a moment the king had him fast in the golden cage, and showed him, with ferocious joy, to the strangers who were visiting his court. The poor captive, when he awoke from his drunken sleep, tried to talk to them, but no one would listen to him, so he shut himself up altogether, and the people who came to stare took him for a dumb man of the woods. He wept and moaned to himself all day, and would hardly touch food, though, in dread that he should die and escape his tormentors, the king ordered his head cook to send him dishes from the royal table.

The gold-bearded man had been in captivity about a month, when the king was forced to make war upon a neighbouring country, and left the palace, to take command of his army. But before he went he called his stepson to him and said:

'Listen, boy, to what I tell you. While I am away I trust the care of my prisoner to you. See that he has plenty to eat and drink, but be careful that he does not escape, or even walk about the room. If I return and find him gone, you will pay for it by a terrible death.'

The young prince was thankful that his stepfather was going to the war, and secretly hoped he might never come back. Directly he had ridden off the boy went to the room where the cage was kept, and never left it night and day. He even played his games beside it.

One day he was shooting at a mark with a silver bow; one of his arrows fell into the golden cage.

The Golden-bearded Man Gives up the Arrow

'Please give me my arrow,' said the prince, running up to him; but the gold-bearded man answered:

'No, I shall not give it to you unless you let me out of my cage.'

'I may not let you out,' replied the boy, 'for if I do my stepfather says that I shall have to die a horrible death when he returns from the war. My arrow can be of no use to you, so give it to me.'

The man handed the arrow through the bars, but when he had done so he begged harder than ever that the prince would open the door and set him free. Indeed, he prayed so earnestly that the prince's heart was touched, for he was a tender-hearted boy who pitied the sorrows of other people. So he shot back the bolt, and the gold-bearded man stepped out into the world.

'I will repay you a thousand fold for that good deed,' said the man, and then he vanished. The prince began to think what he should say to the king when he came back; then he wondered whether it would be wise to wait for his stepfather's return and run the risk of the dreadful death which had been promised him. 'No,' he said to himself, 'I am afraid to stay. Perhaps the world will be kinder to me than he has been.'

Unseen he stole out when twilight fell, and for many days he wandered over mountains and through forests and valleys without knowing where he was going or what he should do. He had only the berries for food, when, one morning, he saw a wood-pigeon sitting on a bough. In an instant he had fitted an arrow to his bow, and was taking aim at the bird, thinking what a good meal he would make off him, when his weapon fell to the ground at the sound of the pigeon's voice:

'Do not shoot, I implore you, noble prince! I have two little sons at home, and they will die of hunger if I am not there to bring them food.'

And the young prince had pity, and unstrung his bow.

'Oh, prince, I will repay your deed of mercy,' said the grateful wood-pigeon.

'Poor thing! how can you repay me?' asked the prince.

'You have forgotten,' answered the wood-pigeon, 'the proverb that runs, "mountain and mountain can never meet, but one living creature can always come across another."' The boy laughed at this speech and went his way.

By-and-by he reached the edge of a lake, and flying towards some rushes which grew near the shore he beheld a wild duck. Now, in the days that the king, his father, was alive, and he had everything to eat he could possibly wish for, the prince always had wild duck for his birthday dinner, so he quickly fitted an arrow to his bow and took a careful aim.

'Do not shoot, I pray you, noble prince!' cried the wild duck; 'I have two little sons at home; they will die of hunger if I am not there to bring them food.'

And the prince had pity, and let fall his arrow and unstrung his bow.

'Oh, prince! I will repay your deed of mercy,' exclaimed the grateful wild duck.

'You poor thing! how can you repay me?' asked the prince.

'You have forgotten,' answered the wild duck, 'the proverb that runs, "mountain and mountain can never meet, but one living creature can always come across another."' The boy laughed at this speech and went his way.

He had not wandered far from the shores of the lake, when he noticed a stork standing on one leg, and again he raised his bow and prepared to take aim.

'Do not shoot, I pray you, noble prince,' cried the stork; 'I have two little sons at home; they will die of hunger if I am not there to bring them food.'

Again the prince was filled with pity, and this time also he did not shoot.

'Oh, prince, I will repay your deed of mercy,' cried the stork.

'You poor stork! how can you repay me?' asked the prince.

'You have forgotten,' answered the stork, 'the proverb that runs, "mountain and mountain can never meet, but one living creature can always come across another."'

The boy laughed at hearing these words again, and walked slowly on. He had not gone far, when he fell in with two discharged soldiers.

'Where are you going, little brother?' asked one.

'I am seeking work,' answered the prince.

'So are we,' replied the soldier. 'We can all go together.'

The boy was glad of company and they went on, and on, and on, through seven kingdoms, without finding anything they were able to do. At length they reached a palace, and there was the king standing on the steps.

'You seem to be looking for something,' said he.

'It is work we want,' they all answered.

So the king told the soldiers that they might become his coachmen; but he made the boy his companion, and gave him rooms near his own. The soldiers were dreadfully angry when they heard this, for of course they did not know that the boy was really a prince; and they soon began to lay their heads together to plot his ruin.

Then they went to the king.

'Your Majesty,' they said, 'we think it our duty to tell you that your new companion has boasted to us that if he were only your steward he would not lose a single grain of corn out of the storehouses. Now, if your Majesty would give orders that a sack of wheat should be mixed with one of barley, and would send for the youth, and command him to separate the grains one from another, in two hours' time, you would soon see what his talk was worth.'

The king, who was weak, listened to what these wicked men had told him, and desired the prince to have the contents of the sack piled into two heaps by the time that he returned from his council. 'If you succeed,' he added, 'you shall be my steward, but if you fail, I will put you to death on the spot.'

The unfortunate prince declared that he had never made any such boast as was reported; but it was all in vain. The king did not believe him, and turning him into an empty room, bade his servants carry in the huge sack filled with wheat and barley, and scatter them in a heap on the floor.

The prince hardly knew where to begin, and indeed if he had had a thousand people to help him, and a week to do it in, he could never have finished his task. So he flung himself on the ground in despair, and covered his face with his hands.

While he lay thus, a wood-pigeon flew in through the window.

'Why are you weeping, noble prince?' asked the wood-pigeon.

'How can I help weeping at the task set me by the king. For he says, if I fail to do it, I shall die a horrible death.'

'Oh, there is really nothing to cry about,' answered the wood-pigeon soothingly. 'I am the king of the wood-pigeons, whose life you spared when you were hungry. And now I will repay my debt, as I promised.' So saying he flew out of the window, leaving the prince with some hope in his heart.

In a few minutes he returned, followed by a cloud of wood-pigeons, so dense that it seemed to fill the room. Their king showed them what they had to do, and they set to work so hard that the grain was sorted into two heaps long before the council was over. When the king came back he could not believe his eyes; but search as he might through the two heaps, he could not find any barley among the wheat, or any wheat amongst the barley. So he praised the prince for his industry and cleverness, and made him his steward at once.

This made the two soldiers more envious still, and they began to hatch another plot.

'Your Majesty,' they said to the king, one day, as he was standing on the steps of the palace, 'that fellow has been boasting again, that if he had the care of your treasures not so much as a gold pin should ever be lost. Put this vain fellow to the proof, we pray you, and throw the ring from the princess's finger into the brook, and bid him find it. We shall soon see what his talk is worth.'

And the foolish king listened to them, and ordered the prince to be brought before him.

'My son,' he said, 'I have heard that you have declared that if I made you keeper of my treasures you would never lose so much as a gold pin. Now, in order to prove the truth of your words, I am going to throw the ring from the princess's finger into the brook, and if you do not find it before I come back from council, you will have to die a horrible death.'

It was no use denying that he had said anything of the kind. The king did not believe him; in fact he paid no attention at all, and hurried off, leaving the poor boy speechless with despair in the corner. However, he soon remembered that though it was very unlikely that he should find the ring in the brook, it was impossible that he should find it by staying in the palace.

For some time the prince wandered up and down peering into the bottom of the stream, but though the water was very clear, nothing could he see of the ring. At length he gave it up in despair, and throwing himself down at the foot of the tree, he wept bitterly.

'What is the matter, dear prince?' said a voice just above him, and raising his head, he saw the wild duck.

'The king of this country declares I must die a

horrible death if I cannot find the princess's ring which he has thrown into the brook,' answered the prince.

'Oh, you must not vex yourself about that, for I can help you,' replied the bird. 'I am the king of the wild ducks, whose life you spared, and now it is my turn to save yours.' Then he flew away, and in a few minutes a great flock of wild ducks were swimming all up and down the stream looking with all their might, and long before the king came back from his council there it was, safe on the grass beside the prince.

At this sight the king was yet more astonished at the cleverness of his steward, and at once promoted him to be the keeper of his jewels.

Now you would have thought that by this time the king would have been satisfied with the prince, and would have left him alone; but people's natures are very hard to change, and when the two envious soldiers came to him with a new falsehood, he was as ready to listen to them as before.

'Gracious Majesty,' said they, 'the youth whom you have made keeper of your jewels has declared to us that a child shall be born in the palace this night, which will be able to speak every language in the world and to play every instrument of music. Is he then become a prophet, or a magician, that he should know things which have not yet come to pass?'

At these words the king became more angry than ever. He had tried to learn magic himself, but somehow or other his spells would never work, and he was furious to hear that the prince claimed a power that he did not possess. Stammering with rage, he ordered the youth to be brought before him, and vowed that unless this miracle was accomplished he would have the prince dragged at a horse's tail until he was dead.

In spite of what the soldiers had said, the boy knew no more magic than the king did, and his task seemed more hopeless than before. He lay weeping in the chamber

The Wonderful Baby

which he was forbidden to leave, when suddenly he heard a sharp tapping at the window, and, looking up, he beheld a stork.

'What makes you so sad, prince?' asked he.

'Someone has told the king that I have prophesied that a child shall be born this night in the palace, who can speak all the languages in the world and play every musical instrument. I am no magician to bring these things to pass, but he says that if it does not happen he will have me dragged through the city at a horse's tail till I die.'

'Do not trouble yourself,' answered the stork. 'I will manage to find such a child, for I am the king of the storks whose life you spared, and now I can repay you for it.'

The stork flew away and soon returned carrying in his beak a baby wrapped in swaddling clothes, and laid it down near a lute. In an instant the baby stretched out its little hands and began to play a tune so beautiful that even the prince forgot his sorrows as he listened. Then he was given a flute and a zither, but he was just as well able to draw music from them; and the prince, whose courage was gradually rising, spoke to him in all the languages he knew. The baby answered him in all, and no one could have told which was his native tongue!

The next morning the king went straight to the prince's room, and saw with his own eyes the wonders that baby could do. 'If your magic can produce such a baby,' he said, 'you must be greater than any wizard that ever lived, and shall have my daughter in marriage.' And, being a king, and therefore accustomed to have everything the moment he wanted it, he commanded the ceremony to be performed without delay, and a splendid feast to be made for the bride and bridegroom. When it was over, he said to the prince:

'Now that you are really my son, tell me by what arts you were able to fulfil the tasks I set you?'

'My noble father-in-law,' answered the prince, 'I am ignorant of all spells and arts. But somehow I have always managed to escape the death which has threatened me.' And he told the king how he had been forced to run away from his stepfather, and how he had spared the three birds, and had joined the two soldiers, who had from envy done their utmost to ruin him.

The king was rejoiced in his heart that his daughter had married a prince, and not a common man, and he chased the two soldiers away with whips, and told them that if they ever dared to show their faces across the borders of his kingdom, they should die the same death he had prepared for the prince.

[From *Ungarische Mährchen.*]

From "Lovely Ilonka." *See p. 5.*

From "The Story of the Seven Simons." *See p. 48.*

From "Little Wildrose." See p. 100.

From "The Gifts of the Magician." See p. 143.

From "The Prince Who Would Seek Immortality." *See p. 191.*

From "The Three Robes." *See p. 222.*

From "Eisenkopf." *See p. 269.*

From "The Horse Gullfaxi and the Sword Gunnföder." *See p. 319.*

TRITILL, LITILL, AND THE BIRDS

ONCE upon a time there lived a princess who was so beautiful and so good that everybody loved her. Her father could hardly bear her out of his sight, and he almost died of grief when, one day, she disappeared, and though the whole kingdom was searched through and through, she could not be found in any corner of it. In despair, the king ordered a proclamation to be made that whoever could bring her back to the palace should have her for his wife. This made the young men start afresh on the search, but they were no more successful than before, and returned sorrowfully to their homes.

Now there dwelt, not far from the palace, an old man who had three sons. The two eldest were allowed by their parents to do just as they liked, but the youngest was always obliged to give way to his brothers. When they were all grown up, the eldest told his father that he was tired of leading such a quiet life, and that he meant to go away and see the world.

The old people were very unhappy at the thought that they must part with him, but they said nothing, and began to collect all that he would want for his travels, and were careful to add a pair of new boots. When everything was ready, he bade them farewell, and started merrily on his way.

For some miles his road lay through a wood, and when he left it he suddenly came out on a bare hillside. Here he sat down to rest, and pulling out his wallet prepared to eat his dinner.

He had only eaten a few mouthfuls when an old man badly dressed passed by, and seeing the food, asked if the young man could not spare him a little.

'Not I, indeed!' answered he; 'why I have scarcely enough for myself. If you want food you must earn it.' And the beggar went on.

After the young man had finished his dinner he rose and walked on for several hours, till he reached a second hill, where he threw himself down on the grass, and took some bread and milk from his wallet. While he was eating and drinking, there came by an old man, yet more wretched than the first, and begged for a few mouthfuls. But instead of food he only got hard words, and limped sadly away.

Towards evening the young man reached an open space in the wood, and by this time he thought he would like some supper. The birds saw the food, and flew round his head in numbers hoping for some crumbs, but he threw stones at them, and frightened them off. Then he began to wonder where he should sleep. Not in the open space he was in, for that was bare and cold, and though he had walked a long way that day, and was tired, he dragged himself up, and went on seeking for a shelter.

At length he saw a deep sort of hole or cave under a great rock, and as it seemed quite empty, he went in, and lay down in a corner. About midnight he was awakened by a noise, and peeping out he beheld a terrible ogress approaching. He implored her not to hurt him, but to let him stay there for the rest of the night, to which she consented, on condition that he should spend the next day in doing any task which she might choose to set him. To this the young man willingly agreed, and turned over and went to sleep again. In the morning, the ogress bade him sweep the dust out of the cave, and to have it clean before her return in the evening, otherwise it would be the worse for him. Then she left the cave.

The young man took the spade, and began to clean

the floor of the cave, but try as he would to move it the dirt still stuck to its place. He soon gave up the task, and sat sulkily in the corner, wondering what punishment the ogress would find for him, and why she had set him to do such an impossible thing.

He had not long to wait, after the ogress came home, before he knew what his punishment was to be! She just gave one look at the floor of the cave, then dealt him a blow on the head which cracked his skull, and there was an end of him.

Meanwhile his next brother grew tired of staying at home, and let his parents have no rest till they had consented that he also should be given some food and some new boots, and go out to see the world. On his road, he also met the two old beggars, who prayed for a little of his bread and milk, but this young man had never been taught to help other people, and had made it a rule through his life to keep all he had to himself. So he turned a deaf ear and finished his dinner.

By-and-by he, too, came to the cave, and was bidden by the ogress to clean the floor, but he was no more successful than his brother, and his fate was the same.

Anyone would have thought that when the old people had only one son left that at least they would have been kind to him, even if they did not love him. But for some reason they could hardly bear the sight of him, though he tried much harder to make them comfortable than his brothers had ever done. So when he asked their leave to go out into the world they gave it at once, and seemed quite glad to be rid of him. They felt it was quite generous of them to provide him with a pair of new boots and some bread and milk for his journey.

Besides the pleasure of seeing the world, the youth was very anxious to discover what had become of his brothers, and he determined to trace, as far as he could, the way that they must have gone. He followed the road that led from his father's cottage to the hill, where he sat down to rest, saying to himself: 'I am sure my brothers must have stopped here, and I will do the same.'

He was hungry as well as tired, and took out some of the food his parents had given him. He was just going to begin to eat when the old man appeared, and asked if he could not spare him a little. The young man at once broke off some of the bread, begging the old man to sit down beside him, and treating him as if he was an old friend. At last the stranger rose, and said to him: 'If ever you are in trouble call me, and I will help you. My name is Tritill.' Then he vanished, and the young man could not tell where he had gone.

However, he felt he had now rested long enough, and that he had better be going his way. At the next hill he met with the second old man, and to him also he gave food and drink. And when this old man had finished he said, like the first: 'If you ever want help in the smallest thing call to me. My name is Litill.'

The young man walked on till he reached the open space in the wood, where he stopped for dinner. In a moment all the birds in the world seemed flying round his head, and he crumbled some of his bread for them and watched them as they darted down to pick it up. When they had cleared off every crumb the largest bird with the gayest plumage said to him: 'If you are in trouble and need help say, "My birds, come to me!" and we will come.' Then they flew away.

Towards evening the young man reached the cave where his brothers had met their deaths, and, like them, he thought it would be a good place to sleep in. Looking round, he saw some pieces of the dead men's clothes and of their bones. The sight made him shiver, but he would not move away, and resolved to await the return of the ogress, for such he knew she must be.

Very soon she came striding in, and he asked politely if she would give him a night's lodging. She answered as before, that he might stay on condition that he should do any work that she might set him to next morning. So the bargain being concluded, the young man curled himself up in his corner and went to sleep.

Litill, Tritill, & the Birds to the rescue

The dirt lay thicker than ever on the floor of the cave when the young man took the spade and began his work. He could not clear it any more than his brothers had done, and at last the spade itself stuck in the earth so that he could not pull it out. The youth stared at it in despair, then the old beggar's words flashed into his mind, and he cried: 'Tritill, Tritill, come and help me!'

And Tritill stood beside him and asked what he wanted. The youth told him all his story, and when he had finished, the old man said: 'Spade and shovel do your duty,' and they danced about the cave till, in a short time, there was not a speck of dust left on the floor. As soon as it was quite clean Tritill went his way.

With a light heart the young man awaited the return of the ogress. When she came in she looked carefully round, and then said to him: 'You did not do that quite alone. However, as the floor is clean I will leave your head on.'

The following morning the ogress told the young man that he must take all the feathers out of her pillows and spread them to dry in the sun. But if one feather was missing when she came back at night his head should pay for it.'

The young man fetched the pillows, and shook out all the feathers, and oh! what quantities of them there were! He was thinking to himself, as he spread them out carefully, how lucky it was that the sun was so bright and that there was no wind, when suddenly a breeze sprang up, and in a moment the feathers were dancing high in the air. At first the youth tried to collect them again, but he soon found that it was no use, and he cried in despair: 'Tritill, Litill, and all my birds, come and help me!'

He had hardly said the words when there they all were; and when the birds had brought all the feathers back again, Tritill, and Litill, and he, put them away in the pillows, as the ogress had bidden him. But one little feather they kept out, and told the young man that if the ogress missed it he was to thrust it up her nose. Then they all vanished, Tritill, Litill, and the birds.

Directly the ogress returned home she flung herself

with all her weight on the bed, and the whole cave quivered under her. The pillows were soft and full instead of being empty, which surprised her, but that did not content her. She got up, shook out the pillow-cases one by one, and began to count the feathers that were in each. 'If one is missing I will have your head,' said she, and at that the young man drew the feather from his pocket and thrust it up her nose, crying . 'If you want your feather, here it is.'

'You did not sort those feathers alone,' answered the ogress calmly; 'however, this time I will let that pass.'

That night the young man slept soundly in his corner, and in the morning the ogress told him that his work that day would be to slay one of her great oxen, to cook its heart, and to make drinking cups of its horns, before she returned home 'There are fifty oxen,' added she, 'and you must guess which of the herd I want killed. If you guess right, to-morrow you shall be free to go where you will, and you shall choose besides three things as a reward for your service. But if you slay the wrong ox your head shall pay for it.'

Left alone, the young man stood thinking for a little. Then he called: 'Tritill, Litill, come to my help!'

In a moment he saw them, far away, driving the biggest ox the youth had ever seen. When they drew near, Tritill killed it, Litill took out its heart for the young man to cook, and both began quickly to turn the horns into drinking cups. The work went merrily on, and they talked gaily, and the young man told his friends of the payment promised him by the ogress if he had done her bidding. The old men warned him that he must ask her for the chest which stood at the foot of her bed, for whatever lay on the top of the bed, and for what lay under the side of the cave. The young man thanked them for their counsel, and Tritill and Litill then took leave of him, saying that for the present he would need them no more.

Scarcely had they disappeared when the ogress came back, and found everything ready just as she had ordered. Before she sat down to eat the bullock's heart she turned to the young man, and said: 'You did not do that all alone, my friend; but, nevertheless, I will keep my word, and to-morrow you shall go your way.' So they went to bed and slept till dawn.

When the sun rose the ogress awoke the young man, and called to him to choose any three things out of her house.

'I choose,' answered he, 'the chest which stands at the foot of your bed; whatever lies on the top of the bed, and whatever is under the side of the cave.'

'You did not choose those things by yourself, my friend,' said the ogress; 'but what I have promised, that will I do.'

And then she gave him his reward.

'The thing which lay on the top of the bed' turned out to be the lost princess. 'The chest which stood at the foot of the bed' proved full of gold and precious stones; and 'what was under the side of the cave' he found to be a great ship, with oars and sails that went of itself as well on land as in the water. 'You are the luckiest man that ever was born,' said the ogress as she went out of the cave as usual.

With much difficulty the youth put the heavy chest on his shoulders and carried it on board the ship, the princess walking by his side. Then he took the helm and steered the vessel back to her father's kingdom. The king's joy at receiving back his lost daughter was so great that he almost fainted, but when he recovered himself he made the young man tell him how everything had really happened. 'You have found her, and you shall marry her,' said the king; and so it was done. And this is the end of the story.

[From *Ungarische Mährchen.*]

THE THREE ROBES

Long, long ago, a king and queen reigned over a large and powerful country. What their names were nobody knows, but their son was called Sigurd, and their daughter Lineik, and these young people were famed throughout the whole kingdom for their wisdom and beauty.

There was only a year between them, and they loved each other so much that they could do nothing apart. When they began to grow up the king gave them a house of their own to live in, with servants and carriages, and everything they could possibly want.

For many years they all lived happily together, and then the queen fell ill, and knew that she would never get better.

'Promise me two things,' she said one day to the king; 'one, that if you marry again, as indeed you must, you will not choose as your wife a woman from some small state or distant island, who knows nothing of the world, and will be taken up with thoughts of her grandeur. But rather seek out a princess of some great kingdom, who has been used to courts all her life, and holds them at their true worth. The other thing I have to ask is, that you will never cease to watch over our children, who will soon become your greatest joy.'

These were the queen's last words, and a few hours later she was dead. The king was so bowed down with sorrow that he would not attend even to the business of the kingdom, and at last his Prime Minister had to tell him that the people were complaining that they had nobody to right their wrongs. 'You must rouse yourself, sir,' went on the minister, 'and put aside your own sorrows for the sake of your country.'

'You do not spare me,' answered the king; 'but what you say is just, and your counsel is good. I have heard that men say, likewise, that it will be for the good of my kingdom for me to marry again, though my heart will never cease to be with my lost wife. But it was her wish also; therefore, to you I entrust the duty of finding a lady fitted to share my throne; only, see that she comes neither from a small town nor a remote island.'

So an embassy was prepared, with the minister at its head, to visit the greatest courts in the world, and to choose out a suitable princess. But the vessel which carried them had not been gone many days when a thick fog came on, and the captain could see neither to the right nor to the left. For a whole month the ship drifted about in darkness, till at length the fog lifted and they beheld a cliff jutting out just in front. On one side of the cliff lay a sheltered bay, in which the vessel was soon anchored, and though they did not know where they were, at any rate they felt sure of fresh fruit and water.

The minister left the rest of his followers on board the ship, and taking a small boat rowed himself to land, in order to look about him and to find out if the island was really as deserted as it seemed.

He had not gone far, when he heard the sound of music, and, turning in its direction, he saw a woman of marvellous beauty sitting on a low stool playing on a harp, while a girl beside her sang. The minister stopped and greeted the lady politely, and she replied with friendliness, asking him why he had come to such an out-of-the-way place. In answer he told her of the object of his journey.

'I am in the same state as your master,' replied the lady; 'I was married to a mighty king who ruled over this land, till Vikings [sea-robbers] came and slew him and put all the people to death. But I managed to escape, and hid myself here with my daughter.'

And the daughter listened, and said softly to her mother: 'Are you speaking the truth now?'

'Remember your promise,' answered the mother angrily, giving her a pinch which was unseen by the minister.

'What is your name, madam?' asked he, much touched by this sad story.

'Blauvor,' she replied, 'and my daughter is called Laufer'; and then she inquired the name of the minister, and of the king his master. After this they talked of many things, and the lady showed herself learned in all that a woman should know, and even in much that men only were commonly taught. 'What a wife she would make for the king,' thought the minister to himself, and before long he had begged the honour of her hand for his master. She declared at first that she was too unworthy to accept the position offered her, and that the minister would soon repent his choice; but this only made him the more eager, and in the end he gained her consent, and prevailed on her to return with him at once to his own country.

The minister then conducted the mother and daughter back to the ship; the anchor was raised, the sails spread, and a fair wind was behind them.

Now that the fog had lifted they could see as they looked back that, except just along the shore, the island was bare and deserted and not fit for men to live in; but about that nobody cared. They had a quick voyage, and in six days they reached the land, and at once set out for the capital, a messenger being sent on first by the minister to inform the king of what had happened.

When his Majesty's eyes fell on the two beautiful women, clad in dresses of gold and silver, he forgot his sorrows and ordered preparations for the wedding to be made without delay. In his joy he never remembered to inquire in what kind of country the future queen had been found. In fact his head was so turned by the beauty of the two ladies that when the invitations were sent by his orders to all the great people in the kingdom, he did not even recollect his two children, who remained shut up in their own house!

After the marriage the king ceased to have any will of his own and did nothing without consulting his wife. She was present at all his councils, and her opinion was asked before making peace or war. But when a few months had passed the king began to have doubts as to whether the minister's choice had really been a wise one, and he noticed that his children lived more and more in their palace and never came near their stepmother.

It always happens that if a person's eyes are once opened they see a great deal more than they ever expected; and soon it struck the king that the members of his court had a way of disappearing one after the other without any reason. At first he had not paid much attention to the fact, but merely appointed some fresh person to the vacant place. As, however, man after man vanished without leaving any trace, he began to grow uncomfortable and to wonder if the queen could have anything to do with it.

Things were in this state when, one day, his wife said to him that it was time for him to make a progress through his kingdom and see that his governors were not cheating him of the money that was his due. 'And you need not be anxious about going,' she added, 'for I will rule the country while you are away as carefully as you could yourself.'

The king had no great desire to undertake this journey, but the queen's will was stronger than his, and he was too lazy to make a fight for it. So he said nothing and set about his preparations, ordering his finest ship to be ready to carry him round the coast. Still his heart was heavy, and he felt uneasy, though he could not have told why; and the night before he was to start he went to the children's palace to take leave of his son and daughter.

He had not seen them for some time, and they gave him a warm welcome, for they loved him dearly and he had always been kind to them. They had much to tell him, but after a while he checked their merry talk and said:

'If I should never come back from this journey I fear that it may not be safe for you to stay here; so directly there are no more hopes of my return go instantly and take the road eastwards till you reach a high mountain, which you must cross. Once over the mountain keep along by the side of a little bay till you come to two trees, one green and the other red, standing in a thicket, and so far back from the road that without looking for them you would never see them. Hide each in the trunk of one of the trees and there you will be safe from all your enemies.'

With these words the king bade them farewell and entered sadly into his ship. For a few days the wind was fair, and everything seemed going smoothly; then, suddenly, a gale sprang up, and a fearful storm of thunder and lightning, such as had never happened within the memory of man. In spite of the efforts of the frightened sailors the vessel was driven on the rocks, and not a man on board was saved.

That very night Prince Sigurd had a dream, in which he thought his father appeared to him in dripping clothes, and, taking the crown from his head, laid it at his son's feet, leaving the room as silently as he had entered it.

Hastily the prince awoke his sister Lineik, and they agreed that their father must be dead, and that they must lose no time in obeying his orders and putting themselves in safety. So they collected their jewels and a few clothes and left the house without being observed by anyone.

They hurried on till they arrived at the mountain without once looking back. Then Sigurd glanced round and saw that their stepmother was following them, with an expression on her face which made her uglier than the ugliest old witch. Between her and them lay a thick wood, and Sigurd stopped for a moment to set it on fire; then he and his sister hastened on more swiftly than before, till they reached the grove with the red and green trees, into which they jumped, and felt that at last they were safe.

Now, at that time there reigned over Greece a king who was very rich and powerful, although his name has somehow been forgotten. He had two children, a son and a daughter, who were more beautiful and accomplished than any Greeks had been before, and they were the pride of their father's heart.

The prince had no sooner grown out of boyhood than he prevailed on his father to make war during the summer months on a neighbouring nation, so as to give him a chance of making himself famous. In winter, however, when it was difficult to get food and horses in that wild country, the army was dispersed, and the prince returned home.

During one of these wars he had heard reports of the Princess Lineik's beauty, and he resolved to seek her out, and to ask for her hand in marriage. All this Blauvor, the queen, found out by means of her black arts, and when the prince drew near the capital she put a splendid dress on her own daughter and then went to meet her guest.

She bade him welcome to her palace, and when they had finished supper she told him of the loss of her husband, and how there was no one left to govern the kingdom but herself.

'But where is the Princess Lineik?' asked the prince when she had ended her tale.

'Here,' answered the queen, bringing forward the girl, whom she had hitherto kept in the background.

The prince looked at her and was rather disappointed. The maiden was pretty enough, but not much out of the common.

'Oh, you must not wonder at her pale face and heavy eyes,' said the queen hastily, for she saw what was passing in his mind. 'She has never got over the loss of both father and mother.'

'That shows a good heart,' thought the prince; 'and when she is happy her beauty will soon come back.' And without any further delay he begged the queen to consent to their betrothal, for the marriage must take place in his own country.

The queen was enchanted. She had hardly expected to succeed so soon, and she at once set about her preparations. Indeed she wished to travel with the young couple, to make sure that nothing should go wrong; but here the prince was firm, that he would take no one with him but Laufer, whom he thought was Lineik.

They soon took leave of the queen, and set sail in a splendid ship; but in a short time a dense fog came on, and in the dark the captain steered out of his course, and they found themselves in a bay which was quite strange to all the crew. The prince ordered a boat to be lowered, and went on shore to look about him, and it was not long before he noticed the two beautiful trees, quite different from any that grew in Greece. Calling one of the sailors, he bade him cut them down, and carry them on board the ship. This was done, and as the sky was now clear they put out to sea, and arrived in Greece without any more adventures.

The news that the prince had brought home a bride had gone before them, and they were greeted with flowery arches and crowns of coloured lights. The king and queen met them on the steps of the palace, and conducted the girl to the women's house, where she would have to remain until her marriage. The prince then went to his own rooms and ordered that the trees should be brought in to him.

The next morning the prince bade his attendants bring his future bride to his own apartments, and when she came he gave her silk which she was to weave into three robes—one red, one green, and one blue—and these must all be ready before the wedding. The blue one was to be done first and the green last, and this was to be the most splendid of all, 'for I will wear it at our marriage,' said he.

Left alone, Laufer sat and stared at the heap of shining silk before her. She did not know how to weave, and burst into tears as she thought that everything would be discovered, for Lineik's skill in weaving was as famous as her beauty. As she sat with her face hidden and her body shaken by sobs, Sigurd in his tree heard her and was moved to pity. 'Lineik, my sister,' he called, softly, 'Laufer is weeping; help her, I pray you.'

'Have you forgotten the wrongs her mother did to us?' answered Lineik, 'and that it is owing to her that we are banished from home?'

But she was not really unforgiving, and very soon she slid quietly out of her hiding-place, and taking the silk from Laufer's hands began to weave it. So quick and clever was she that the blue dress was not only woven but embroidered, and Lineik was safe back in her tree before the prince returned.

'It is the most beautiful work I have ever seen,' said he, taking up a bit. 'And I am sure that the red one will be still better, because the stuff is richer,' and with a low bow he left the room.

Laufer had hoped secretly that when the prince had seen the blue dress finished he would have let her off the other two; but when she found she was expected to fulfil the whole task, her heart sank and she began to cry loudly. Again Sigurd heard her, and begged Lineik to come to her help, and Lineik, feeling sorry for her distress, wove and embroidered the second dress as she had done

LINEIK CAUGHT BY THE PRINCE

the first, mixing gold thread and precious stones till you could hardly see the red of the stuff. When it was done she glided into her tree just as the prince came in.

'You are as quick as you are clever,' said he, admiringly. 'This looks as if it had been embroidered by the fairies! But as the green robe must outshine the other two I will give you three days in which to finish it. After it is ready we will be married at once.'

Now, as he spoke, there rose up in Laufer's mind all the unkind things that she and her mother had done to Lineik. Could she hope that they would be forgotten, and that Lineik would come to her rescue for the third time? And perhaps Lineik, who had not forgotten the past either, might have left her alone, to get on as best she could, had not Sigurd, her brother, implored her to help just once more. So Lineik again slid out of her tree, and, to Laufer's great relief, set herself to work. When the shining green silk was ready she caught the sun's rays and the moon's beams on the point of her needle and wove them into a pattern such as no man had ever seen. But it took a long time, and on the third morning, just as she was putting the last stitches into the last flower the prince came in.

Lineik jumped up quickly, and tried to get past him back to her tree; but the folds of the silk were wrapped round her, and she would have fallen had not the prince caught her.

'I have thought for some time that all was not quite straight here,' said he. 'Tell me who you are, and where you come from?'

Lineik then told her name and her story. When she had ended the prince turned angrily to Laufer, and declared that, as a punishment for her wicked lies, she deserved to die a shameful death.

But Laufer fell at his feet and begged for mercy. It was her mother's fault, she said: 'It was she, and not I, who passed me off as the Princess Lineik. The only lie

I have ever told you was about the robes, and I do not deserve death for that.'

She was still on her knees when Prince Sigurd entered the room. He prayed the Prince of Greece to forgive Laufer, which he did, on condition that Lineik would consent to marry him. 'Not till my stepmother is dead,' answered she, 'for she has brought misery to all that came near her.' Then Laufer told them that Blauvor was not the wife of a king, but an ogress who had stolen her from a neighbouring palace and had brought her up as her daughter. And besides being an ogress she was also a witch, and by her black arts had sunk the ship in which the father of Sigurd and Lineik had set sail. It was she who had caused the disappearance of the courtiers, for which no one could account, by eating them during the night, and she hoped to get rid of all the people in the country, and then to fill the land with ogres and ogresses like herself.

So Prince Sigurd and the Prince of Greece collected an army swiftly, and marched upon the town where Blauvor had her palace. They came so suddenly that no one knew of it, and if they had, Blauvor had eaten most of the strong men ; and others, fearful of something they could not tell what, had secretly left the place. Therefore she was easily captured, and the next day was beheaded in the market-place. Afterwards the two princes marched back to Greece.

Lineik had no longer any reason for putting off her wedding, and married the Prince of Greece at the same time that Sigurd married the princess. And Laufer remained with Lineik as her friend and sister, till they found a husband for her in a great nobleman ; and all three couples lived happily until they died.

[From *Isländische Mährchen Poestion Wien.*]

THE SIX HUNGRY BEASTS

Once upon a time there lived a man who dwelt with his wife in a little hut, far away from any neighbours. But they did not mind being alone, and would have been quite happy, if it had not been for a marten, who came every night to their poultry yard, and carried off one of their fowls. The man laid all sorts of traps to catch the thief, but instead of capturing the foe, it happened that one day he got caught himself, and falling down, struck his head against a stone, and was killed.

Not long after the marten came by on the look out for his supper. Seeing the dead man lying there, he said to himself: 'That is a prize, this time I have done well'; and dragging the body with great difficulty to the sledge which was waiting for him, drove off with his booty. He had not driven far when he met a squirrel, who bowed and said: 'Good-morning, godfather! what have you got behind you?'

The marten laughed and answered: 'Did you ever hear anything so strange? The old man that you see here set traps about his hen-house, thinking to catch me; but he fell into his own trap, and broke his own neck. He is very heavy; I wish you would help me to draw the sledge.' The squirrel did as he was asked, and the sledge moved slowly along.

By-and-by a hare came running across a field, but stopped to see what wonderful thing was coming. 'What have you got there?' she asked, and the marten told his story and begged the hare to help them pull.

The hare pulled her hardest, and after a while they were joined by a fox, and then by a wolf, and at length a bear was added to the company, and *he* was of more use than all the other five beasts put together. Besides, when the whole six had supped off the man he was not so heavy to draw.

The worst of it was that they soon began to get hungry again, and the wolf, who was the hungriest of all, said to the rest:

'What shall we eat now, my friends, as there is no more man?'

'I suppose we shall have to eat the smallest of us,' replied the bear, and the marten turned round to seize the squirrel who was much smaller than any of the rest. But the squirrel ran up a tree like lightning, and the marten remembering, just in time, that *he* was the next in size, slipped quick as thought into a hole in the rocks.

'What shall we eat *now*?' asked the wolf again, when he had recovered from his surprise.

'We must eat the smallest of us,' repeated the bear, stretching out a paw towards the hare; but the hare was not a hare for nothing, and before the paw had touched her, she had darted deep into the wood.

Now that the squirrel, the marten, and the hare had all gone, the fox was the smallest of the three who were left, and the wolf and the bear explained that they were very sorry, but they would have to eat *him*. Michael, the fox, did not run away as the others had done, but smiled in a friendly manner, and remarked: 'Things taste so stale in a valley; one's appetite is so much better up on a mountain.' The wolf and the bear agreed, and they turned out of the hollow where they had been walking, and chose a path that led up the mountain side. The fox trotted cheerfully by his two big companions, but on the way he managed to whisper to the wolf: 'Tell me, Peter, when I am eaten, what will you have for your next dinner?'

This simple question seemed to put out the wolf very much. What *would* they have for their next dinner, and, what was more important still, who would there be to eat it? They had made a rule always to dine off the smallest

MICHAEL THE FOX DID NOT RUN AWAY AS THE OTHERS HAD DONE.

of the party, and when the fox was gone, why of course, *he* was smaller than the bear.

These thoughts flashed quickly through his head, and he said hastily:

'Dear brothers, would it not be better for us to live together as comrades, and everyone to hunt for the common dinner? Is not my plan a good one?'

'It is the best thing I have ever heard,' answered the fox; and as they were two to one the bear had to be content, though in his heart he would much have preferred a good dinner at once to any friendship.

For a few days all went well; there was plenty of game in the forest, and even the wolf had as much to eat as he could wish. One morning the fox as usual was going his rounds when he noticed a tall, slender tree, with a magpie's nest in one of the top branches. Now the fox was particularly fond of young magpies, and he set about making a plan by which he could have one for dinner. At last he hit upon something which he thought would do, and accordingly he sat down near the tree and began to stare hard at it.

'What are you looking at, Michael?' asked the magpie, who was watching him from a bough.

'I'm looking at this tree. It has just struck me what a good tree it would be to cut my new snow-shoes out of.' But at this answer the magpie screeched loudly, and exclaimed: 'Oh, not this tree, dear brother, I implore you! I have built my nest on it, and my young ones are not yet old enough to fly.'

'It will not be easy to find another tree that would make such good snow-shoes,' answered the fox, cocking his head on one side, and gazing at the tree thoughtfully; 'but I do not like to be ill-natured, so if you will give me one of your young ones I will seek my snow-shoes elsewhere.'

Not knowing what to do the poor magpie had to agree, and flying back, with a heavy heart, he threw one of his young ones out of the nest. The fox seized it in his mouth and ran off in triumph, while the magpie, though deeply grieved for the loss of his little one, found some comfort in the thought that only a bird of extraordinary wisdom would have dreamed of saving the rest by the sacrifice of the one. But what do you think happened? Why, a few days later, Michael the fox might have been seen sitting under the very same tree, and a dreadful pang shot through the heart of the magpie as he peeped at him from a hole in the nest.

'What are you looking at?' he asked in a trembling voice.

'At this tree. I was just thinking what good snow-shoes it would make,' answered the fox in an absent voice, as if he was not thinking of what he was saying.

'Oh, my brother, my dear little brother, don't do that,' cried the magpie, hopping about in his anguish. 'You know you promised only a few days ago that you would get your snow-shoes elsewhere.'

'So I did; but though I have searched through the whole forest, there is not a single tree that is as good as this. I am very sorry to put you out, but really it is not my fault. The only thing I can do for you is to offer to give up my snow-shoes altogether if you will throw me down one of your young ones in exchange.'

And the poor magpie, in spite of his wisdom, was obliged to throw another of his little ones out of the nest; and this time he was not able to console himself with the thought that he had been much cleverer than other people.

He sat on the edge of his nest, his head drooping and his feathers all ruffled, looking the picture of misery. Indeed he was so different from the gay, jaunty magpie whom every creature in the forest knew, that a crow who was flying past, stopped to inquire what was the matter. 'Where are the two young ones who are not in the nest?' asked he.

'I had to give them to the fox,' replied the magpie in a quivering voice; 'he has been here twice in the last week, and wanted to cut down my tree for the purpose of making snow-shoes out of it, and the only way I could buy him off was by giving him two of my young ones.'

Oh, you fool,' cried the crow, 'the fox was only trying to frighten you. He could not have cut down the tree, for he has neither axe nor knife. Dear me, to think that you have sacrificed your young ones for nothing! Dear, dear! how could you be so very foolish!' And the crow flew away, leaving the magpie overcome with shame and sorrow.

The next morning the fox came to his usual place in front of the tree, for he was hungry, and a nice young magpie would have suited him very well for dinner. But this time there was no cowering, timid magpie to do his bidding, but a bird with his head erect and a determined voice.

'My good fox,' said the magpie—putting his head on one side and looking very wise—'my good fox, if you take my advice, you will go home as fast as you can. There is no use your talking about making snow-shoes out of this tree, when you have neither knife nor axe to cut it down with!'

'Who has been teaching you wisdom?' asked the fox, forgetting his manners in his surprise at this new turn of affairs.

'The crow, who paid me a visit yesterday,' answered the magpie.

'The crow was it?' said the fox, 'well, the crow had better not meet me for the future, or it may be the worse for him.'

As Michael, the cunning beast, had no desire to continue the conversation, he left the forest; but when he came to the high road he laid himself at full length on the ground, stretching himself out, just as if he was dead. Very soon he noticed, out of the corner of his eye, that the crow was flying towards him, and he kept stiller and stiffer than ever, with his tongue hanging out of his mouth. The crow, who wanted her supper very badly, hopped quickly towards him, and was stooping forward to peck at his tongue when the fox gave a snap, and caught him by the wing. The crow knew that it was of no use struggling, so he said:

'Ah, brother, if you are really going to eat me, do it, I beg of you, in good style. Throw me first over this precipice, so that my feathers may be strewn here and there, and that all who see them may know that your cunning is greater than mine.' This idea pleased the fox, for he had not yet forgiven the crow for depriving him of the young magpies, so he carried the crow to the edge of the precipice and threw him over, intending to go round by a path he knew and pick him up at the bottom. But no sooner had the fox let the crow go than he soared up into the air, and hovering just out of reach of his enemy's jaws, he cried with a laugh: 'Ah, fox! you know well how to catch, but you cannot keep.'

With his tail between his legs, the fox slunk into the forest. He did not know where to look for a dinner, as he guessed that the crow would have flown back before him, and put every one on their guard. The notion of going to bed supperless was very unpleasant to him, and he was wondering what in the world he should do, when he chanced to meet with his old friend the bear.

This poor animal had just lost his wife, and was going to get some one to mourn over her, for he felt her loss greatly. He had hardly left his comfortable cave when he had come across the wolf, who inquired where he was going. 'I am going to find a mourner,' answered the bear, and told his story.

'Oh, let me mourn for you,' cried the wolf.

'Do you understand how to howl?' said the bear.

'Oh, certainly, godfather, certainly,' replied the wolf; but the bear said he should like to have a specimen of his howling, to make sure that he knew his business. So the wolf broke forth in his song of lament: 'Hu, hu, hu, hum, hoh,' he shouted, and he made such a noise that the bear put up his paws to his ears, and begged him to stop.

'You have no idea how it is done. Be off with you,' said he angrily.

A little further down the road the hare was resting in a ditch, but when she saw the bear, she came out and spoke to him, and inquired why he looked so sad. The bear told her of the loss of his wife, and of his search after a mourner that could lament over her in the proper style. The hare instantly offered her services, but the bear took care to ask her to give him a proof of her talents, before he accepted them. 'Pu, pu, pu, pum, poh,' piped the hare; but this time her voice was so small that the bear could hardly hear her. 'That is not what I want,' he said, 'I will bid you good morning.'

It was after this that the fox came up, and he also was struck with the bear's altered looks, and stopped. 'What is the matter with you, godfather?' asked he, 'and where are you going?'

'I am going to find a mourner for my wife,' answered the bear.

'Oh, do choose me,' cried the fox, and the bear looked at him thoughtfully.

'Can you howl well?' he said.

'Yes, beautifully, just listen,' and the fox lifted up his voice and sang—weeping: 'Lou, lou, lou! the famous spinner, the baker of good cakes, the prudent housekeeper is torn from her husband! Lou, lou, lou! she is gone! she is gone!'

'Now at last I have found some one who knows the art of lamentation,' exclaimed the bear, quite delighted; and he led the fox back to his cave, and bade him begin his lament over the dead wife who was lying stretched out on her bed of grey moss. But this did not suit the fox at all.

'One cannot wail properly in this cave,' he said, 'it is much too damp. You had better take the body to the storehouse. It will sound much finer there.' So the bear carried his wife's body to the storehouse, while he himself went back to the cave to cook some pap for the mourner. From time to time he paused and listened for the sound of wailing, but he heard nothing. At last he went to the door of the storehouse, and called to the fox:

'Why don't you howl, godfather? What are you about?'

WHY THE TIP OF HIS TAIL IS WHITE

And the fox, who, instead of weeping over the dead bear, had been quietly eating her, answered:

'There only remain now her legs and the soles of her feet. Give me five minutes more and they will be gone also!'

When the bear heard that he ran back for the kitchen ladle, to give the traitor the beating he deserved. But as he opened the door of the storehouse, Michael was ready for him, and slipping between his legs, dashed straight off into the forest. The bear, seeing that the traitor had escaped, flung the ladle after him, and it just caught the tip of his tail, and that is how there comes to be a spot of white on the tails of all foxes.

[From *Finnische Mährchen.*]

HOW THE BEGGAR BOY TURNED INTO COUNT PIRO

ONCE upon a time there lived a man who had only one son, a lazy, stupid boy, who would never do anything he was told. When the father was dying, he sent for his son and told him that he would soon be left alone in the world, with no possessions but the small cottage they lived in and a pear tree which grew behind it, and that, whether he liked it or not, he would have to work, or else he would starve. Then the old man died.

But the boy did not work; instead, he idled about as before, contenting himself with eating the pears off his tree, which, unlike other pear trees before or since, bore fruit the whole year round. Indeed, the pears were so much finer than any you could get even in the autumn, that one day, in the middle of the winter, they attracted the notice of a fox who was creeping by.

'Dear me; what lovely pears!' he said to the youth. 'Do give me a basket of them. It will bring you luck!'

'Ah, little fox, but if I give you a basketful, what am I to eat?' asked the boy.

'Oh, trust me, and do what I tell you,' said the fox; 'I know it will bring you luck.' So the boy got up and picked some of the ripest pears and put them into a rush basket. The fox thanked him, and, taking the basket in his mouth, trotted off to the king's palace and made his way straight to the king.

'Your Majesty, my master sends you a few of his best

pears, and begs you will graciously accept them,' he said, laying the basket at the feet of the king.

'Pears! at this season?' cried the king, peering down to look at them; 'and, pray, who is your master?'

'The Count Piro,' answered the fox.

'But how does he manage to get pears in mid-winter?' asked the king.

'Oh, he has everything he wants,' replied the fox; 'he is richer even than you are, your Majesty.'

'Then what can I send him in return for his pears?' said the king.

'Nothing, your Majesty, or you would hurt his feelings,' answered the fox.

'Well, tell him how heartily I thank him, and how much I shall enjoy them.' And the fox went away.

He trotted back to the cottage with his empty basket and told his tale, but the youth did not seem as pleased to hear as the fox was to tell.

'But, my dear little fox,' said he, 'you have brought me nothing in return, and I am so hungry!'

'Let me alone,' replied the fox; 'I know what I am doing. You will see, it will bring you luck.'

A few days after this the fox came back again.

'I must have another basket of pears,' said he.

'Ah, little fox, what shall I eat if you take away all my pears?' answered the youth.

'Be quiet, it will be all right,' said the fox; and taking a bigger basket than before, he filled it quite full of pears. Then he picked it up in his mouth, and trotted off to the palace.

'Your Majesty, as you seemed to like the first basket of pears, I have brought you some more,' said he, 'with my master, the Count Piro's humble respects.'

'Now, surely it is not possible to grow such pears with deep snow on the ground?' cried the king.

'Oh, that never affects them,' answered the fox lightly; 'he is rich enough to do anything. But to-day he sends me to ask if you will give him your daughter in marriage?'

'If he is so much richer than I am,' said the king, 'I shall be obliged to refuse. My honour would not permit me to accept his offer.'

'Oh, your Majesty, you must not think that,' replied the fox; 'and do not let the question of a dowry trouble you. The Count Piro would not dream of asking anything but the hand of the princess.'

'Is he really so rich that he can do without a dowry?' asked the king.

'Did I not tell your Majesty that he was richer than you?' answered the fox reproachfully.

'Well, beg him to come here, that we may talk together,' said the king.

So the fox went back to the young man and said: 'I have told the king that you are Count Piro, and have asked his daughter in marriage.'

'Oh, little fox, what have you done?' cried the youth in dismay; 'when the king sees me he will order my head to be cut off.'

'Oh, no, he won't!' replied the fox; 'just do as I tell you.' And he went off to the town, and stopped at the house of the best tailor.

'My master, the Count Piro, begs that you will send him at once the finest coat that you have in your shop,' said the fox, putting on his grandest air, 'and if it fits him I will call and pay for it to-morrow! Indeed, as he is in a great hurry, perhaps it might be as well if I took it round myself.' The tailor was not accustomed to serve counts, and he at once got out all the coats he had ready. The fox chose out a beautiful one of white and silver, bade the tailor tie it up in a parcel, and carrying the string in his teeth, he left the shop, and went to a horse-dealer's, whom he persuaded to send his finest horse round to the cottage, saying that the king had bidden his master to the palace.

Very unwillingly the young man put on the coat and mounted the horse, and rode up to meet the king, with the fox running before him.

'What am I to say to his Majesty, little fox?' he asked anxiously; 'you know that I have never spoken to a king before.'

'Say nothing,' answered the fox, 'but leave the talking to me. "Good morning, your Majesty," will be all that is necessary for you.'

By this time they had reached the palace, and the king came to the door to receive Count Piro, and led him to the great hall, where a feast was spread. The princess was already seated at the table, but was as dumb as Count Piro himself.

'The Count speaks very little,' the king said at last to the fox, and the fox answered: 'He has so much to think about in the management of his property that he cannot afford to talk like ordinary people.' The king was quite satisfied, and they finished dinner, after which Count Piro and the fox took leave.

The next morning the fox came round again.

'Give me another basket of pears,' he said.

'Very well, little fox; but remember it may cost me my life,' answered the youth.

'Oh, leave it to me, and do as I tell you, and you will see that in the end it will bring you luck,' answered the fox; and plucking the pears he took them up to the king.

'My master, Count Piro, sends you these pears,' he said, 'and asks for an answer to his proposal.'

'Tell the count that the wedding can take place whenever he pleases,' answered the king, and, filled with pride, the fox trotted back to deliver his message.

'But I can't bring the princess here, little fox?' cried the young man in dismay.

'You leave everything to me,' answered the fox; 'have I not managed well so far?'

The little fox frightens the Ogre & his wife

And up at the palace preparations were made for a grand wedding, and the youth was married to the princess.

After a week of feasting, the fox said to the king: 'My master wishes to take his young bride home to his own castle.'

'Very well, I will accompany them,' replied the king; and he ordered his courtiers and attendants to get ready, and the best horses in his stable to be brought out for himself, Count Piro and the princess. So they all set out, and rode across the plain, the little fox running before them.

He stopped at the sight of a great flock of sheep, which was feeding peacefully on the rich grass. 'To whom do these sheep belong?' asked he of the shepherd. 'To an ogre,' replied the shepherd.

'Hush,' said the fox in a mysterious manner. 'Do you see that crowd of armed men riding along? If you were to tell them that those sheep belonged to an ogre, they would kill them, and then the ogre would kill *you*! If they ask, just say the sheep belong to Count Piro; it will be better for everybody.' And the fox ran hastily on, as he did not wish to be seen talking to the shepherd.

Very soon the king came up.

'What beautiful sheep!' he said, drawing up his horse. 'I have none so fine in my pastures. Whose are they?'

'Count Piro's,' answered the shepherd, who did not know the king.

'Well, he must be a very rich man,' thought the king to himself, and rejoiced that he had such a wealthy son-in-law.

Meanwhile the fox had met with a huge herd of pigs, snuffling about the roots of some trees.

'To whom do these pigs belong?' he asked of the swineherd.

'To an ogre,' replied he.

'Hush!' whispered the fox, though nobody could hear him; 'do you see that troop of armed men riding towards us? If you tell them that the pigs belong to the ogre they will kill them, and then the ogre will kill *you*! If they ask, just say that the pigs belong to Count Piro; it will be better for everybody.' And he ran hastily on.

Soon after the king rode up.

'What fine pigs!' he said, reining in his horse. 'They are fatter than any I have got on my farms. Whose are they?'

'Count Piro's,' answered the swineherd, who did not know the king; and again the king felt he was lucky to have such a rich son-in-law.

This time the fox ran faster than before, and in a flowery meadow he found a troop of horses feeding. 'Whose horses are these?' he asked of the man who was watching them.

'An ogre's,' replied he.

'Hush!' whispered the fox, 'do you see that crowd of armed men coming towards us? If you tell them the horses belong to an ogre they will drive them off, and then the ogre will kill you! If they ask, just say they are Count Piro's; it will be better for everybody.' And he ran on again.

In a few minutes the king rode up.

'Oh, what lovely creatures! how I wish they were mine!' he exclaimed. 'Whose are they?'

'Count Piro's,' answered the man, who did not know the king; and the king's heart leapt as he thought that if they belonged to his rich son-in-law they were as good as his.

At last the fox came to the castle of the ogre himself. He ran up the steps, with tears falling from his eyes, and crying:

'Oh, you poor, poor people, what a sad fate is yours!'

'What has happened?' asked the ogre, trembling with fright.

'Do you see that troop of horsemen who are riding along the road? They are sent by the king to kill you!'

'Oh, dear little fox, help us, we implore you!' cried the ogre and his wife.

'Well, I will do what I can,' answered the fox. 'The best place is for you both to hide in the big oven, and when the soldiers have gone by I will let you out.'

The ogre and ogress scrambled into the oven as quick as thought, and the fox banged the door on them; just as he did so the king came up.

'Do us the honour to dismount, your Majesty,' said the fox, bowing low. 'This is the palace of Count Piro!'

'Why it is more splendid than my own!' exclaimed the king, looking round on all the beautiful things that filled the hall. But why are there no servants?'

'His Excellency the Count Piro wished the princess to choose them for herself,' answered the fox, and the king nodded his approval. He then rode on, leaving the bridal pair in the castle. But when it was dark and all was still, the fox crept downstairs and lit the kitchen fire, and the ogre and his wife were burned to death. The next morning the fox said to Count Piro:

'Now that you are rich and happy, you have no more need of me; but, before I go, there is one thing I must ask of you in return: when I die, promise me that you will give me a magnificent coffin, and bury me with due honours.'

'Oh, little, little fox, don't talk of dying,' cried the princess, nearly weeping, for she had taken a great liking to the fox.

After some time the fox thought he would see if the Count Piro was really grateful to him for all he had done, and went back to the castle, where he lay down on the door-step, and pretended to be dead. The princess was just going out for a walk, and directly she saw him lying there, she burst into tears and fell on her knees beside him.

'My dear little fox, you are not dead,' she wailed; 'you poor, poor little creature, you shall have the finest coffin in the world!'

'A coffin for an animal?' said Count Piro. 'What nonsense! just take him by the leg and throw him into the ditch.'

Then the fox sprang up and cried: 'You wretched, thankless beggar; have you forgotten that you owe all your riches to me?'

Count Piro was frightened when he heard these words, as he thought that perhaps the fox might have power to take away the castle, and leave him as poor as when he had nothing to eat but the pears off his tree. So he tried to soften the fox's anger, saying that he had only spoken in joke, as he had known quite well that he was not really dead. For the sake of the princess, the fox let himself be softened, and he lived in the castle for many years, and played with Count Piro's children. And when he actually did die, his coffin was made of silver, and Count Piro and his wife followed him to the grave.

[From *Siciliänische Mährchen.*]

THE ROGUE AND THE HERDSMAN

In a tiny cottage near the king's palace there once lived an old man, his wife, and his son, a very lazy fellow, who would never do a stroke of work. He could not be got even to look after their one cow, but left her to look after herself, while he lay on a bank and went to sleep in the sun. For a long time his father bore with him, hoping that as he grew older he might gain more sense; but at last the old man's patience was worn out, and he told his son that he should not stay at house in idleness, and must go out into the world to seek his fortune.

The young man saw that there was no help for it, and he set out with a wallet full of food over his shoulder. At length he came to a large house, at the door of which he knocked.

'What do you want?' asked the old man who opened it. And the youth told him how his father had turned him out of his house because he was so lazy and stupid, and he needed shelter for the night.

'That you shall have,' replied the man; 'but to-morrow I shall give you some work to do, for you must know that I am the chief herdsman of the king.'

The youth made no answer to this. He felt, if he was to be made to work after all, that he might as well have stayed where he was. But as he did not see any other way of getting a bed, he went slowly in.

The herdsman's two daughters and their mother were sitting at supper, and invited him to join them. Nothing more was said about work, and when the meal was over they all went to bed.

In the morning, when the young man was dressed, the herdsman called to him and said:

'Now listen, and I will tell you what you have to do.'

'What is it?' asked the youth, sulkily.

'Nothing less than to look after two hundred pigs,' was the reply.

'Oh, I am used to that,' answered the youth.

'Yes; but this time you will have to do it properly,' said the herdsman; and he took the youth to the place where the pigs were feeding, and told him to drive them to the woods on the side of the mountain. This the young man did, but as soon as they reached the outskirts of the mountain they grew quite wild, and would have run away altogether, had they not luckily gone towards a narrow ravine, from which the youth easily drove them home to his father's cottage.

'Where do all these pigs come from, and how did you get them?' asked the old man in surprise, when his son knocked at the door of the hut he had left only the day before.

'They belong to the king's chief herdsman,' answered his son. 'He gave them to me to look after, but I knew I could not do it, so I drove them straight to you. Now make the best of your good fortune, and kill them and hang them up at once.'

'What are you talking about?' cried the father, pale with horror. 'We should certainly both be put to death if I did any such thing.'

'No, no; do as I tell you, and I will get out of it somehow,' replied the young man. And in the end he had his way. The pigs were killed, and laid side by side in a row. Then he cut off the tails and tied them together with a piece of cord, and swinging the bundle over his back, he returned to the place where they should have been feeding. Here there was a small swamp, which was just what he wanted, and finding a large stone, he fastened the rope to it, and sank it in the swamp, after which he arranged the tails carefully one by one, so that only their points were seen sticking out of the water. When everything was in order, he hastened home to his master with such a sorrowful face that the herdsman saw at once that something dreadful had happened.

'Where are the pigs?' asked he.

'Oh, don't speak of them!' answered the young man; 'I really can hardly tell you. The moment they got into the field they became quite mad, and each ran in a different direction. I ran too, hither and thither, but as fast as I caught one, another was off, till I was in despair. At last, however, I collected them all and was about to drive them back, when suddenly they rushed down the hill into the swamp, where they vanished completely, leaving only the points of their tails, which you can see for yourself.'

'You have made up that story very well,' replied the herdsman.

'No, it is the real truth; come with me and I'll prove it.' And they went together to the spot, and there sure enough were the points of the tails sticking up out of the water. The herdsman laid hold of the nearest, and pulled at it with all his might, but it was no use, for the stone and the rope held them all fast. He called to the young man to help him, but the two did not succeed any better than the one had done.

'Yes, your story was true after all; it is a wonderful thing,' said the herdsman. 'But I see it is no fault of yours, and I must put up with my loss as well as I can. Now let us return home, for it is time for supper.

Next morning the herdsman said to the young man: 'I have got some other work for you to do. To-day you must take a hundred sheep to graze; but be careful that no harm befalls them.'

'I will do my best,' replied the youth. And he opened the gate of the fold, where the sheep had been all night, and drove them out into the meadow. But in a short time they grew as wild as the pigs had done, and scattered in all directions. The young man could not collect them, try as he would, and he thought to himself that this was the punishment for his laziness in refusing to look after his father's one cow.

At last, however, the sheep seemed tired of running about, and then the youth managed to gather them together, and drove them, as before, straight to his father's house.

'Whose sheep are these, and what are they doing here?' asked the old man in wonder, and his son told him. But when the tale was ended the father shook his head.

'Give up these bad ways and take them back to your master,' said he.

'No, no,' answered the youth; 'I am not so stupid as that! We will kill them and have them for dinner.'

'You will lose your life if you do,' replied the father.

'Oh, I am not sure of that!' said the son, 'and, anyway, I will have my will for once.' And he killed all the sheep and laid them on the grass. But he cut off the head of the ram which always led the flock and had bells round its horns. This he took back to the place where they should have been feeding, for here he had noticed a high rock, with a patch of green grass in the middle and two or three thick bushes growing on the edge. Up this rock he climbed with great difficulty, and fastened the ram's head to the bushes with a cord, leaving only the tips of the horns with the bells visible. As there was a soft breeze blowing, the bushes to which the head was tied moved gently, and the bells rang. When all was done to his liking he hastened quickly back to his master.

'Where are the sheep?' asked the herdsman as the young man ran panting up the steps.

'Oh! don't speak of them,' answered he. 'It is only by a miracle that I am here myself.'

'Tell me at once what has happened,' said the herdsman sternly.

The youth began to sob, and stammered out: 'I—I hardly know how to tell you! They—they—they were so—so troublesome—that I could not manage them at all. They—ran about in—in all directions, and I—I—ran after them and nearly died of fatigue. Then I heard a—a noise, which I—I thought was the wind. But—but—it was the sheep, which, be-before my very eyes, were carried straight up—up into the air. I stood watching them as if I was turned to stone, but there kept ringing in my ears the sound of the bells on the ram which led them.'

'That is nothing but a lie from beginning to end,' said the herdsman.

'No, it is as true as that there is a sun in heaven,' answered the young man.

'Then give me a proof of it,' cried his master.

'Well, come with me,' said the youth. By this time it was evening and the dusk was falling. The young man brought the herdsman to the foot of the great rock, but it was so dark you could hardly see. Still the sound of sheep bells rang softly from above, and the herdsman knew them to be those he had hung on the horns of his ram.

'Do you hear?' asked the youth.

'Yes, I hear; you have spoken the truth, and I cannot blame you for what has happened. I must bear the loss as best as I can.'

He turned and went home, followed by the young man, who felt highly pleased with his own cleverness.

'I should not be surprised if the tasks I set you were too difficult, and that you were tired of them,' said the herdsman next morning; 'but to-day I have something quite easy for you to do. You must look after forty oxen, and be sure you are very careful, for one of them has gold-tipped horns and hoofs, and the king reckons it among his greatest treasures.'

The young man drove out the oxen into the meadow, and no sooner had they got there than, like the sheep and the pigs, they began to scamper in all directions, the precious bull being the wildest of all. As the youth stood watching them, not knowing what to do next, it came into his head that his father's cow was put out to grass at no great distance ; and he forthwith made such a noise that he quite frightened the oxen, who were easily persuaded to take the path he wished. When they heard the cow lowing they galloped all the faster, and soon they all arrived at his father's house.

The old man was standing before the door of his hut when the great herd of animals dashed round a corner of the road, with his son and his own cow at their head.

'Whose cattle are these, and why are they here?' he asked; and his son told him the story.

'Take them back to your master as soon as you can,' said the old man; but the son only laughed, and said:

'No, no; they are a present to you! They will make you fat!'

For a long while the old man refused to have anything to do with such a wicked scheme; but his son talked him over in the end, and they killed the oxen as they had killed the sheep and the pigs. Last of all they came to the king's cherished ox.

The son had a rope ready to cast round its horns, and throw it to the ground, but the ox was stronger than the rope, and soon tore it in pieces. Then it dashed away to the wood, the youth following; over hedges and ditches they both went, till they reached the rocky pass which bordered the herdsman's land. Here the ox, thinking itself safe, stopped to rest, and thus gave the young man a chance to come up with it. Not knowing how to catch it, he collected all the wood he could find and made a circle of fire round the ox, who by this time had fallen asleep, and did not wake till the fire had caught its head, and it was too late for it to escape. Then the young man, who had been watching, ran home to his master.

'You have been away a long while,' said the herdsman. 'Where are the cattle?'

The young man gasped, and seemed as if he was unable to speak. At last he answered:

'It is always the same story! The oxen are—gone—gone!'

'G-g-gone?' cried the herdsman. 'Scoundrel, you lie!'

'I am telling you the exact truth,' answered the young man. 'Directly we came to the meadow they grew so wild that I could not keep them together. Then the big ox broke away, and the others followed till they all disappeared down a deep hole into the earth. It seemed to me that I heard sounds of bellowing, and I thought I recognised the voice of the golden horned ox; but when I got to the place from which the sounds had come, I could neither see nor hear anything in the hole itself, though there were traces of a fire all round it.'

'Wretch!' cried the herdsman, when he had heard this story, 'even if you did not lie before, you are lying now.'

'No, master, I am speaking the truth. Come and see for yourself.'

'If I find you have deceived me, you are a dead man, said the herdsman; and they went out together.

'What do you call that?' asked the youth. And the herdsman looked and saw the traces of a fire, which seemed to have sprung up from under the earth.

'Wonder upon wonder,' he exclaimed, 'so you really did speak the truth after all! Well, I cannot reproach you, though I shall have to pay heavily to my royal master for the value of that ox. But come, let us go home! I will never set you to herd cattle again, henceforward I will give you something easier to do.'

'I have thought of exactly the thing for you,' said the herdsman as they walked along, 'and it is so simple that you cannot make a mistake. Just make me ten scythes, one for every man, for I want the grass mown in one of my meadows to-morrow.'

At these words the youth's heart sank, for he had never been trained either as a smith or a joiner. However, he dared not say no, but smiled and nodded.

Slowly and sadly he went to bed, but he could not sleep, for wondering how the scythes were to be made. All the skill and cunning he had shown before was of no use to him now, and after thinking about the scythes for many hours, there seemed only one way open to him. So, listening to make sure that all was still, he stole away to his parents, and told them the whole story. When they had heard everything, they hid him where no one could find him.

Time passed away, and the young man stayed at home doing all his parents bade him, and showing himself very different from what he had been before he went out to see the world; but one day he said to his father that he should like to marry, and have a house of his own.

'When I served the king's chief herdsman,' added he, 'I saw his daughter, and I am resolved to try if I cannot win her for my wife.'

'It will cost you your life, if you do,' answered the father, shaking his head.

'Well, I will do my best,' replied his son; 'but first give me the sword which hangs over your bed!'

The old man did not understand what good the sword would do, however he took it down, and the young man went his way.

Late in the evening he arrived at the house of the herdsman, and knocked at the door, which was opened by a little boy.

'I want to speak to your master,' said he.

'So it is you?' cried the herdsman, when he had received the message. 'Well, you can sleep here to-night if you wish.'

'I have come for something else besides a bed,' replied the young man, drawing his sword, 'and if you do not promise to give me your youngest daughter as my wife I will stab you through the heart.'

What could the poor man do but promise? And he fetched his youngest daughter, who seemed quite pleased at the proposed match, and gave the youth her hand.

Then the young man went home to his parents, and bade them get ready to welcome his bride. And when the wedding was over he told his father-in-law, the herdsman, what he had done with the sheep, and pigs, and cattle. By-and-by the story came to the king's ears, and he thought that a man who was so clever was just the man to govern the country; so he made him his minister, and after the king himself there was no one so great as he.

[From *Isländische Mährchen.*]

EISENKOPF

ONCE upon a time there lived an old man who had only one son, whom he loved dearly; but they were very poor, and often had scarcely enough to eat. Then the old man fell ill, and things grew worse than ever, so he called his son and said to him:

'My dear boy, I have no longer any food to give you, and you must go into the world and get it for yourself. It does not matter what work you do, but remember if you do it well and are faithful to your master, you will always have your reward.'

So Peter put a piece of black bread in his knapsack, and strapping it on his back, took a stout stick in his hand, and set out to seek his fortune. For a long while he travelled on and on, and nobody seemed to want him; but one day he met an old man, and being a polite youth, he took off his hat and said: 'Good morning,' in a pleasant voice. 'Good morning,' answered the old man; 'and where are you going?'

'I am wandering through the country trying to get work,' replied Peter.

'Then stay with me, for I can give you plenty,' said the old man, and Peter stayed.

His work did not seem hard, for he had only two horses and a cow to see after, and though he had been hired for a year, the year consisted of but three days, so that it was not long before he received his wages. In payment the old man gave him a nut, and offered to keep him for another year; but Peter was home-sick; and, besides, he would rather have been paid ever so small a piece of money than a nut; for, thought he, nuts grow on every tree, and I can gather as many as I like. However, he did not say this to the old man, who had been kind to him, but just bade him farewell.

The nearer Peter drew to his father's house the more ashamed he felt at having brought back such poor wages. What could one nut do for him? Why, it would not buy even a slice of bacon. It was no use taking it home, he might as well eat it. So he sat down on a stone and cracked it with his teeth, and then took it out of his mouth to break off the shell. But who could ever guess what came out of that nut? Why horses and oxen and sheep stepped out in such numbers that they seemed as if they would stretch to the world's end! The sight gave Peter such a shock that he wrung his hands in dismay. What was he to do with all these creatures, where was he to put them? He stood and gazed in terror, and at this moment Eisenkopf came by.

'What is the matter, young man?' asked he.

'Oh, my friend, there is plenty the matter,' answered Peter. 'I have gained a nut as my wages, and when I cracked it this crowd of beasts came out, and I don't know what to do with them all!'

'Listen to me, my son,' said Eisenkopf. 'If you will promise never to marry I will drive them all back into the nut again.'

In his trouble Peter would have promised far harder things than this, so he gladly gave the promise Eisenkopf asked for; and at a whistle from the stranger the animals all began crowding into the nut again, nearly tumbling over each other in their haste. When the last foot had got inside, the two halves of the shell shut close. Then Peter put it in his pocket and went on to the house.

No sooner had he reached it than he cracked his nut for the second time, and out came the horses, sheep, and oxen again. Indeed Peter thought that there were even more of them than before. The old man could not believe his eyes when he saw the multitudes of horses, oxen and sheep standing before his door.

'How did you come by all these?' he gasped, as soon as he could speak; and the son told him the whole story, and of the promise he had given Eisenkopf.

The next day some of the cattle were driven to market and sold, and with the money the old man was able to buy some of the fields and gardens round his house, and in a few months had grown the richest and most prosperous man in the whole village. Everything seemed to turn to gold in his hands, till one day, when he and his son were sitting in the orchard watching their herds of cattle grazing in the meadows, he suddenly said: 'Peter, my boy, it is time that you were thinking of marrying.'

'But, my dear father, I told you I can never marry, because of the promise I gave to Eisenkopf.'

'Oh, one promises here and promises there, but no one ever thinks of keeping such promises. If Eisenkopf does not like your marrying, he will have to put up with it all the same! Besides, there stands in the stable a grey horse which is saddled night and day; and if Eisenkopf should show his face, you have only got to jump on the horse's back and ride away, and nobody on earth can catch you. When all is safe you will come back again, and we shall live as happily as two fish in the sea.'

And so it all happened. The young man found a pretty, brown-skinned girl who was willing to have him for a husband, and the whole village came to the wedding feast. The music was at its gayest, and the dance at its merriest, when Eisenkopf looked in at the window.

'Oh, ho, my brother! what is going on here? It has the air of being a wedding feast. Yet I fancied—was I mistaken?—that you had given me a promise that you never would marry.' But Peter had not waited for the end of this speech. Scarcely had he seen Eisenkopf than he darted like the wind to the stable and flung himself on

EISENKOPF COMES TO THE WEDDING.

the horse's back. In another moment he was away over the mountain, with Eisenkopf running fast behind him.

On they went through thick forests where the sun never shone, over rivers so wide that it took a whole day to sail across them, up hills whose sides were all of glass; on they went through seven times seven countries till Peter reined in his horse before the house of an old woman.

'Good day, mother,' said he, jumping down and opening the door.

'Good day, my son,' answered she, 'and what are you doing here, at the world's end?'

'I am flying for my life, mother, flying to the world which is beyond all worlds; for Eisenkopf is at my heels.'

'Come in and rest then, and have some food, for I have a little dog who will begin to howl when Eisenkopf is still seven miles off.'

So Peter went in and warmed himself and ate and drank, till suddenly the dog began to howl.

'Quick, my son, quick, you must go,' cried the old woman. And the lightning itself was not quicker than Peter.

'Stop a moment,' cried the old woman again, just as he was mounting his horse, 'take this napkin and this cake, and put them in your bag where you can get hold of them easily.' Peter took them and put them into his bag, and waving his thanks for her kindness, he was off like the wind.

Round and round he rode, through seven times seven countries, through forests still thicker, and rivers still wider, and mountains still more slippery than the others he had passed, till at length he reached a house where dwelt another old woman.

'Good day, mother,' said he.

'Good day, my son! What are you seeking here at the world's end?'

'I am flying for my life, mother, flying to the world that is beyond all worlds, for Eisenkopf is at my heels.'

'Come in, my son, and have some food. I have a little dog who will begin to howl when Eisenkopf is still seven miles off; so lie on this bed and rest yourself in peace.'

Then she went to the kitchen and baked a number of cakes, more than Peter could have eaten in a whole month. He had not finished a quarter of them, when the dog began to howl.

'Now, my son, you must go,' cried the old woman; 'but first put these cakes and this napkin in your bag, where you can easily get at them.' So Peter thanked her and was off like the wind.

On he rode, through seven times seven countries, till he came to the house of a third old woman, who welcomed him as the others had done. But when the dog howled, and Peter sprang up to go, she said, as she gave him the same gifts for his journey: 'You have now three cakes and three napkins, for I know that my sisters have each given you one. Listen to me, and do what I tell you. Ride seven days and nights straight before you, and on the eighth morning you will see a great fire. Strike it three times with the three napkins and it will part in two. Then ride into the opening, and when you are in the middle of the opening, throw the three cakes behind your back with your left hand.'

Peter thanked her for her counsel, and was careful to do exactly all the old woman had told him. On the eighth morning he reached a fire so large that he could see nothing else on either side, but when he struck it with the napkins it parted, and stood on each hand like a wall. As he rode through the opening he threw the cakes behind him. From each cake there sprang a huge dog, and he gave them the names of World's-weight, Iron-strong, and Quick-ear. They bayed with joy at the sight of him, and as Peter turned to pat them, he beheld

Eisenkopf at the edge of the fire, but the opening had closed up behind Peter, and he could not get through.

'Stop, you promise-breaker,' shrieked he; 'you have slipped through my hands once, but wait till I catch you again!'

Then he lay down by the fire and watched to see what would happen.

When Peter knew that he had nothing more to fear from Eisenkopf, he rode on slowly till he came to a small white house. Here he entered and found himself in a room where a grey-haired woman was spinning and a beautiful girl was sitting in the window combing her golden hair.

'What brings you here, my son?' asked the old woman.

'I am seeking for a place, mother,' answered Peter.

'Stay with me, then, for I need a servant,' said the old woman.

'With pleasure, mother,' replied he.

After that Peter's life was a very happy one. He sowed and ploughed all day, except now and then when he took his dogs and went to hunt. And whatever game he brought back the maiden with the golden hair knew how to dress it.

One day the old woman had gone to the town to buy some flour, and Peter and the maiden were left alone in the house. They fell into talk, and she asked him where his home was, and how he had managed to come through the fire. Peter then told her the whole story, and of his striking the flames with the three napkins as he had been told to do. The maiden listened attentively and wondered in herself whether what he said was true. So after Peter had gone out to the fields, she crept up to his room and stole the napkins and then set off as fast as she could to the fire by a path she knew of over the hill.

At the third blow she gave the flames divided, and Eisenkopf, who had been watching and hoping for a chance of this kind, ran down the opening and stood before her. At this sight the maiden was almost frightened to death, but with a great effort she recovered herself and ran home as fast as her legs would carry her, closely pursued by Eisenkopf. Panting for breath she rushed into the house and fell fainting on the floor; but Eisenkopf entered behind her, and hid himself in the kitchen under the hearth.

Not long after, Peter came in and picked up the three napkins which the maiden had dropped on the threshold. He wondered how they got there, for he knew he had left them in his room; but what was his horror when he saw the form of the fainting girl lying where she had dropped, as still and white as if she had been dead. He lifted her up and carried her to her bed, where she soon revived, but she did not tell Peter about Eisenkopf, who had been almost crushed to death under the hearth-stone by the body of World's-weight.

The next morning Peter locked up his dogs and went out into the forest alone. Eisenkopf, however, had seen him go, and followed so closely at his heels that Peter had barely time to clamber up a tall tree, where Eisenkopf could not reach him. 'Come down at once, you gallows-bird,' he cried. 'Have you forgotten your promise that you never would marry?'

'Oh, I know it is all up with me,' answered Peter, 'but let me call out three times.'

'You can call a hundred times if you like,' returned Eisenkopf, 'for now I have got you in my power, and you shall pay for what you have done.'

'Iron-strong, World's-weight, Quick-ear, fly to my help!' cried Peter; and Quick-ear heard, and said to his brothers: 'Listen, our master is calling us.'

'You are dreaming, fool,' answered World's-weight; 'why he has not finished his breakfast.' And he gave Quick-ear a slap with his paw, for he was young and needed to be taught sense.

'Iron-strong, World's-weight, Quick-ear, fly to my help!' cried Peter again.

This time World's-weight heard also, and he said, 'Ah, now our master is really calling.'

'How silly you are!' answered Iron-strong; 'you know that at this hour he is always eating.' And he gave World's-weight a cuff, because he was old enough to know better.

Peter sat trembling on the tree dreading lest his dogs had never heard, or else that, having heard, they had refused to come. It was his last chance, so making a mighty effort he shrieked once more:

'Iron-strong, World's-weight, Quick-ear, fly to my help, or I am a dead man!'

And Iron-strong heard, and said: 'Yes, he is certainly calling, we must go at once.' And in an instant he had burst open the door, and all three were bounding away in the direction of the voice. When they reached the foot of the tree Peter just said: 'At him!' And in a few minutes there was nothing left of Eisenkopf.

As soon as his enemy was dead Peter got down and returned to the house, where he bade farewell to the old woman and her daughter, who gave him a beautiful ring, all set with diamonds. It was really a magic ring, but neither Peter nor the maiden knew that.

Peter's heart was heavy as he set out for home. He had ceased to love the wife whom he had left at his wedding feast, and his heart had gone out to the golden-haired girl. However, it was no use thinking of that, so he rode forward steadily.

The fire had to be passed through before he had gone very far, and when he came to it, Peter shook the napkins three times in the flames and a passage opened for him. But then a curious thing happened; the three dogs, who had followed at his heels all the way, now became three cakes again, which Peter put into his bag with the napkins. After that he stopped at the houses of the three old women, and gave each one back her napkin and her cake.

'Where is my wife?' asked Peter, when he reached home.

'Oh, my dear son, why did you ever leave us? After you had vanished, no one knew where, your poor wife grew more and more wretched, and would neither eat nor drink. Little by little she faded away, and a month ago we laid her in her grave, to hide her sorrows under the earth.'

At this news Peter began to weep, for he had loved his wife before he went away and had seen the golden-haired maiden.

He went sorrowfully about his work for the space of half a year, when, one night, he dreamed that he moved the diamond ring given him by the maiden from his right hand and put it on the wedding finger of the left. The dream was so real that he awoke at once and changed the ring from one hand to the other. And as he did so guess what he saw? Why, the golden-haired girl standing before him. And he sprang up and kissed her, and said: 'Now you are mine for ever and ever, and when we die we will both be buried in one grave.'

And so they were.

[From *Ungarische Mährchen.*]

THE DEATH OF ABU NOWAS AND OF HIS WIFE

ONCE upon a time there lived a man whose name was Abu Nowas, and he was a great favourite with the Sultan of the country, who had a palace in the same town where Abu Nowas dwelt.

One day Abu Nowas came weeping into the hall of the palace where the Sultan was sitting, and said to him: 'Oh, mighty Sultan, my wife is dead.'

'That is bad news,' replied the Sultan; 'I must get you another wife.' And he bade his Grand Vizir send for the Sultana.

'This poor Abu Nowas has lost his wife,' said he, when she entered the hall.

'Oh, then we must get him another,' answered the Sultana; 'I have a girl that will suit him exactly,' and clapped her hands loudly. At this signal a maiden appeared and stood before her.

'I have got a husband for you,' said the Sultana.

'Who is he?' asked the girl.

'Abu Nowas, the jester,' replied the Sultana.

'I will take him,' answered the maiden; and as Abu Nowas made no objection, it was all arranged. The Sultana had the most beautiful clothes made for the bride, and the Sultan gave the bridegroom his wedding suit, and a thousand gold pieces into the bargain, and soft carpets for the house.

So Abu Nowas took his wife home, and for some time they were very happy, and spent the money freely which the Sultan had given them, never thinking what they should do for more when that was gone. But come to an end it did, and they had to sell their fine things one by one, till at length nothing was left but a cloak apiece, and one blanket to cover them. 'We have run through our fortune,' said Abu Nowas, 'what are we to do now? I am afraid to go back to the Sultan, for he will command his servants to turn me from the door. But you shall return to your mistress, and throw yourself at her feet and weep, and perhaps she will help us.'

'Oh, you had much better go,' said the wife. 'I shall not know what to say.'

'Well, then, stay at home, if you like,' answered Abu Nowas, 'and I will ask to be admitted to the Sultan's presence, and will tell him, with sobs, that my wife is dead, and that I have no money for her burial. When he hears that perhaps he will give us something.'

'Yes, that is a good plan,' said the wife; and Abu Nowas set out.

The Sultan was sitting in the hall of justice when Abu Nowas entered, his eyes streaming with tears, for he had rubbed some pepper into them. They smarted dreadfully, and he could hardly see to walk straight, and everyone wondered what was the matter with him.

'Abu Nowas! What has happened?' cried the Sultan.

'Oh, noble Sultan, my wife is dead,' wept he.

'We must all die,' answered the Sultan; but this was not the reply for which Abu Nowas had hoped.

'True, O Sultan, but I have neither shroud to wrap her in, nor money to bury her with,' went on Abu Nowas, in no wise abashed by the way the Sultan had received his news.

'Well, give him a hundred pieces of gold,' said the Sultan, turning to the Grand Vizir. And when the money was counted out Abu Nowas bowed low, and left the hall, his tears still flowing, but with joy in his heart.

'Have you got anything?' cried his wife, who was waiting for him anxiously.

'Yes, a hundred gold pieces,' said he, throwing down the bag, 'but that will not last us any time. Now you must go to the Sultana, clothed in sackcloth and robes of mourning, and tell her that your husband, Abu Nowas, is dead, and you have no money for his burial. When she hears that, she will be sure to ask you what has become of the money and the fine clothes she gave us on our marriage, and you will answer, "before he died he sold everything."'

The wife did as she was told, and wrapping herself in sackcloth went up to the Sultana's own palace, and as she was known to have been one of Subida's favourite attendants, she was taken without difficulty into the private apartments.

'What is the matter?' inquired the Sultana, at the sight of the dismal figure.

'My husband lies dead at home, and he has spent all our money, and sold everything, and I have nothing left to bury him with,' sobbed the wife.

Then Subida took up a purse containing two hundred gold pieces, and said: 'Your husband served us long and faithfully. You must see that he has a fine funeral.'

The wife took the money, and, kissing the feet of the Sultana, she joyfully hastened home. They spent some happy hours planning how they should spend it, and thinking how clever they had been. 'When the Sultan goes this evening to Subida's palace,' said Abu Nowas, 'she will be sure to tell him that Abu Nowas is dead. "Not Abu Nowas, it is his wife," he will reply, and they will quarrel over it, and all the time we shall be sitting here enjoying ourselves. Oh, if they only knew, how angry they would be!'

As Abu Nowas had foreseen, the Sultan went, in the evening after his business was over, to pay his usual visit to the Sultana.

'Poor Abu Nowas is dead!' said Subida when he entered the room.

'It is not Abu Nowas, but his wife who is dead,' answered the Sultan.

'No; really you are quite wrong. She came to tell me herself only a couple of hours ago,' replied Subida, 'and as he had spent all their money, I gave her something to bury him with.'

'You must be dreaming,' exclaimed the Sultan. 'Soon after midday Abu Nowas came into the hall, his eyes streaming with tears, and when I asked him the reason he answered that his wife was dead, and they had sold everything they had, and he had nothing left, not so much as would buy her a shroud, far less for her burial.'

For a long time they talked, and neither would listen to the other, till the Sultan sent for the door-keeper and bade him go instantly to the house of Abu Nowas and see if it was the man or his wife who was dead. But Abu Nowas happened to be sitting with his wife behind the latticed window, which looked on the street, and he saw the man coming, and sprang up at once. 'There is the Sultan's door-keeper! They have sent him here to find out the truth. Quick! throw yourself on the bed and pretend that you are dead.' And in a moment the wife was stretched out stiffly, with a linen sheet spread across her, like a corpse.

She was only just in time, for the sheet was hardly drawn across her when the door opened and the porter came in. 'Has anything happened?' asked he.

'My poor wife is dead,' replied Abu Nowas. 'Look! she is laid out here.' And the porter approached the bed, which was in a corner of the room, and saw the stiff form lying underneath.

'We must all die,' said he, and went back to the Sultan.

'Well, have you found out which of them is dead?' asked the Sultan.

'Yes, noble Sultan; it is the wife,' replied the porter.

'He only says that to please you,' cried Subida in a rage; and calling to her chamberlain, she ordered him to go at once to the dwelling of Abu Nowas and see which of the two was dead. 'And be sure you tell the truth about it,' added she, 'or it will be the worse for you.'

As her chamberlain drew near the house, Abu Nowas caught sight of him. 'There is the Sultana's chamberlain,' he exclaimed in a fright. 'Now it is my turn to die. Be quick and spread the sheet over me.' And he laid himself on the bed, and held his breath when the chamberlain came in. 'What are you weeping for?' asked the man, finding the wife in tears.

'My husband is dead,' answered she, pointing to the bed; and the chamberlain drew back the sheet and beheld Abu Nowas lying stiff and motionless. Then he gently replaced the sheet and returned to the palace.

'Well, have you found out this time?' asked the Sultan.

'My lord, it is the husband who is dead.'

'But I tell you he was with me only a few hours ago,' cried the Sultan angrily. 'I must get to the bottom of this before I sleep! Let my golden coach be brought round at once.'

The coach was before the door in another five minutes, and the Sultan and Sultana both got in. Abu Nowas had ceased being a dead man, and was looking into the street when he saw the coach coming. 'Quick! quick!' he called to his wife. 'The Sultan will be here directly, and we must both be dead to receive him.' So they laid themselves down, and spread the sheet over them, and held their breath. At that instant the Sultan entered, followed by the Sultana and the chamberlain, and he went up to the bed and found the corpses stiff and motionless. 'I would give a thousand gold pieces to anyone who would tell me the truth about this,' cried he, and at the words Abu Nowas sat up. 'Give them to me, then,' said he, holding out his hand. 'You cannot give them to anyone who needs them more.'

'Oh, Abu Nowas, you impudent dog!' exclaimed the Sultan, bursting into a laugh, in which the Sultana joined. 'I might have known it was one of your tricks!' But he sent Abu Nowas the gold he had promised, and let us hope that it did not fly so fast as the last had done.

[From *Tünische Mährchen.*]

MOTIKATIKA

ONCE upon a time, in a very hot country, a man lived with his wife in a little hut, which was surrounded by grass and flowers. They were perfectly happy together till, by-and-by, the woman fell ill and refused to take any food. The husband tried to persuade her to eat all sorts of delicious fruits that he had found in the forest, but she would have none of them, and grew so thin he feared she would die. 'Is there *nothing* you would like?' he said at last in despair.

'Yes, I think I could eat some wild honey,' answered she. The husband was overjoyed, for he thought this sounded easy enough to get, and he went off at once in search of it.

He came back with a wooden pan quite full, and gave it to his wife. 'I can't eat *that*,' she said, turning away in disgust. 'Look! there are some dead bees in it! I want honey that is quite pure.' And the man threw the rejected honey on the grass, and started off to get some fresh. When he got back he offered it to his wife, who treated it as she had done the first bowlful. 'That honey has got ants in it: throw it away,' she said, and when he brought her some more, she declared it was full of earth. In his fourth journey he managed to find some that she would eat, and then she begged him to get her some water. This took him some time, but at length he came to a lake whose waters were sweetened with sugar. He filled a pannikin quite full, and carried it home to his wife, who drank it eagerly, and said that she now felt quite well.

When she was up and had dressed herself, her husband lay down in her place, saying: 'You have given me a great deal of trouble, and now it is my turn!'

'What is the matter with you?' asked the wife.

'I am thirsty and want some water,' answered he; and she took a large pot and carried it to the nearest spring, which was a good way off. 'Here is the water,' she said to her husband, lifting the heavy pot from her head; but he turned away in disgust.

'You have drawn it from the pool that is full of frogs and willows; you must get me some more.' So the woman set out again and walked still further to another lake.

'This water tastes of rushes,' he exclaimed, 'go and get some fresh.' But when she brought back a third supply he declared that it seemed made up of water-lilies, and that he must have water that was pure, and not spoilt by willows, or frogs, or rushes. So for the fourth time she put her jug on her head, and passing all the lakes she had hitherto tried, she came to another, where the water was golden like honey. She stooped down to drink, when a horrible head bobbed up on the surface.

'How dare you steal my water?' cried the head.

'It is my husband who has sent me,' she replied, trembling all over. 'But do not kill me! You shall have my baby, if you will only let me go.'

'How am I to know which is your baby?' asked the ogre.

'Oh, that is easily managed. I will shave both sides of his head, and hang some white beads round his neck. And when you come to the hut you have only to call "Motikatika!" and he will run to meet you, and you can eat him.'

'Very well,' said the ogre, 'you can go home.' And after filling the pot she returned, and told her husband of the dreadful danger she had been in.

Now, though his mother did not know it, the baby was a magician, and he had heard all that his mother had promised the ogre; and he laughed to himself as he planned how to outwit her.

The next morning she shaved his head on both sides, and hung the white beads round his neck, and said to him: 'I am going to the fields to work, but you must

THE WOMAN AND THE OGRE

stay at home. Be sure you do not go outside, or some wild beast may eat you.'

'Very well,' answered he.

As soon as his mother was out of sight, the baby took out some magic bones, and placed them in a row before him. 'You are my father,' he told one bone, 'and you are my mother. You are the biggest,' he said to the third, 'so you shall be the ogre who wants to eat me; and you,' to another, 'are very little, therefore you shall be me. Now, then, tell me what I am to do.'

'Collect all the babies in the village the same size as yourself,' answered the bones; 'shave the sides of their heads, and hang white beads round their necks, and tell them that when anybody calls "Motikatika," they are to answer to it. And be quick for you have no time to lose.'

Motikatika went out directly, and brought back quite a crowd of babies, and shaved their heads and hung white beads round their little black necks, and just as he had finished, the ground began to shake, and the huge ogre came striding along, crying: 'Motikatika! Motikatika!'

'Here we are! here we are!' answered the babies, all running to meet him.

'It is Motikatika I want,' said the ogre.

'We are all Motikatika,' they replied. And the ogre sat down in bewilderment, for he dared not eat the children of people who had done him no wrong, or a heavy punishment would befall him. The children waited for a little, wondering, and then they went away.

The ogre remained where he was, till the evening, when the woman returned from the fields.

'I have not seen Motikatika,' said he.

'But why did you not call him by his name, as I told you?' she asked.

'I did, but all the babies in the village seemed to be named Motikatika,' answered the ogre; 'you cannot think the number who came running to me.'

The woman did not know what to make of it, so, to keep him in a good temper, she entered the hut and prepared a bowl of maize, which she brought him.

'I do not want maize, I want the baby,' grumbled he, 'and I will have him.'

'Have patience,' answered she ; 'I will call him, and you can eat him at once.' And she went into the hut and cried, 'Motikatika!'

'I am coming, mother,' replied he; but first he took out his bones, and, crouching down on the ground behind the hut, asked them how he should escape the ogre.

'Change yourself into a mouse,' said the bones; and so he did, and the ogre grew tired of waiting, and told the woman she must invent some other plan.

'To-morrow I will send him into the field to pick some beans for me, and you will find him there, and can eat him.'

'Very well,' replied the ogre, 'and this time I will take care to have him,' and he went back to his lake.

Next morning Motikatika was sent out with a basket, and told to pick some beans for dinner. On the way to the field he took out his bones and asked them what he was to do to escape from the ogre. 'Change yourself into a bird and snap off the beans,' said the bones. And the ogre chased away the bird, not knowing that it was Motikatika.

The ogre went back to the hut and told the woman that she had deceived him again, and that he would not be put off any longer.

'Return here this evening,' answered she, 'and you will find him in bed under this white coverlet. Then you can carry him away, and eat him at once.'

But the boy heard, and consulted his bones, which said: 'Take the red coverlet from your father's bed, and put yours on his,' and so he did. And when the ogre came, he seized Motikatika's father and carried him outside the hut and ate him. When his wife found out the mistake, she cried bitterly; but Motikatika said: 'It is only just that he should be eaten, and not I; for it was he, and not I, who sent you to fetch the water.'

[Adapted from the *Ba-Ronga* (H. Junod).]

NIELS AND THE GIANTS

On one of the great moors over in Jutland, where trees won't grow because the soil is so sandy and the wind so strong, there once lived a man and his wife, who had a little house and some sheep, and two sons who helped them to herd them. The elder of the two was called Rasmus, and the younger Niels. Rasmus was quite content to look after sheep, as his father had done before him, but Niels had a fancy to be a hunter, and was not happy till he got hold of a gun and learned to shoot. It was only an old muzzle-loading flint-lock after all, but Niels thought it a great prize, and went about shooting at everything he could see. So much did he practise that in the long run he became a wonderful shot, and was heard of even where he had never been seen. Some people said there was very little in him beyond this, but that was an idea they found reason to change in the course of time.

The parents of Rasmus and Niels were good Catholics, and when they were getting old the mother took it into her head that she would like to go to Rome and see the Pope. The others didn't see much use in this, but she had her way in the end: they sold all the sheep, shut up the house, and set out for Rome on foot. Niels took his gun with him.

'What do you want with that?' said Rasmus; 'we have plenty to carry without it.' But Niels could not be happy without his gun, and took it all the same.

It was in the hottest part of summer that they began their journey, so hot that they could not travel at all in the middle of the day, and they were afraid to do it by night lest they might lose their way or fall into the hands of robbers. One day, a little before sunset, they came to an inn which lay at the edge of a forest.

'We had better stay here for the night,' said Rasmus.

'What an idea!' said Niels, who was growing impatient at the slow progress they were making. 'We can't travel by day for the heat, and we remain where we are all night. It will be long enough before we get to Rome if we go on at this rate.'

Rasmus was unwilling to go on, but the two old people sided with Niels, who said, 'The nights aren't dark, and the moon will soon be up. We can ask at the inn here, and find out which way we ought to take.'

So they held on for some time, but at last they came to a small opening in the forest, and here they found that the road split in two. There was no sign-post to direct them, and the people in the inn had not told them which of the two roads to take.

'What's to be done now?' said Rasmus. 'I think we had better have stayed at the inn.'

'There's no harm done,' said Niels. 'The night is warm, and we can wait here till morning. One of us will keep watch till midnight, and then waken the other.'

Rasmus chose to take the first watch, and the others lay down to sleep. It was very quiet in the forest, and Rasmus could hear the deer and foxes and other animals moving about among the rustling leaves. After the moon rose he could see them occasionally, and when a big stag came quite close to him he got hold of Niels' gun and shot it.

Niels was wakened by the report. 'What's that?' he said.

'I've just shot a stag,' said Rasmus, highly pleased with himself.

'That's nothing,' said Niels. 'I've often shot a sparrow, which is a much more difficult thing to do.'

It was now close on midnight, so Niels began his watch, and Rasmus went to sleep. It began to get colder, and Niels began to walk about a little to keep himself warm. He soon found that they were not far from the edge of the forest, and when he climbed up one of the trees there he could see out over the open country beyond. At a little distance he saw a fire, and beside it there sat three giants, busy with broth and beef. They were so huge that the spoons they used were as large as spades, and their forks as big as hay-forks: with these they lifted whole bucketfuls of broth and great joints of meat out of an enormous pot which was set on the ground between them. Niels was startled and rather scared at first, but he comforted himself with the thought that the giants were a good way off, and that if they came nearer he could easily hide among the bushes. After watching them for a little, however, he began to get over his alarm, and finally slid down the tree again, resolved to get his gun and play some tricks with them.

When he had climbed back to his former position, he took good aim, and waited till one of the giants was just in the act of putting a large piece of meat into his mouth. *Bang!* went Niels' gun, and the bullet struck the handle of the fork so hard that the point went into the giant's chin, instead of his mouth.

'None of your tricks,' growled the giant to the one who sat next him. 'What do you mean by hitting my fork like that, and making me prick myself?'

'I never touched your fork,' said the other. 'Don't try to get up a quarrel with me.'

'Look at it, then,' said the first. 'Do you suppose I stuck it into my own chin for fun?'

The two got so angry over the matter that each offered to fight the other there and then, but the third giant acted as peace-maker, and they again fell to their eating.

While the quarrel was going on, Niels had loaded the gun again, and just as the second giant was about to put a nice tit-bit into his mouth, *bang!* went the gun again, and the fork flew into a dozen pieces.

This giant was even more furious than the first had been, and words were just coming to blows, when the third giant again interposed.

'Don't be fools,' he said to them; 'what's the good of beginning to fight among ourselves, when it is so necessary for the three of us to work together and get the upper hand over the king of this country. It will be a hard enough task as it is, but it will be altogether hopeless if we don't stick together. Sit down again, and let us finish our meal; I shall sit between you, and then neither of you can blame the other.'

Niels was too far away to hear their talk, but from their gestures he could guess what was happening, and thought it good fun.

'Thrice is lucky,' said he to himself; 'I'll have another shot yet.'

This time it was the third giant's fork that caught the bullet, and snapped in two.

'Well,' said he, 'if I were as foolish as you two, I would also fly into a rage, but I begin to see what time of day it is, and I'm going off this minute to see who it is that's playing these tricks with us.'

So well had the giant made his observations, that though Niels climbed down the tree as fast as he could, so as to hide among the bushes, he had just got to the ground when the enemy was upon him.

'Stay where you are,' said the giant, 'or I'll put my foot on you, and there won't be much of you left after that.'

Niels gave in, and the giant carried him back to his comrades.

'You don't deserve any mercy at our hands,' said his captor, 'but as you are such a good shot you may be of great use to us, so we shall spare your life, if you will do us a service. Not far from here there stands a castle, in which the king's daughter lives; we are at war with the king, and want to get the upper hand of him by carrying off the princess, but the castle is so well guarded that there is no getting into it. By our skill in magic we have cast sleep on every living thing in the castle, except a little black dog, and, as long as he is awake, we are no better off than before; for, as soon as we begin to climb over the wall, the little dog will hear us, and its barking will waken all the others again. Having got you, we can place you where you will be able to shoot the dog before it begins to bark, and then no one can hinder us from getting the princess into our hands. If you do that, we shall not only let you off, but reward you handsomely.'

Niels had to consent, and the giants set out for the castle at once. It was surrounded by a very high rampart, so high that even the giants could not touch the top of it. 'How am I to get over that?' said Niels.

'Quite easily,' said the third giant; 'I'll throw you up on it.'

'No, thanks,' said Niels. 'I might fall down on the other side, or break my leg or neck, and then the little dog wouldn't get shot after all.'

'No fear of that,' said the giant; 'the rampart is quite wide on the top, and covered with long grass, so that you will come down as softly as though you fell on a feather-bed.'

Niels had to believe him, and allowed the giant to throw him up. He came down on his feet quite unhurt, but the little black dog heard the dump, and rushed out of its kennel at once. It was just opening its mouth to bark, when Niels fired, and it fell dead on the spot.

'Go down on the inside now,' said the giant, 'and see if you can open the gate to us.'

Niels made his way down into the courtyard, but on his way to the outer gate he found himself at the entrance to the large hall of the castle. The door was open, and the hall was brilliantly lighted, though there was no one to be seen. Niels went in here and looked round him: on the wall there hung a huge sword without a sheath, and beneath it was a large drinking-horn, mounted with silver. Niels went closer to look at these, and saw that the horn had letters engraven on the silver rim: when he took it down and turned it round, he found that the inscription was:—

> Whoever drinks the wine I hold
> Can wield the sword that hangs above;
> Then let him use it for the right,
> And win a royal maiden's love.

Niels took out the silver stopper of the horn, and drank some of the wine, but when he tried to take down the sword he found himself unable to move it. So he hung up the horn again, and went further in to the castle. 'The giants can wait a little,' he said.

Before long he came to an apartment in which a beautiful princess lay asleep in a bed, and on a table by her side there lay a gold-hemmed handkerchief. Niels tore this in two, and put one half in his pocket, leaving the other half on the table. On the floor he saw a pair of gold-embroidered slippers, and one of these he also put in his pocket. After that he went back to the hall, and took down the horn again. 'Perhaps I have to drink all that is in it before I can move the sword,' he thought; so he put it to his lips again and drank till it was quite empty. When he had done this, he could wield the sword with the greatest of ease, and felt himself strong enough to do anything, even to fight the giants he had left outside, who were no doubt wondering why he had not opened the gate to them before this time. To kill the giants, he thought, would be using the sword for the right; but as to winning the love of the princess, that was a thing which the son of a poor sheep-farmer need not hope for.

When Niels came to the gate of the castle, he found that there was a large door and a small one, so he opened the latter.

'Can't you open the big door?' said the giants; 'we shall hardly be able to get in at this one.'

'The bars are too heavy for me to draw,' said Niels; 'if you stoop a little you can quite well come in here.' The first giant accordingly bent down and entered in a stooping posture, but before he had time to straighten his back again Niels made a sweep with the sword, and off went the giant's head. To push the body aside as it fell was quite easy for Niels, so strong had the wine made him, and the second giant as he entered met the same reception. The third was slower in coming, so Niels called out to him: 'Be quick,' he said, 'you are surely the oldest of the three, since you are so slow in your movements, but I can't wait here long; I must get back to my own people as soon as possible.' So the third also came in, and was served in the same way. It appears from the story that giants were not given fair play!

By this time day was beginning to break, and Niels thought that his folks might already be searching for him, so, instead of waiting to see what took place at the castle, he ran off to the forest as fast as he could, taking the sword with him. He found the others still asleep, so he woke them up, and they again set out on their journey. Of the night's adventures he said not a word, and when they asked where he got the sword, he only pointed in the direction of the castle, and said, 'Over that way.' They thought he had found it, and asked no more questions.

When Niels left the castle, he shut the door behind him, and it closed with such a bang that the porter woke up. He could scarcely believe his eyes when he saw the three headless giants lying in a heap in the courtyard, and could not imagine what had taken place. The whole castle was soon aroused, and then everybody wondered at the affair: it was soon seen that the bodies were those of the king's great enemies, but how they came to be there and in that condition was a perfect mystery. Then it was noticed that the drinking-horn was empty and the sword gone, while the princess reported that half of her handkerchief and one of her slippers had been taken away. *How* the giants had been killed seemed a little clearer now, but *who* had done it was as great a puzzle as before. The old knight who had charge of the castle said that in his opinion it must have been some young knight, who had immediately set off to the king to claim the hand of the princess. This sounded likely, but the messenger who was sent to the Court returned with the news that no one there knew anything about the matter.

'We must find him, however,' said the princess; 'for if he is willing to marry me I cannot in honour refuse him, after what my father put on the horn.' She took council with her father's wisest men as to what ought to be done, and among other things they advised her to build a house beside the highway, and put over the door this inscription:—'Whoever will tell the story of his life, may stay here three nights for nothing.' This was done, and many strange tales were told to the princess, but none of the travellers said a word about the three giants.

In the meantime Niels and the others tramped on towards Rome. Autumn passed, and winter was just beginning when they came to the foot of a great range of mountains, towering up to the sky. 'Must we go over these?' said they. 'We shall be frozen to death or buried in the snow.'

'Here comes a man,' said Niels; 'let us ask him the way to Rome.' They did so, and were told that there was no other way.

'And is it far yet?' said the old people, who were beginning to be worn out by the long journey. The man held up his foot so that they could see the sole of his shoe; it was worn as thin as paper, and there was a hole in the middle of it.

'These shoes were quite new when I left Rome,' he said, 'and look at them now; that will tell you whether you are far from it or not.'

This discouraged the old people so much that they gave up all thought of finishing the journey, and only wished to get back to Denmark as quickly as they could. What with the winter and bad roads they took longer to return than they had taken to go, but in the end they found themselves in sight of the forest where they had slept before.

'What's this?' said Rasmus. 'Here's a big house built since we passed this way before.'

'So it is,' said Peter; 'let's stay all night in it.'

'No, we can't afford that,' said the old people; 'it will be too dear for the like of us.'

However, when they saw what was written above the door, they were all well pleased to get a night's lodging for nothing. They were well received, and had so much attention given to them, that the old people were quite put out by it. After they had got time to rest themselves, the princess's steward came to hear their story.

'You saw what was written above the door,' he said to the father. 'Tell me who you are and what your history has been.'

'Dear me, I have nothing of any importance to tell you,' said the old man, 'and I am sure we should never have made so bold as to trouble you at all if it hadn't been for the youngest of our two sons here.'

'Never mind that,' said the steward; 'you are very welcome if you will only tell me the story of your life.'

'Well, well, I will,' said he, 'but there is nothing to tell about it. I and my wife have lived all our days on a moor in North Jutland, until this last year, when she took a fancy to go to Rome. We set out with our two sons, but turned back long before we got there, and are now on our way home again. That's all my own story, and our two sons have lived with us all their days, so there is nothing more to be told about them either.'

'Yes there is,' said Rasmus; 'when we were on our way south, we slept in the wood near here one night, and I shot a stag.'

The steward was so much accustomed to hearing stories of no importance that he thought there was no use going further with this, but reported to the princess that the newcomers had nothing to tell.

'Did you question them all?' she said.

'Well, no; not directly,' said he; 'but the father said that none of them could tell me any more than he had done.'

'You are getting careless,' said the princess; 'I shall go and talk to them myself.'

Niels knew the princess again as soon as she entered the room, and was greatly alarmed, for he immediately supposed that all this was a device to discover the person who had run away with the sword, the slipper and the half of the handkerchief, and that it would fare badly with him if he were discovered. So he told his story much the same as the others did (Niels was not very particular), and thought he had escaped all further trouble, when Rasmus put in his word. 'You've forgotten something, Niels,' he said; 'you remember you found a sword near here that night I shot the stag.'

'Where is the sword?' said the princess.

'I know,' said the steward, 'I saw where he laid it down when they came in;' and off he went to fetch it, while Niels wondered whether he could make his escape in the meantime. Before he had made up his mind, however, the steward was back with the sword, which the princess recognised at once.

'Where did you get this?' she said to Niels.

Niels was silent, and wondered what the usual penalty

was for a poor sheep-farmer's son who was so unfortunate as to deliver a princess and carry off things from her bedroom.

'See what else he has about him,' said the princess to the steward, and Niels had to submit to be searched: out of one pocket came a gold-embroidered slipper, and out of another the half of a gold-hemmed handkerchief.

'That is enough,' said the princess; '*now* we needn't ask any more questions. Send for my father the king at once.'

'Please let me go,' said Niels; 'I did you as much good as harm, at any rate.'

'Why, who said anything about doing harm?' said the princess. 'You must stay here till my father comes.'

The way in which the princess smiled when she said this gave Niels some hope that things might not be bad for him after all, and he was yet more encouraged when he thought of the words engraven on the horn, though the last line still seemed too good to be true. However, the arrival of the king soon settled the matter: the princess was willing and so was Niels, and in a few days the wedding bells were ringing. Niels was made an earl by that time, and looked as handsome as any of them when dressed in all his robes. Before long the old king died, and Niels reigned after him; but whether his father and mother stayed with him, or went back to the moor in Jutland, or were sent to Rome in a carriage and four, is something that all the historians of his reign have forgotten to mention.

SHEPHERD PAUL

Once upon a time a shepherd was taking his flock out to pasture, when he found a little baby lying in a meadow, left there by some wicked person, who thought it was too much trouble to look after it. The shepherd was fond of children, so he took the baby home with him and gave it plenty of milk, and by the time the boy was fourteen he could tear up oaks as if they were weeds. Then Paul, as the shepherd had called him, grew tired of living at home, and went out into the world to try his luck.

He walked on for many miles, seeing nothing that surprised him, but in an open space of the wood he was astonished at finding a man combing trees as another man would comb flax.

'Good morning, friend,' said Paul; 'upon my word, you must be a strong man!'

The man stopped his work and laughed. 'I am Tree Comber,' he answered proudly; 'and the greatest wish of my life is to wrestle with Shepherd Paul.'

'May all your wishes be fulfilled as easily, for I am Shepherd Paul, and can wrestle with you at once,' replied the lad; and he seized Tree Comber and flung him with such force to the ground that he sank up to his knees in the earth. However, in a moment he was up again, and catching hold of Paul, threw him so that he sank up to his waist; but then it was Paul's turn again, and this time the man was buried up to his neck. 'That is enough,' cried he; 'I see you are a smart fellow, let us become friends.'

'Very good,' answered Paul, and they continued their journey together.

By-and-by they reached a man who was grinding stones to powder in his hands, as if they had been nuts.

'Good morning,' said Paul politely; 'upon my word, you must be a strong fellow!'

'I am Stone Crusher,' answered the man, and the greatest wish of my life is to wrestle with Shepherd Paul.'

'May all your wishes be as easily fulfilled, for I am Shepherd Paul, and will wrestle with you at once,' and the sport began. After a short time the man declared himself beaten, and begged leave to go with them; so they all three travelled together.

A little further on they came upon a man who was kneading iron as if it had been dough. 'Good morning,' said Paul, 'you must be a strong fellow.'

'I am Iron Kneader, and should like to fight Shepherd Paul,' answered he.

'Let us begin at once then,' replied Paul; and on this occasion also, Paul got the better of his foe, and they all four continued their journey.

At midday they entered a forest, and Paul stopped suddenly. 'We three will go and look for game,' he said, 'and you, Tree Comber, will stay behind and prepare a good supper for us.' So Tree Comber set to work to boil and roast, and when dinner was nearly ready, a little dwarf with a pointed beard strolled up to the place. 'What are you cooking?' asked he, 'give me some of it.'

'I'll give you some on your back, if you like,' answered Tree Comber rudely. The dwarf took no notice, but waited patiently till the dinner was cooked, then suddenly throwing Tree Comber on the ground, he ate up the contents of the saucepan and vanished. Tree Comber felt rather ashamed of himself, and set about boiling some more vegetables, but they were still very hard when the hunters returned, and though they complained of his bad cooking, he did not tell them about the dwarf.

Next day Stone Crusher was left behind, and after him Iron Kneader, and each time the dwarf appeared, and they fared no better than Tree Comber had done. The fourth day Paul said to them: 'My friends, there must be some reason why your cooking has always been so bad, now you shall go and hunt and I will stay behind.' So they went off, amusing themselves by thinking what was in store for Paul.

He set to work at once, and had just got all his vegetables simmering in the pot when the dwarf appeared as before, and asked to have some of the stew. 'Be off,' cried Paul, snatching up the saucepan as he spoke. The dwarf tried to get hold of his collar, but Paul seized him by the beard, and tied him to a big tree so that he could not stir, and went on quietly with his cooking. The hunters came back early, longing to see how Paul had got on, and, to their surprise, dinner was quite ready for them.

'You are great useless creatures,' said he, 'who couldn't even outwit that little dwarf. When we have finished supper I will show you what I have done with him!' But when they reached the place where Paul had left the dwarf, neither he nor the tree was to be seen, for the little fellow had pulled it up by the roots and run away, dragging it after him. The four friends followed the track of the tree and found that it ended in a deep hole. 'He must have gone down here,' said Paul, 'and I will go after him. See! there is a basket that will do for me to sit in, and a cord to lower me with. But when I pull the cord again, lose no time in drawing the basket up.'

And he stepped into the basket, which was lowered by his friends.

At last it touched the ground and he jumped out and looked about him. He was in a beautiful valley, full of meadows and streams, with a splendid castle standing by. As the door was open he walked in, but a lovely maiden met him and implored him to go back, for the owner of the castle was a dragon with six heads, who had stolen her from her home and brought her down to this underground spot. But Paul refused to listen to all her entreaties, and declared that he was not afraid of the dragon, and did not care how many heads he had ; and he sat down calmly to wait for him.

In a little while the dragon came in, and all the long teeth in his six heads chattered with anger at the sight of the stranger.

'I am Shepherd Paul,' said the young man, 'and I have come to fight you, and as I am in a hurry we had better begin at once.'

'Very good,' answered the dragon. 'I am sure of my supper, but let us have a mouthful of something first, just to give us an appetite.'

Whereupon he began to eat some huge boulders as if they had been cakes, and when he had quite finished, he offered Paul one. Paul was not fond of boulders, but he took a wooden knife and cut one in two, then he snatched up both halves in his hands and threw them with all his strength at the dragon, so that two out of the six heads were smashed in. At this the dragon, with a mighty roar, rushed upon Paul, but he sprang on one side, and with a swinging blow cut off two of the other heads. Then, seizing the monster by the neck, he dashed the remaining heads against the rock.

When the maiden heard that the dragon was dead, she thanked her deliverer with tears in her eyes, but told him that her two younger sisters were in the power of dragons still fiercer and more horrible than this one. He vowed that his sword should never rest in its sheath till they were set free, and bade the girl come with him, and show him the way.

The maiden gladly consented to go with him, but first she gave him a golden rod, and bade him strike the castle with it. He did so, and it instantly changed into a golden

SHEPHERD PAUL CONQUERS THE SIX-HEADED DRAGON

apple, which he put in his pocket. After that, they started on their search.

They had not gone far before they reached the castle where the second girl was confined by the power of the dragon with twelve heads, who had stolen her from her home. She was overjoyed at the sight of her sister and of Paul, and brought him a shirt belonging to the dragon, which made every one who wore it twice as strong as they were before. Scarcely had he put it on when the dragon came back, and the fight began. Long and hard was the struggle, but Paul's sword and his shirt helped him, and the twelve heads lay dead upon the ground.

Then Paul changed the castle into an apple, which he put into his pocket, and set out with the two girls in search of the third castle.

It was not long before they found it, and within the walls was the third sister, who was younger and prettier than either of the other two. *Her* husband had eighteen heads, but when he quitted the lower regions for the surface of the earth, he left them all at home except one, which he changed for the head of a little dwarf, with a pointed beard.

The moment that Paul knew that this terrible dragon was no other than the dwarf whom he had tied to the tree, he longed more than ever to fly at his throat. But the thought of the eighteen heads warned him to be careful, and the third sister brought him a silk shirt which would make him ten times stronger than he was before.

He had scarcely put it on, when the whole castle began to shake violently, and the dragon flew up the steps into the hall.

'Well, my friend, so we meet once more! Have you forgotten me? I am Shepherd Paul, and I have come to wrestle with you, and to free your wife from your clutches.'

'Ah, I am glad to see you again,' said the dragon. 'Those were my two brothers whom you killed, and now your blood shall pay for them.' And he went into his room to look for his shirt and to drink some magic wine, but the shirt was on Paul's back, and as for the wine, the girl had given a cupful to Paul and then had allowed the rest to run out of the cask.

At this the dragon grew rather frightened, but in a moment had recollected his eighteen heads, and was bold again.

'Come on,' he cried, rearing himself up and preparing to dart all his heads at once at Paul. But Paul jumped underneath, and gave an upward cut so that six of the heads went rolling down. They were the best heads too, and very soon the other twelve lay beside them. Then Paul changed the castle into an apple, and put it in his pocket. Afterwards he and the three girls set off for the opening which led upwards to the earth.

The basket was still there, dangling from the rope, but it was only big enough to hold the three girls, so Paul sent them up, and told them to be sure and let down the basket for him. Unluckily, at the sight of the maidens' beauty, so far beyond anything they had ever seen, the friends forgot all about Paul, and carried the girls straight away into a far country, so that they were not much better off than before. Meanwhile Paul, mad with rage at the ingratitude of the three sisters, vowed he would be revenged upon them, and set about finding some way of getting back to earth. But it was not very easy, and for months, and months, and months, he wandered about underground, and, at the end, seemed no nearer to fulfilling his purpose than he was at the beginning.

At length, one day, he happened to pass the nest of a huge griffin, who had left her young ones all alone. Just as Paul came along a cloud containing fire instead of rain burst overhead, and all the little griffins would certainly have been killed had not Paul spread his cloak over the nest and saved them. When their father returned the young ones told him what Paul had done,

THE - MAIDENS - ASCEND -

and he lost no time in flying after Paul, and asking how he could reward him for his goodness.

'By carrying me up to the earth,' answered Paul; and the griffin agreed, but first went to get some food to eat on the way, as it was a long journey.

'Now get on my back,' he said to Paul, 'and when I turn my head to the right, cut a slice off the bullock that hangs on that side, and put it in my mouth, and when I turn my head to the left, draw a cupful of wine from the cask that hangs on that side, and pour it down my throat.'

For three days and three nights Paul and the griffin flew upwards, and on the fourth morning it touched the ground just outside the city where Paul's friends had gone to live. Then Paul thanked him and bade him farewell, and he returned home again.

At first Paul was too tired to do anything but sleep, but as soon as he was rested he started off in search of the three faithless ones, who almost died from fright at the sight of him, for they had thought he would never come back to reproach them for their wickedness.

'You know what to expect,' Paul said to them quietly. 'You shall never see me again. Off with you!' He next took the three apples out of his pocket and placed them all in the prettiest places he could find; after which he tapped them with his golden rod, and they became castles again. He gave two of the castles to the eldest sisters, and kept the other for himself and the youngest, whom he married, and there they are living still.

[From *Ungarische Mährchen.*]

HOW THE WICKED TANUKI WAS PUNISHED

THE hunters had hunted the wood for so many years that no wild animal was any more to be found in it. You might walk from one end to the other without ever seeing a hare, or a deer, or a boar, or hearing the cooing of the doves in their nest. If they were not dead, they had flown elsewhere. Only three creatures remained alive, and they had hidden themselves in the thickest part of the forest, high up the mountain. These were a grey-furred, long-tailed tanuki, his wife the fox, who was one of his own family, and their little son.

The fox and the tanuki were very clever, prudent beasts, and they also were skilled in magic, and by this means had escaped the fate of their unfortunate friends. If they heard the twang of an arrow or saw the glitter of a spear, ever so far off, they lay very still, and were not to be tempted from their hiding-place, if their hunger was ever so great, or the game ever so delicious. '*We* are not so foolish as to risk our lives,' they said to each other proudly. But at length there came a day when, in spite of their prudence, they seemed likely to die of starvation, for no more food was to be had. Something had to be done, but they did not know what.

Suddenly a bright thought struck the tanuki. 'I have got a plan,' he cried joyfully to his wife. 'I will pretend to be dead, and you must change yourself into a man, and take me to the village for sale. It will be easy to find a buyer, tanukis' skins are always wanted; then buy some food with the money and come home again. I will manage to escape somehow, so do not worry about me.'

The fox laughed with delight, and rubbed her paws together with satisfaction. 'Well, next time *I* will go,' she said, 'and you can sell *me*.' And then she changed herself into a man, and picking up the stiff body of the tanuki, set off towards the village. She found him rather heavy, but it would never have done to let him walk through the wood and risk his being seen by somebody.

As the tanuki had foretold, buyers were many, and the fox handed him over to the person who offered the largest price, and hurried to get some food with the money. The buyer took the tanuki back to his house, and throwing him into a corner went out. Directly the tanuki found he was alone, he crept cautiously through a chink of the window, thinking, as he did so, how lucky it was that *he* was not a fox, and was able to climb. Once outside, he hid himself in a ditch till it grew dusk, and then galloped away into the forest.

While the food lasted they were all three as happy as kings ; but there soon arrived a day when the larder was as empty as ever. 'It is my turn now to pretend to be dead,' cried the fox. So the tanuki changed himself into a peasant, and started for the village, with his wife's body hanging over his shoulder. A buyer was not long in coming forward, and while they were making the bargain a wicked thought darted into the tanuki's head, that if he got rid of the fox there would be more food for him and his son. So as he put the money in his pocket he whispered softly to the buyer that the fox was not really dead, and that if he did not take care she might run away from him. The man did not need twice telling. He gave the poor fox a blow on the head, which put an end to her, and the wicked tanuki went smiling to the nearest shop.

In former times he had been very fond of his little

son; but since he had betrayed his wife he seemed to have changed all in a moment, for he would not give him as much as a bite, and the poor little fellow would have starved had he not found some nuts and berries to eat, and he waited on, always hoping that his mother would come back.

At length some notion of the truth began to dawn on him; but he was careful to let the old tanuki see nothing, though in his own mind he turned over plans from morning till night, wondering how best he might avenge his mother.

One morning, as the little tanuki was sitting with his father, he remembered, with a start, that his mother had taught him all she knew of magic, and that he could work spells as well as his father, or perhaps better. 'I am as good a wizard as you,' he said suddenly, and a cold chill ran through the tanuki as he heard him, though he laughed, and pretended to think it a joke. But the little tanuki stuck to his point, and at last the father proposed they should have a wager.

'Change yourself into any shape you like,' said he, 'and I will undertake to know you. I will go and wait on the bridge which leads over the river to the village, and you shall transform yourself into anything you please, but I will know you through any disguise.' The little tanuki agreed, and went down the road which his father had pointed out. But instead of transforming himself into a different shape, he just hid himself in a corner of the bridge, where he could see without being seen.

He had not been there long when his father arrived and took up his place near the middle of the bridge, and soon after the king came by, followed by a troop of guards and all his court.

'Ah! he thinks that now he has changed himself into a king I shall not know him,' thought the old tanuki, and as the king passed in his splendid carriage, borne by his servants, he jumped upon it crying: 'I have won my wager ; you cannot deceive me.' But in reality it was he who had deceived himself. The soldiers, conceiving that their king was being attacked, seized the tanuki by the legs and flung him over into the river, and the water closed over him.

And the little tanuki saw it all, and rejoiced that his mother's death had been avenged. Then he went back to the forest, and if he has not found it too lonely, he is probably living there still.

[From *Japanische Mährchen.*]

THE CRAB AND THE MONKEY

There was once a crab who lived in a hole on the shady side of a mountain. She was a very good housewife, and so careful and industrious that there was no creature in the whole country whose hole was so neat and clean as hers, and she took great pride in it.

One day she saw lying near the mouth of her hole a handful of cooked rice which some pilgrim must have let fall when he was stopping to eat his dinner. Delighted at this discovery, she hastened to the spot, and was carrying the rice back to her hole when a monkey, who lived in some trees near by, came down to see what the crab was doing. His eyes shone at the sight of the rice, for it was his favourite food, and like the sly fellow he was, he proposed a bargain to the crab. She was to give him half the rice in exchange for the kernel of a sweet red kaki fruit which he had just eaten. He half expected that the crab would laugh in his face at this impudent proposal, but instead of doing so she only looked at him for a moment with her head on one side and then said that she would agree to the exchange. So the monkey went off with his rice, and the crab returned to her hole with the kernel.

For some time the crab saw no more of the monkey, who had gone to pay a visit on the sunny side of the mountain; but one morning he happened to pass by her hole, and found her sitting under the shadow of a beautiful kaki tree.

'Good day,' he said politely, 'you have some very fine

fruit there! I am very hungry, could you spare me one or two?'

'Oh, certainly,' replied the crab, 'but you must forgive me if I cannot get them for you myself. I am no tree-climber.'

'Pray do not apologise,' answered the monkey. 'Now that I have your permission I can get them myself quite easily.' And the crab consented to let him go up, merely saying that he must throw her down half the fruit.

In another moment he was swinging himself from branch to branch, eating all the ripest kakis and filling his pockets with the rest, and the poor crab saw to her disgust that the few he threw down to her were either not ripe at all or else quite rotten.

'You are a shocking rogue,' she called in a rage; but the monkey took no notice, and went on eating as fast as he could. The crab understood that it was no use her scolding, so she resolved to try what cunning would do.

'Sir Monkey,' she said, 'you are certainly a very good climber, but now that you have eaten so much, I am quite sure you would never be able to turn one of your somersaults.' The monkey prided himself on turning better somersaults than any of his family, so he instantly went head over heels three times on the bough on which he was sitting, and all the beautiful kakis that he had in his pockets rolled to the ground. Quick as lightning the crab picked them up and carried a quantity of them into her house, but when she came up for another the monkey sprang on her, and treated her so badly that he left her for dead. When he had beaten her till his arm ached he went his way.

It was a lucky thing for the poor crab that she had some friends to come to her help or she certainly would have died then and there. The wasp flew to her, and took her back to bed and looked after her, and then he consulted with a rice-mortar and an egg which had fallen out of a nest near by, and they agreed that when the monkey returned, as he was sure to do, to steal the rest of the fruit, that they would punish him severely for the manner in which he had behaved to the crab. So the mortar climbed up to the beam over the front door, and the egg lay quite still on the ground, while the wasp set down the water-bucket in a corner. Then the crab dug itself a deep hole in the ground, so that not even the tip of her claws might be seen.

The Monkey's Punishment

Soon after everything was ready the monkey jumped down from his tree, and creeping to the door began a long hypocritical speech, asking pardon for all he had done. He waited for an answer of some sort, but none came. He listened, but all was still; then he peeped, and saw no one; then he went in. He peered about for the crab, but in vain ; however, his eyes fell on the egg, which he snatched up and set on the fire. But in a moment the egg had burst into a thousand pieces, and its sharp shell struck him in the face and scratched him horribly. Smarting with pain he ran to the bucket and stooped down to throw some water over his head. As he stretched out his hand up started the wasp and stung him on the nose. The monkey shrieked and ran to the door, but as he passed through down fell the mortar and struck him dead. After that the crab lived happily for many years, and at length died in peace under her own kaki tree.

[From *Japanische Mährchen.*]

THE HORSE GULLFAXI AND THE SWORD GUNNFÖDER

Many, many years ago there lived a king and queen who had one only son, called Sigurd. When the little boy was only ten years old the queen, his mother, fell ill and died, and the king, who loved her dearly, built a splendid monument to his wife's memory, and day after day he sat by it and bewailed his sad loss.

One morning, as he sat by the grave, he noticed a richly dressed lady close to him. He asked her name and she answered that it was Ingiborg, and seemed surprised to see the king there all alone. Then he told her how he had lost his queen, and how he came daily to weep at her grave. In return, the lady informed him that she had lately lost her husband, and suggested that they might both find it a comfort if they made friends.

This pleased the king so much that he invited her to his palace, where they saw each other often; and after a time he married her.

After the wedding was over he soon regained his good spirits, and used to ride out hunting as in old days; but Sigurd, who was very fond of his stepmother, always stayed at home with her.

One evening Ingiborg said to Sigurd: 'To-morrow your father is going out hunting, and you must go with him.' But Sigurd said he would much rather stay at home, and the next day when the king rode off Sigurd refused to accompany him. The stepmother was very angry, but he would not listen, and at last she assured him that he would be sorry for his disobedience, and that in future he had better do as he was told.

After the hunting party had started she hid Sigurd under her bed, and bade him be sure to lie there till she called him.

Sigurd lay very still for a long while, and was just thinking it was no good staying there any more, when he felt the floor shake under him as if there were an earthquake, and peeping out he saw a great giantess wading along ankle deep through the ground and ploughing it up as she walked.

'Good morning, Sister Ingiborg,' cried she as she entered the room, 'is Prince Sigurd at home?'

'No,' said Ingiborg; 'he rode off to the forest with his father this morning.' And she laid the table for her sister and set food before her. After they had both done eating the giantess said: 'Thank you, sister, for your good dinner—the best lamb, the best can of beer and the best drink I have ever had; but—is not Prince Sigurd at home?'

Ingiborg again said 'No'; and the giantess took leave of her and went away. When she was quite out of sight Ingiborg told Sigurd to come out of his hiding-place.

The king returned home at night, but his wife told him nothing of what had happened, and the next morning she again begged the prince to go out hunting with his father. Sigurd, however, replied as before, that he would much rather stay at home.

So once more the king rode off alone. This time Ingiborg hid Sigurd under the table, and scolded him well for not doing as she bade him. For some time he lay quite still, and then suddenly the floor began to shake, and a giantess came along wading half way to her knees through the ground.

As she entered the house she asked, as the first one

had done: 'Well, Sister Ingiborg, is Prince Sigurd at home?'

'No,' answered Ingiborg, 'he rode off hunting with his father this morning'; and going to the cupboard she laid the table for her sister. When they had finished their meal the giantess rose and said: 'Thank you for all these nice dishes, and for the best lamb, the best can of beer and the nicest drink I have ever had; but—is Prince Sigurd *really* not at home?'

'No, certainly not!' replied Ingiborg; and with that they took leave of each other.

When she was well out of sight Sigurd crept from under the table, and his stepmother declared that it was most important that he should not stay at home next day; but he said he did not see what harm could come of it, and he did not mean to go out hunting, and the next morning, when the king prepared to start, Ingiborg implored Sigurd to accompany his father. But it was all no use, he was quite obstinate and would not listen to a word she said. 'You will have to hide me again,' said he, so no sooner had the king gone than Ingiborg hid Sigurd between the wall and the panelling, and by-and-by there was heard once more a sound like an earthquake, as a great giantess, wading knee deep through the ground, came in at the door.

'Good day, Sister Ingiborg!' she cried, in a voice like thunder; 'is Prince Sigurd at home?'

'Oh, no,' answered Ingiborg, 'he is enjoying himself out there in the forest. I expect it will be quite dark before he comes back again.'

'That's a lie!' shouted the giantess. And they squabbled about it till they were tired, after which Ingiborg laid the table; and when the giantess had done eating she said: 'Well, I must thank you for all these good things, and for the best lamb, the best can of beer and the best drink I have had for a long time; but—are you *quite* sure Prince Sigurd is not at home?'

'Quite,' said Ingiborg. 'I've told you already that he rode off with his father this morning to hunt in the forest.'

At this the giantess roared out with a terrible voice: 'If he is near enough to hear my words, I lay this spell on him: Let him be half scorched and half withered; and may he have neither rest nor peace till he finds me.' And with these words she stalked off.

For a moment Ingiborg stood as if turned to stone, then she fetched Sigurd from his hiding-place, and, to her horror, there he was, half scorched and half withered.

'Now you see what has happened through your own obstinacy,' said she; 'but we must lose no time, for your father will soon be coming home.'

Going quickly into the next room she opened a chest and took out a ball of string and three gold rings, and gave them to Sigurd, saying: 'If you throw this ball on the ground it will roll along till it reaches some high cliffs. There you will see a giantess looking out over the rocks. She will call down to you and say: "Ah, this is just what I wanted! Here is Prince Sigurd. He shall go into the pot to-night"; but don't be frightened by her. She will draw you up with a long boat-hook, and you must greet her from me, and give her the smallest ring as a present. This will please her, and she will ask you to wrestle with her. When you are exhausted, she will offer you a horn to drink out of, and though she does not know it, the wine will make you so strong that you will easily be able to conquer her. After that she will let you stay there all night. The same thing will happen with my two other sisters. But, above all, remember this: should my little dog come to you and lay his paws on you, with tears running down his face, then hurry home, for my life will be in danger. Now, good-bye, and don't forget your stepmother.'

Then Ingiborg dropped the ball on the ground, and Sigurd bade her farewell.

That same evening the ball stopped rolling at the foot of some high rocks, and on glancing up, Sigurd saw the giantess looking out at the top.

'Ah, just what I wanted!' she cried out when she saw him; 'here is Prince Sigurd. He shall go into the pot to-night. Come up, my friend, and wrestle with me.'

With these words she reached out a long boat hook and hauled him up the cliff. At first Sigurd was rather frightened, but he remembered what Ingiborg had said, and gave the giantess her sister's message and the ring.

The giantess was delighted, and challenged him to wrestle with her. Sigurd was fond of all games, and began to wrestle with joy; but he was no match for the giantess, and as she noticed that he was getting faint she gave him a horn to drink out of, which was very foolish on her part, as it made Sigurd so strong that he soon overthrew her.

'You may stay here to-night,' said she; and he was glad of the rest.

Next morning Sigurd threw down the ball again and away it rolled for some time, till it stopped at the foot of another high rock. Then he looked up and saw another giantess, even bigger and uglier than the first one, who called out to him: 'Ah, this is just what I wanted! Here is Prince Sigurd. He shall go into the pot to-night. Come up quickly and wrestle with me.' And she lost no time in hauling him up.

The prince gave her his stepmother's message and the second largest ring. The giantess was greatly pleased when she saw the ring, and at once challenged Sigurd to wrestle with her.

They struggled for a long time, till at last Sigurd grew faint; so she handed him a horn to drink from, and when he had drunk he became so strong that he threw her down with one hand.

On the third morning Sigurd once more laid down his ball, and it rolled far away, till at last it stopped under a very high rock indeed, over the top of which the most hideous giantess that ever was seen looked down.

When she saw who was there she cried out: 'Ah, this is just what I wanted! Here comes Prince Sigurd. Into the pot he goes this very night. Come up here, my friend, and wrestle with me.' And she hauled him up just as her sisters had done.

Sigurd then gave her his stepmother's message and the last and largest ring. The sight of the red gold delighted the giantess, and she challenged Sigurd to a wrestling match. This time the fight was fierce and long, but when at length Sigurd's strength was failing the giantess gave him something to drink, and after he had drunk it he soon brought her to her knees. 'You have beaten me,' she gasped, so now, listen to me. 'Not far from here is a lake. Go there; you will find a little girl playing with a boat. Try to make friends with her, and give her this little gold ring. You are stronger than ever you were, and I wish you good luck.'

With these words they took leave of each other, and Sigurd wandered on till he reached the lake, where he found the little girl playing with a boat, just as he had been told. He went up to her and asked what her name was.

She was called Helga, she answered, and she lived near by.

So Sigurd gave her the little gold ring, and proposed that they should have a game. The little girl was delighted, for she had no brothers or sisters, and they played together all the rest of the day.

When evening came Sigurd asked leave to go home with her, but Helga at first forbade him, as no stranger had ever managed to enter their house without being found out by her father, who was a very fierce giant.

However, Sigurd persisted, and at length she gave way; but when they came near the door she held her glove over him and Sigurd was at once transformed into a bundle of wool. Helga tucked the bundle under her arm and threw it on the bed in her room.

Almost at the same moment her father rushed in and hunted round in every corner, crying out: 'This place smells of men. What's that you threw on the bed, Helga?'

'A bundle of wool,' said she.

'Oh, well, perhaps it was that I smelt,' said the old man, and troubled himself no more.

The following day Helga went out to play and took the bundle of wool with her under her arm. When she reached the lake she held her glove over it again and Sigurd resumed his own shape.

They played the whole day, and Sigurd taught Helga all sorts of games she had never even heard of. As they walked home in the evening she said: 'We shall be able to play better still to-morrow, for my father will have to go to the town, so we can stay at home.'

When they were near the house Helga again held her glove over Sigurd, and once more he was turned into a bundle of wool, and she carried him in without his being seen.

Very early next morning Helga's father went to the town, and as soon as he was well out of the way the girl held up her glove and Sigurd was himself again. Then she took him all over the house to amuse him, and opened every room, for her father had given her the keys before he left; but when they came to the last room Sigurd noticed one key on the bunch which had not been used and asked which room it belonged to.'

Helga grew red and did not answer.

'I suppose you don't mind my seeing the room which it opens?' asked Sigurd, and as he spoke he saw a heavy iron door and begged Helga to unlock it for him. But she told him she dared not do so, at least if she *did* open the door it must only be a *very* tiny chink ; and Sigurd declared that would do quite well.

The door was so heavy, that it took Helga some time to open it, and Sigurd grew so impatient that he pushed it wide open and walked in. There he saw a splendid horse, all ready saddled, and just above it hung a richly ornamented sword on the handle of which was engraved these words : 'He who rides this horse and wears this sword will find happiness.'

At the sight of the horse Sigurd was so filled with wonder that he was not able to speak, but at last he gasped out : 'Oh, do let me mount him and ride him round the house ! Just once ; I promise not to ask any more.'

'Ride him round the house !' cried Helga, growing pale at the mere idea. 'Ride Gullfaxi ! Why father would never, *never* forgive me, if I let you do that.'

'But it can't do him any harm,' argued Sigurd ; 'you don't know *how* careful I will be. I have ridden all sorts of horses at home, and have never fallen off—not *once.* Oh, Helga, do !'

'Well, perhaps, if you come back *directly,*' replied Helga, doubtfully ; 'but you must be very quick, or father will find out !'

But, instead of mounting Gullfaxi, as she expected, Sigurd stood still.

'And the sword,' he said, looking fondly up to the place where it hung. 'My father is a king, but he has not got any sword so beautiful as that. Why, the jewels in the scabbard are more splendid than the big ruby in his crown ! Has it got a name ? Some swords have, you know.'

'It is called "Gunnfjöder," the "Battle Plume,"' answered Helga, 'and "Gullfaxi" means "Golden Mane." I don't suppose, if you *are* to get on the horse at all, it would matter your taking the sword too. And if you take the sword you will have to carry the stick and the stone and the twig as well.'

'They are easily carried,' said Sigurd, gazing at them with scorn; 'what wretched dried-up things! Why in the world do you keep them?'

'Father says that he would rather lose Gullfaxi than lose them,' replied Helga, 'for if the man who rides the horse is pursued he has only to throw the twig behind him and it will turn into a forest, so thick that even a bird could hardly fly through. But if his enemy happens to know magic, and can throw down the forest, the man has only to strike the stone with the stick, and hailstones as large as pigeons' eggs will rain down from the sky and will kill every one for twenty miles round.'

Having said all this she allowed Sigurd to ride 'just once' round the house, taking the sword and other things with him. But when he had ridden round, instead of dismounting, he suddenly turned the horse's head and galloped away.

Soon after this Helga's father came home and found his daughter in tears. He asked what was the matter, and when he heard all that had happened, he rushed off as fast as he could to pursue Sigurd.

Now, as Sigurd happened to look behind him he saw the giant coming after him with great strides, and in all haste he threw the twig behind him. Immediately such a thick wood sprang up at once between him and his enemy that the giant was obliged to run home for an axe with which to cut his way through.

The next time Sigurd glanced round, the giant was so near that he almost touched Gullfaxi's tail. In an agony of fear Sigurd turned quickly in his saddle and hit the stone with the stick. No sooner had he done this than a terrible hailstorm burst behind, and the giant was killed on the spot.

But had Sigurd struck the stone without turning round, the hail would have driven right into his face and killed him instead.

THE DEADLY HAILSTORM

After the giant was dead Sigurd rode on towards his own home, and on the way he suddenly met his stepmother's little dog, running to meet him, with tears pouring down its face. He galloped on as hard as he could, and on arriving found nine men-servants in the act of tying Queen Ingiborg to a post in the courtyard of the palace, where they intended to burn her.

Wild with anger Prince Sigurd sprang from his horse and, sword in hand, fell on the men and killed them all. Then he released his stepmother, and went in with her to see his father.

The king lay in bed sick with sorrow, and neither eating nor drinking, for he thought that his son had been killed by the queen. He could hardly believe his own eyes for joy when he saw the prince, and Sigurd told him all his adventures.

After that Prince Sigurd rode back to fetch Helga, and a great feast was made which lasted three days ; and every one said no bride was ever seen so beautiful as Helga, and they lived happily for many, many years, and everybody loved them.

[From *Isländische Mährchen.*]

THE STORY OF THE SHAM PRINCE, OR THE AMBITIOUS TAILOR

Once upon a time there lived a respectable young tailor called Labakan, who worked for a clever master in Alexandria. No one could call Labakan either stupid or lazy, for he could work extremely well and quickly—when he chose; but there was something not altogether right about him. Sometimes he would stitch away as fast as if he had a red-hot needle and a burning thread, and at other times he would sit lost in thought, and with such a queer look about him that his fellow-workmen used to say, 'Labakan has got on his aristocratic face to-day.'

On Fridays he would put on his fine robe which he had bought with the money he had managed to save up, and go to the mosque. As he came back, after prayers, if he met any friend who said 'Good-day,' or 'How are you, friend Labakan?' he would wave his hand graciously or nod in a condescending way; and if his master happened to say to him, as he sometimes did, 'Really, Labakan, you look like a prince,' he was delighted, and would answer, 'Have *you* noticed it too?' or 'Well, so I have long thought.'

Things went on like this for some time, and the master put up with Labakan's absurdities because he was, on the whole, a good fellow and a clever workman.

One day, the sultan's brother happened to be passing through Alexandria, and wanted to have one of his state robes altered, so he sent for the master tailor, who handed the robe over to Labakan as his best workman.

In the evening, when every one had left the workshop and gone home, a great longing drove Labakan back to the place where the royal robe hung. He stood a long time gazing at it, admiring the rich material and the splendid embroidery in it. At last he could hold out no longer. He felt he *must* try it on, and lo! and behold, it fitted as though it had been made for him.

'Am not I as good a prince as any other?' he asked himself, as he proudly paced up and down the room. 'Has not the master often said that I seemed born to be a prince?'

It seemed to him that he must be the son of some unknown monarch, and at last he determined to set out at once and travel in search of his proper rank.

He felt as if the splendid robe had been sent him by some kind fairy, and he took care not to neglect such a precious gift. He collected all his savings, and, concealed by the darkness of the night, he passed through the gates of Alexandria.

The new prince excited a good deal of curiosity whereever he went, for his splendid robe and majestic manner did not seem quite suitable to a person travelling on foot. If anyone asked questions, he only replied with an important air of mystery that he had his own reasons for not riding.

However, he soon found out that walking made him ridiculous, so at last he bought a quiet, steady old horse, which he managed to get cheap.

One day, as he was ambling along upon Murva (that was the horse's name), a horseman overtook him and asked leave to join him, so that they might both beguile the journey with pleasant talk. The newcomer was a bright, cheerful, good-looking young man, who soon plunged into conversation and asked many questions. He told Labakan that his own name was Omar, that he was a nephew of Elfi Bey, and was travelling in order to carry out a command given him by his uncle on his deathbed. Labakan was not quite so open in his confidences, but hinted that he too was of noble birth and was travelling for pleasure.

The two young men took a fancy to each other and rode on together. On the second day of their journey Labakan questioned Omar as to the orders he had to carry out, and to his surprise heard this tale.

Elfi Bey, Pacha of Cairo, had brought up Omar from his earliest childhood, and the boy had never known his parents. On his deathbed Elfi Bey called Omar to him, and then told him that he was not his nephew, but the son of a great king, who, having been warned of coming dangers by his astrologers, had sent the young prince away and made a vow not to see him till his twenty-second birthday.

Elfi Bey did not tell Omar his father's name, but expressly desired him to be at a great pillar four days' journey east of Alexandria on the fourth day of the coming month, on which day he would be twenty-two years old. Here he would meet some men, to whom he was to hand a dagger which Elfi Bey gave him, and to say:

'Here am I for whom you seek.'

If they answered: 'Praised be the Prophet who has preserved you,' he was to follow them, and they would take him to his father.

Labakan was greatly surprised and interested by this story, but after hearing it he could not help looking on Prince Omar with envious eyes, angry that his friend should have the position he himself longed so much for. He began to make comparisons between the prince and himself, and was obliged to confess that he was a fine-looking young man with very good manners and a pleasant expression.

At the same time, he felt sure that had he been in the prince's place any royal father might have been glad to own him.

These thoughts haunted him all day, and he dreamt them all night. He woke very early, and as he saw Omar sleeping quietly, with a happy smile on his face, a wish arose in his mind to take by force or by cunning the things which an unkind fate had denied him.

The dagger which was to act as a passport was sticking in Omar's girdle. Labakan drew it gently out, and hesitated for a moment whether or not to plunge it into the heart of the sleeping prince. However, he shrank from the idea of murder, so he contented himself with placing the dagger in his own belt, and, saddling Omar's swift horse for himself, was many miles away before the prince woke up to realise his losses.

For two days Labakan rode on steadily, fearing lest, after all, Omar might reach the meeting place before him. At the end of the second day he saw the great pillar at a distance. It stood on a little hill in the middle of a plain, and could be seen a very long way off. Labakan's heart beat fast at the sight. Though he had had some time in which to think over the part he meant to play his conscience made him rather uneasy. However, the thought that he must certainly have been born to be a king supported him, and he bravely rode on.

The neighbourhood was quite bare and desert, and it was a good thing that the new prince had brought food for some time with him, as two days were still wanting till the appointed time.

Towards the middle of the next day he saw a long procession of horses and camels coming towards him. It halted at the bottom of the hill, and some splendid tents were pitched. Everything looked like the escort of some great man. Labakan made a shrewd guess that all these people had come here on his account; but he checked his impatience, knowing that only on the fourth day could his wishes be fulfilled.

The first rays of the rising sun woke the happy tailor. As he began to saddle his horse and prepare to ride to the pillar, he could not help having some remorseful thoughts of the trick he had played and the blighted hopes of the real prince. But the die was cast, and his vanity whispered that he was as fine looking a young man as the proudest king might wish his son to be, and that, moreover, what had happened had happened.

With these thoughts he summoned up all his courage, sprang on his horse, and in less than a quarter of an hour was at the foot of the hill. Here he dismounted, tied the horse to a bush, and, drawing out Prince Omar's dagger, climbed up the hill.

At the foot of the pillar stood six men round a tall and stately person. His superb robe of cloth of gold was girt round him by a white cashmere shawl, and his white, richly jewelled turban showed that he was a man of wealth and high rank.

Labakan went straight up to him, and, bending low, handed him the dagger, saying: 'Here am I whom you seek.'

'Praised be the Prophet who has preserved you!' replied the old man with tears of joy. 'Embrace me, my dear son Omar!'

The proud tailor was deeply moved by these solemn words, and with mingled shame and joy sank into the old king's arms.

But his happiness was not long unclouded. As he raised his head he saw a horseman who seemed trying to urge a tired or unwilling horse across the plain.

Only too soon Labakan recognised his own old horse, Murva, and the real Prince Omar, but having once told a lie he made up his mind not to own his deceit.

At last the horseman reached the foot of the hill. Here he flung himself from the saddle and hurried up to the pillar.

'Stop!' he cried, 'whoever you may be, and do not let a disgraceful impostor take you in. *My* name is Omar, and let no one attempt to rob me of it.'

This turn of affairs threw the standers-by into great surprise. The old king in particular seemed much moved as he looked from one face to the other. At last Labakan spoke with forced calmness, 'Most gracious lord and father, do not let yourself be deceived by this man. As far as I know, he is a half-crazy tailor's apprentice from Alexandria, called Labakan, who really deserves more pity than anger.'

These words infuriated the prince. Foaming with rage, he tried to press towards Labakan, but the attendants threw themselves upon him and held him fast, whilst the king said, 'Truly, my dear son, the poor fellow is quite mad. Let him be bound and placed on a dromedary. Perhaps we may be able to get some help for him.'

The prince's first rage was over, and with tears he cried to the king, 'My heart tells me that you are my father, and in my mother's name I entreat you to hear me.'

'Oh! heaven forbid!' was the reply. 'He is talking nonsense again. How can the poor man have got such notions into his head?'

With these words the king took Labakan's arm to support him down the hill. They both mounted richly caparisoned horses and rode across the plain at the head of their followers.

The unlucky prince was tied hand and foot, and fastened on a dromedary, a guard riding on either side and keeping a sharp look-out on him.

The old king was Sached, Sultan of the Wachabites. For many years he had had no children, but at length the son he had so long wished for was born. But the soothsayers and magicians whom he consulted as to the child's future all said that until he was twenty-two years old he stood in danger of being injured by an enemy. So, to make all safe, the sultan had confided the prince to his trusty friend Elfi Bey, and deprived himself of the happiness of seeing him for twenty-two years.

All this the sultan told Labakan, and was much pleased by his appearance and dignified manner.

When they reached their own country they were received with every sign of joy, for the news of the prince's safe return had spread like wildfire, and every town and village was decorated, whilst the inhabitants thronged to greet them with cries of joy and thankfulness. All this filled Labakan's proud heart with rapture, whilst the unfortunate Omar followed in silent rage and despair.

At length they arrived in the capital, where the public rejoicings were grander and more brilliant than anywhere else. The queen awaited them in the great hall of the palace, surrounded by her entire court. It was getting dark, and hundreds of coloured hanging lamps were lit to turn night into day.

The brightest hung round the throne on which the queen sat, and which stood above four steps of pure gold inlaid with great amethysts. The four greatest nobles in the kingdom held a canopy of crimson silk over the queen, and the Sheik of Medina fanned her with a peacock-feather fan.

In this state she awaited her husband and her son. She, too, had not seen Omar since his birth, but so many dreams had shown her what he would look like that she felt she would know him among a thousand.

And now the sound of trumpets and drums and of shouts and cheers outside announced the long looked for moment. The doors flew open, and between rows of low-bending courtiers and servants the king approached the throne, leading his pretended son by the hand.

'Here,' said he, 'is he for whom you have been longing so many years.'

But the queen interrupted him, 'That is not my son!' she cried. 'That is not the face the Prophet has shown me in my dreams!'

Just as the king was about to reason with her, the door was thrown violently open, and Prince Omar rushed in, followed by his keepers, whom he had managed to get away from. He flung himself down before the throne, panting out, 'Here will I die; kill me at once, cruel father, for I cannot bear this shame any longer.'

Everyone pressed round the unhappy man, and the guards were about to seize him, when the queen, who at first was dumb with surprise, sprang up from her throne.

'Hold!' cried she. 'This and no other is the right one; this is the one whom my eyes have never yet seen, but whom my heart recognises.'

The guards had stepped back, but the king called to them in a furious voice to secure the madman.

'It is I who must judge,' he said in tones of command; 'and this matter cannot be decided by women's dreams, but by certain unmistakable signs. This one' (pointing to Labakan) 'is my son, for it was he who brought me the token from my friend Elfi—the dagger.'

'He stole it from me,' shrieked Omar; 'he betrayed my unsuspicious confidence.'

But the king would not listen to his son's voice, for he had always been accustomed to depend on his own judgment. He let the unhappy Omar be dragged from the hall, whilst he himself retired with Labakan to his own rooms, full of anger with the queen his wife, in spite of their many years of happy life together.

The queen, on her side, was plunged in grief, for she felt certain that an impostor had won her husband's heart and taken the place of her real son.

When the first shock was over she began to think how she could manage to convince the king of his mistake. Of course it would be a difficult matter, as the man who declared he was Omar had produced the dagger as a token, besides talking of all sorts of things which happened when he was a child. She called her oldest and wisest ladies about her and asked their advice, but none of them had any to give. At last one very clever old woman said: 'Did not the young man who brought the dagger call him whom your majesty believes to be your son Labakan, and say he was a crazy tailor?'

'Yes,' replied the queen; 'but what of that?'

'Might it not be,' said the old lady, 'that the impostor has called your real son by his own name? If this should be the case, I know of a capital way to find out the truth.'

And she whispered some words to the queen, who seemed much pleased, and went off at once to see the king.

Now the queen was a very wise woman, so she pretended to think she might have made a mistake, and only begged to be allowed to put a test to the two young men to prove which was the real prince.

The king, who was feeling much ashamed of the rage he had been in with his dear wife, consented at once, and she said: 'No doubt others would make them ride or shoot, or something of that sort, but every one learns these things. I wish to set them a task which requires sharp wits and clever hands, and I want them to try which of them can best make a kaftan and pair of trousers.'

The king laughed. 'No, no, that will never do. Do you suppose my son would compete with that crazy tailor as to which could make the best clothes? Oh, dear, no, that won't do at all.'

But the queen claimed his promise, and as he was a man of his word the king gave in at last. He went to his son and begged that he would humour his mother, who had set her heart on his making a kaftan.

The worthy Labakan laughed to himself. 'If that is all she wants,' thought he, 'her majesty will soon be pleased to own me.'

Two rooms were prepared, with pieces of material, scissors, needles and threads, and each young man was shut up in one of them.

The king felt rather curious as to what sort of

garment his son would make, and the queen, too, was very anxious as to the result of her experiment.

On the third day they sent for the two young men and their work. Labakan came first and spread out his kaftan before the eyes of the astonished king. 'See, father,' he said; 'see, my honoured mother, if this is not a masterpiece of work. I'll bet the court tailor himself cannot do better.'

The queen smiled and turned to Omar: 'And what have you done, my son?'

Impatiently he threw the stuff and scissors down on the floor. 'I have been taught how to manage a horse, to draw a sword, and to throw a lance some sixty paces, but I never learnt to *sew*, and such a thing would have been thought beneath the notice of the pupil of Elfi Bey, the ruler of Cairo.'

'Ah, true son of your father,' cried the queen; 'if only I might embrace you and call you son! Forgive me, my lord and husband,' she added, turning to the king, 'for trying to find out the truth in this way. Do you not see yourself now which is the prince and which the tailor? Certainly this kaftan is a very fine one, but I should like to know what master taught this young man how to make clothes.'

The king sat deep in thought, looking now at his wife and now at Labakan, who was doing his best to hide his vexation at his own stupidity. At last the king said: 'Even this trial does not satisfy me; but happily I know of a sure way to discover whether or not I have been deceived.'

He ordered his swiftest horse to be saddled, mounted, and rode off alone into a forest at some little distance. Here lived a kindly fairy called Adolzaide, who had often helped the kings of his race with her good advice, and to her he betook himself.

In the middle of the forest was a wide open space surrounded by great cedar trees, and this was supposed to be the fairy's favourite spot. When the king reached this place he dismounted, tied his horse to the tree, and standing in the middle of the open place said: 'If it is true that you have helped my ancestors in their time of need, do not despise their descendant, but give me counsel, for that of men has failed me.'

He had hardly finished speaking when one of the cedar trees opened, and a veiled figure all dressed in white stepped from it.

'I know your errand, King Sached,' she said; 'it is an honest one, and I will give you my help. Take these two little boxes and let the two men who claim to be your son choose between them. I know that the real prince will make no mistake.'

She then handed him two little boxes made of ivory set with gold and pearls. On the lid of each (which the king vainly tried to open) was an inscription in diamonds. On one stood the words 'Honour and Glory,' and on the other 'Wealth and Happiness.'

'It would be a hard choice,' thought the king as he rode home.

He lost no time in sending for the queen and for all his court, and when all were assembled he made a sign, and Labakan was led in. With a proud air he walked up to the throne, and kneeling down, asked:

'What does my lord and father command?'

The king replied: 'My son, doubts have been thrown on your claim to that name. One of these boxes contains the proofs of your birth. Choose for yourself. No doubt you will choose right.'

He then pointed to the ivory boxes, which were placed on two little tables near the throne.

Labakan rose and looked at the boxes. He thought for some minutes, and then said: 'My honoured father, what can be better than the happiness of being your son, and what nobler than the riches of your love. I choose the box with the words "Wealth and Happiness."'

'We shall see presently if you have chosen the right one. For the present take a seat there beside the Pacha of Medina,' replied the king.

Omar was next led in, looking sad and sorrowful. He threw himself down before the throne and asked what was the king's pleasure. The king pointed out the two boxes to him, and he rose and went to the tables. He carefully read the two mottoes and said: 'The last few days have shown me how uncertain is happiness and how easily riches vanish away. Should I lose a crown by it I make my choice of "Honour and Glory."'

He laid his hand on the box as he spoke, but the king signed to him to wait, and ordered Labakan to come to the other table and lay his hand on the box he had chosen.

Then the king rose from his throne, and in solemn silence all present rose too, whilst he said: 'Open the boxes, and may Allah show us the truth.'

The boxes were opened with the greatest ease. In the one Omar had chosen lay a little gold crown and sceptre on a velvet cushion. In Labakan's box was found —a large needle with some thread!

The king told the two young men to bring him their boxes. They did so. He took the crown in his hand, and as he held it, it grew bigger and bigger, till it was as large as a real crown. He placed it on the head of his son Omar, kissed him on the forehead, and placed him on his right hand. Then, turning to Labakan, he said: 'There is an old proverb, "The cobbler sticks to his last." It seems as though you were to stick to your needle. You have not deserved any mercy, but I cannot be harsh on this day. I give you your life, but I advise you to leave this country as fast as you can.'

Full of shame, the unlucky tailor could not answer. He flung himself down before Omar, and with tears in his eyes asked: 'Can you forgive me, prince?'

'Go in peace,' said Omar as he raised him.

'Oh, my true son!' cried the king as he clasped the

prince in his arms, whilst all the pachas and emirs shouted, 'Long live Prince Omar!'

In the midst of all the noise and rejoicing Labakan slipped off with his little box under his arm. He went to the stables, saddled his old horse, Murva, and rode out of the gate towards Alexandria. Nothing but the ivory box with its diamond motto was left to show him that the last few weeks had not been a dream.

When he reached Alexandria he rode up to his old master's door. When he entered the shop, his master came forward to ask what was his pleasure, but as soon as he saw who it was he called his workmen, and they all fell on Labakan with blows and angry words, till at last he fell, half fainting, on a heap of old clothes.

The master then scolded him soundly about the stolen robe, but in vain Labakan told him he had come to pay for it and offered three times its price. They only fell to beating him again, and at last pushed him out of the house more dead than alive.

He could do nothing but remount his horse and ride to an inn. Here he found a quiet place in which to rest his bruised and battered limbs and to think over his many misfortunes. He fell asleep fully determined to give up trying to be great, but to lead the life of an honest workman.

Next morning he set to work to fulfil his good resolutions. He sold his little box to a jeweller for a good price, bought a house and opened a workshop. Then he hung up a sign with, 'Labakan, Tailor,' over his door, and sat down to mend his own torn clothes with the very needle which had been in the ivory box.

After a while he was called away, and when he went back to his work he found a wonderful thing had happened! The needle was sewing away all by itself and making the neatest little stitches, such as Labakan had never been able to make even at his best.

Certainly even the smallest gift of a kind fairy is of

great value, and this one had yet another advantage, for the thread never came to an end, however much the needle sewed.

Labakan soon got plenty of customers. He used to cut out the clothes, make the first stitch with the magic needle, and then leave it to do the rest. Before long the whole town went to him, for his work was both so good and so cheap. The only puzzle was how he could do so much, working all alone, and also why he worked with closed doors.

And so the promise on the ivory box of 'Wealth and Happiness' came true for him, and when he heard of all the brave doings of Prince Omar, who was the pride and darling of his people and the terror of his enemies, the ex-prince thought to himself, 'After all, I am better off as a tailor, for "Honour and Glory" are apt to be very dangerous things.'

THE COLONY OF CATS

Long, long ago, as far back as the time when animals spoke, there lived a community of cats in a deserted house they had taken possession of not far from a large town. They had everything they could possibly desire for their comfort, they were well fed and well lodged, and if by any chance an unlucky mouse was stupid enough to venture in their way, they caught it, not to eat it, but for the pure pleasure of catching it. The old people of the town related how they had heard their parents speak of a time when the whole country was so overrun with rats and mice that there was not so much as a grain of corn nor an ear of maize to be gathered in the fields; and it might be out of gratitude to the cats who had rid the country of these plagues that their descendants were allowed to live in peace. No one knows where they got the money to pay for everything, nor who paid it, for all this happened so very long ago. But one thing is certain, they were rich enough to keep a servant; for though they lived very happily together, and did not scratch nor fight more than human beings would have done, they were not clever enough to do the housework themselves, and preferred at all events to have some one to cook their meat, which they would have scorned to eat raw. Not only were they very difficult to please about the housework, but most women quickly tired of living alone with only cats for companions, consequently they never kept a servant long; and it had become a saying in the town, when anyone found herself reduced to her last penny: 'I will go and live with the cats,' and so many a poor woman actually did.

Now Lizina was not happy at home, for her mother, who was a widow, was much fonder of her elder daughter; so that often the younger one fared very badly, and had not enough to eat, while the elder could have everything she desired, and if Lizina dared to complain she was certain to have a good beating.

At last the day came when she was at the end of her courage and patience, and exclaimed to her mother and sister:

'As you hate me so much you will be glad to be rid of me, so I am going to live with the cats!'

'Be off with you!' cried her mother, seizing an old broom-handle from behind the door. Poor Lizina did not wait to be told twice, but ran off at once and never stopped till she reached the door of the cats' house. Their cook had left them that very morning, with her face all scratched, the result of such a quarrel with the head of the house that he had very nearly scratched out her eyes. Lizina therefore was warmly welcomed, and she set to work at once to prepare the dinner, not without many misgivings as to the tastes of the cats, and whether she would be able to satisfy them.

Going to and fro about her work, she found herself frequently hindered by a constant succession of cats who appeared one after another in the kitchen to inspect the new servant; she had one in front of her feet, another perched on the back of her chair while she peeled the vegetables, a third sat on the table beside her, and five or six others prowled about among the pots and pans on the shelves against the wall. The air resounded with their purring, which meant that they were pleased with their new maid, but Lizina had not yet learned to understand their language, and often she did not know what they wanted her to do. However, as she was a good, kind-hearted girl, she set to work to pick up the little kittens which tumbled about on the floor, she patched up quarrels, and nursed on her lap a big tabby—the oldest of the community—which had a lame paw. All these kindnesses could hardly fail to make a favourable impression on the cats, and it was even better after a while, when she had had time to grow accustomed to their strange ways. Never had the house been kept so clean, the meats so well served, nor the sick cats so well cared for. After a time they had a visit from an old cat, whom they called their father, who lived by himself in a barn at the top of the hill, and came down from time to time to inspect the little colony. He too was much taken with Lizina, and inquired, on first seeing her: 'Are you well served by this nice, black-eyed little person?' and the cats answered with one voice: 'Oh, yes, Father Gatto, we have never had so good a servant!'

At each of his visits the answer was always the same; but after a time the old cat, who was very observant, noticed that the little maid had grown to look sadder and sadder. 'What is the matter, my child—has any one been unkind to you?' he asked one day, when he found her crying in her kitchen. She burst into tears and answered between her sobs: 'Oh, no! they are all very good to me; but I long for news from home, and I pine to see my mother and my sister.'

Old Gatto, being a sensible old cat, understood the little servant's feelings. 'You shall go home,' he said, 'and you shall not come back here unless you please. But first you must be rewarded for all your kind services to my children. Follow me down into the inner cellar, where you have never yet been, for I always keep it locked and carry the key away with me.'

Lizina looked round her in astonishment as they went down into the great vaulted cellar underneath the kitchen. Before her stood the big earthenware water jars, one of which contained oil, the other a liquid shining like gold. 'In which of these jars shall I dip you?' asked

· LIZINA · COMES · OUT · OF · THE · JAR ·

Father Gatto, with a grin that showed all his sharp white teeth, while his moustaches stood out straight on either side of his face. The little maid looked at the two jars from under her long dark lashes: 'In the oil jar!' she answered timidly, thinking to herself: 'I could not ask to be bathed in gold.'

But Father Gatto replied: 'No, no; you have deserved something better than that.' And seizing her in his strong paws he plunged her into the liquid gold. Wonder of wonders! when Lizina came out of the jar she shone from head to foot like the sun in the heavens on a fine summer's day. Her pretty pink cheeks and long black hair alone kept their natural colour, otherwise she had become like a statue of pure gold. Father Gatto purred loudly with satisfaction. 'Go home,' he said, 'and see your mother and sisters; but take care if you hear the cock crow to turn towards it; if on the contrary the ass brays, you must look the other way.'

The little maid, having gratefully kissed the white paw of the old cat, set off for home; but just as she got near her mother's house the cock crowed, and quickly she turned towards it. Immediately a beautiful golden star appeared on her forehead, crowning her glossy black hair. At the same time the ass began to bray, but Lizina took care not to look over the fence into the field where the donkey was feeding. Her mother and sister, who were in front of their house, uttered cries of admiration and astonishment when they saw her, and their cries became still louder when Lizina, taking her handkerchief from her pocket, drew out also a handful of gold.

For some days the mother and her two daughters lived very happily together, for Lizina had given them everything she had brought away except her golden clothing, for that would not come off, in spite of all the efforts of her sister, who was madly jealous of her good fortune. The golden star, too, could not be removed from her forehead. But all the gold pieces she drew from her pockets had found their way to her mother and sister.

'I will go now and see what *I* can get out of the pussies,' said Peppina, the elder girl, one morning, as she took Lizina's basket and fastened her pockets into her own skirt. 'I should like some of the cats' gold for myself,' she thought, as she left her mother's house before the sun rose.

The cat colony had not yet taken another servant, for they knew they could never get one to replace Lizina, whose loss they had not yet ceased to mourn. When they heard that Peppina was her sister, they all ran to meet her. 'She is not the least like her,' the kittens whispered among themselves.

'Hush, be quiet!' the older cats said; 'all servants cannot be pretty.'

No, decidedly she was not at all like Lizina. Even the most reasonable and large-minded of the cats soon acknowledged that.

The very first day she shut the kitchen door in the face of the tom-cats who used to enjoy watching Lizina at her work, and a young and mischievous cat who jumped in by the open kitchen window and alighted on the table got such a blow with the rolling-pin that he squalled for an hour.

With every day that passed the household became more and more aware of its misfortune.

The work was as badly done as the servant was surly and disagreeable; in the corners of the rooms there were collected heaps of dust; spiders' webs hung from the ceilings and in front of the window-panes; the beds were hardly ever made, and the feather beds, so beloved by the old and feeble cats, had never once been shaken since Lizina left the house. At Father Gatto's next visit he found the whole colony in a state of uproar.

'Cæsar has one paw so badly swollen that it looks as if it were broken,' said one. 'Peppina kicked him with her great wooden shoes on. Hector has an abscess in his back where a wooden chair was flung at him; and Agrippina's three little kittens have died of hunger beside their mother, because Peppina forgot them in their basket up in the attic. There is no putting up with the creature —do send her away, Father Gatto! Lizina herself would not be angry with us; she must know very well what her sister is like.'

'Come here,' said Father Gatto, in his most severe tones to Peppina. And he took her down into the cellar and showed her the same two great jars that he had showed Lizina. 'In which of these shall I dip you?' he asked; and she made haste to answer: 'In the liquid gold,' for she was no more modest than she was good and kind.

Father Gatto's yellow eyes darted fire. 'You have not deserved it,' he uttered, in a voice like thunder, and seizing her he flung her into the jar of oil, where she was nearly suffocated. When she came to the surface screaming and struggling, the vengeful cat seized her again and rolled her in the ash-heap on the floor; then when she rose, dirty, blinded, and disgusting to behold, he thrust her from the door, saying: 'Begone, and when you meet a braying ass be careful to turn your head towards it.'

Stumbling and raging, Peppina set off for home, thinking herself fortunate to find a stick by the wayside with which to support herself. She was within sight of her mother's house when she heard in the meadow on the right, the voice of a donkey loudly braying. Quickly she turned her head towards it, and at the same time put her hand up to her forehead, where, waving like a plume, was a donkey's tail. She ran home to her mother at the top of her speed, yelling with rage and despair; and it took Lizina two hours with a big basin of hot water and two cakes of soap to get rid of the layer of ashes with which Father Gatto had adorned her. As for the donkey's tail, it was impossible to get rid of that; it was as firmly fixed on her forehead as was the golden star on Lizina's. Their mother was furious. She first beat Lizina unmercifully with the broom, then she took her to the mouth of the well and lowered her into it, leaving her at the bottom weeping and crying for help.

Before this happened, however, the king's son in passing the mother's house had seen Lizina sitting sewing in the parlour, and had been dazzled by her beauty. After coming back two or three times, he at last ventured to approach the window and to whisper in the softest voice: 'Lovely maiden, will you be my bride?' and she had answered: 'I will.'

Next morning, when the prince arrived to claim his bride, he found her wrapped in a large white veil. 'It is so that maidens are received from their parents' hands,' said the mother, who hoped to make the king's son marry Peppina in place of her sister, and had fastened the donkey's tail round her head like a lock of hair under the veil. The prince was young and a little timid, so he made no objections, and seated Peppina in the carriage beside him.

Their way led past the old house inhabited by the cats, who were all at the window, for the report had got about that the prince was going to marry the most beautiful maiden in the world, on whose forehead shone a golden star, and they knew that this could only be their adored Lizina. As the carriage slowly passed in front of the old house, where cats from all parts of world seemed to be gathered, a song burst from every throat:

> Mew, mew, mew!
> Prince, look quick behind you!
> In the well is fair Lizina,
> And you've got nothing but Peppina.

When he heard this the coachman, who understood the cat's language better than the prince, his master, stopped his horses and asked:

'Does your highness know what the grimalkins are

saying?' and the song broke forth again louder than ever.

With a turn of his hand the prince threw back the veil, and discovered the puffed-up, swollen face of Peppina, with the donkey's tail twisted round her head. 'Ah, traitress!' he exclaimed, and ordering the horses to be turned round, he drove the elder daughter, quivering with rage, to the old woman who had sought to deceive him. With his hand on the hilt of his sword he demanded Lizina in so terrific a voice that the mother hastened to the well to draw her prisoner out. Lizina's clothing and her star shone so brilliantly that when the prince led her home to the king, his father, the whole palace was lit up. Next day they were married, and lived happy ever after; and all the cats, headed by old Father Gatto, were present at the wedding.

HOW TO FIND OUT A TRUE FRIEND

ONCE upon a time there lived a king and queen who longed to have a son. As none came, one day they made a vow at the shrine of St. James that if their prayers were granted the boy should set out on a pilgrimage as soon as he had passed his eighteenth birthday. And fancy their delight when one evening the king returned home from hunting and saw a baby lying in the cradle.

All the people came crowding round to peep at it, and declared it was the most beautiful baby that ever was seen. Of course that is what they always say, but this time it happened to be true. And every day the boy grew bigger and stronger till he was twelve years old, when the king died, and he was left alone to take care of his mother.

In this way six years passed by, and his eighteenth birthday drew near. When she thought of this the queen's heart sank within her, for he was the light of her eyes, and how was she to send him forth to the unknown dangers that beset a pilgrim? So day by day she grew more and more sorrowful, and when she was alone wept bitterly.

Now the queen imagined that no one but herself knew how sad she was, but one morning her son said to her, 'Mother, why do you cry the whole day long?'

'Nothing, nothing, my son; there is only one thing in the world that troubles me.'

'What *is* that one thing?' asked he. 'Are you afraid

your property is badly managed? Let me go and look into the matter.'

This pleased the queen, and he rode off to the plain country, where his mother owned great estates; but everything was in beautiful order, and he returned with a joyful heart, and said, 'Now, mother, you can be happy again, for your lands are better managed than anyone else's I have seen. The cattle are thriving; the fields are thick with corn, and soon they will be ripe for harvest.'

'That is good news indeed,' answered she; but it did not seem to make any difference to her, and the next morning she was weeping and wailing as loudly as ever.

'Dear mother,' said her son in despair, 'if you will not tell me what is the cause of all this misery I shall leave home and wander far through the world.'

'Ah, my son, my son,' cried the queen, 'it is the thought that I must part from you which causes me such grief; for before you were born we vowed a vow to St. James that when your eighteenth birthday was passed you should make a pilgrimage to his shrine, and very soon you will be eighteen, and I shall lose you. And for a whole year my eyes will never be gladdened by the sight of you, for the shrine is far away.'

'Will it take no longer than that to reach it?' said he. 'Oh, don't be so wretched; it is only dead people who never return. As long as I am alive you may be sure I will come back to you.'

After this manner he comforted his mother, and on his eighteenth birthday his best horse was led to the door of the palace, and he took leave of the queen in these words, 'Dear mother, farewell, and by the help of fate I shall return to you as soon as I can.'

The queen burst into tears and wept sore; then amidst her sobs she drew three apples from her pocket and held them out, saying, 'My son, take these apples and give heed unto my words. You will need a companion in the long journey on which you are going. If you come across a young man who pleases you beg him to accompany you, and when you get to an inn invite him to have dinner with you. After you have eaten cut one of these apples in two unequal parts, and ask him to take one. If he takes the larger bit, then part from him, for he is no true friend to you. But if he takes the smaller bit treat him as your brother, and share with him all you have.' Then she kissed her son once more, and blessed him, and let him go.

The young man rode a long way without meeting a single creature, but at last he saw a youth in the distance about the same age as himself, and he spurred his horse till he came up with the stranger, who stopped and asked:

'Where are you going, my fine fellow?'

'I am making a pilgrimage to the shrine of St. James, for before I was born my mother vowed that I should go forth with a thank offering on my eighteenth birthday.'

'That is my case too,' said the stranger, 'and, as we must both travel in the same direction, let us bear each other company.'

The young man agreed to this proposal, but he took care not to get on terms of familiarity with the new comer until he had tried him with the apple.

By-and-by they reached an inn, and at sight of it the king's son said, 'I am very hungry. Let us enter and order something to eat.' The other consented, and they were soon sitting before a good dinner.

When they had finished the king's son drew an apple from his pocket, and cut it into a big half and a little half, and offered both to the stranger, who took the biggest bit. 'You are no friend of mine,' thought the king's son, and in order to part company with him he pretended to be ill and declared himself unable to proceed on his journey.

'Well, I can't wait for you,' replied the other; 'I am in haste to push on, so farewell.'

'Farewell,' said the king's son, glad in his heart to get rid of him so easily. The king's son remained in the inn for some time, so as to let the young man have a good start; them he ordered his horse and rode after him. But he was very sociable and the way seemed long and dull by himself. 'Oh, if I could only meet with a true friend,' he thought, 'so that I should have some one to speak to. I hate being alone.'

Soon after he came up with a young man, who stopped and asked him, 'Where are you going, my fine fellow?' The king's son explained the object of his journey, and the young man answered, as the other had done, that he also was fulfilling the vow of his mother made at his birth.

'Well, we can ride on together,' said the king's son, and the road seemed much shorter now that he had some one to talk to.

At length they reached an inn, and the king's son exclaimed, 'I am very hungry; let us go in and get something to eat.'

When they had finished the king's son drew an apple out of his pocket and cut it in two; he held the big bit and the little bit out to his companion, who took the big bit at once and soon ate it up. 'You are no friend of mine,' thought the king's son, and began to declare he felt so ill he could not continue his journey. When he had given the young man a good start he set off himself, but the way seemed even longer and duller than before. 'Oh, if I could only meet with a true friend he should be as a brother to me,' he sighed sadly; and as the thought passed through his mind, he noticed a youth going the same road as himself.

The youth came up to him and said, 'Which way are you going, my fine fellow?' And for the third time the king's son explained all about his mother's vow. 'Why, that is just like me,' cried the youth.

'Then let us ride on together,' answered the king's son.

Now the miles seemed to slip by, for the new comer was so lively and entertaining that the king's son could not help hoping that he indeed might prove to be the true friend.

More quickly than he could have thought possible they reached an inn by the road-side, and turning to his companion the king's son said, 'I am hungry; let us go in and have something to eat.' So they went in and ordered dinner, and when they had finished the king's son drew out of his pocket the last apple, and cut it into two unequal parts, and held both out to the stranger. And the stranger took the little piece, and the heart of the king's son was glad within him, for at last he had found the friend he had been looking for. 'Good youth,' he cried, 'we will be brothers, and what is mine shall be thine, and what is thine shall be mine. And together we will push on to the shrine, and if one of us dies on the road the other shall carry his body there.' And the stranger agreed to all he said, and they rode forward together.

It took them a whole year to reach the shrine, and they passed through many different lands on their way. One day they arrived tired and half-starved in a big city, and said to one another, 'Let us stay here for a little and rest before we set forth again.' So they hired a small house close to the royal castle, and took up their abode there.

The following morning the king of the country happened to step on to his balcony, and saw the young men in the garden, and said to himself, 'Dear me, those are wonderfully handsome youths; but one is handsomer than the other, and to him will I give my daughter to wife;' and indeed the king's son excelled his friend in beauty.

In order to set about his plan the king asked both the young men to dinner, and when they arrived at the castle he received them with the utmost kindness, and sent for his daughter, who was more lovely than both the sun and moon put together. But at bed-time the king caused the other young man to be given a poisoned drink, which killed him in a few minutes, for he thought to himself, 'If his friend dies the other will forget his pilgrimage, and will stay here and marry my daughter.'

When the king's son awoke the next morning he inquired of the servants where his friend had gone, as he did not see him. 'He died suddenly last night,' said they, 'and is to be buried immediately.'

But the king's son sprang up, and cried, 'If my friend is dead I can stay here no longer, and cannot linger an hour in this house.'

'Oh, give up your journey and remain here,' exclaimed the king, 'and you shall have my daughter for your wife.' 'No,' answered the king's son, 'I cannot stay; but, I pray you, grant my request, and give me a good horse, and let me go in peace, and when I have fulfilled my vow then I will return and marry your daughter.'

So the king, seeing no words would move him, ordered a horse to be brought round, and the king's son mounted it, and took his dead friend before him on the saddle, and rode away.

Now the young man was not really dead, but only in a deep sleep.

When the king's son reached the shrine of St. James he got down from his horse, took his friend in his arms as if he had been a child, and laid him before the altar. 'St. James,' he said, 'I have fulfilled the vow my parents made for me. I have come myself to your shrine, and have brought my friend. I place him in your hands. Restore him to life, I pray, for though he be dead yet has he fulfilled his vow also.' And, behold! while he yet prayed his friend got up and stood before him as well as ever. And both the young men gave thanks, and set their faces towards home.

When they arrived at the town where the king

dwelt they entered the small house over against the castle. The news of their coming spread very soon, and the king rejoiced greatly that the handsome young prince had come back again, and commanded great feasts to be prepared, for in a few days his daughter should marry the king's son. The young man himself could imagine no greater happiness, and when the marriage was over they spent some months at the court making merry.

At length the king's son said, 'My mother awaits me at home, full of care and anxiety. Here I must remain no longer, and to-morrow I will take my wife and my friend and start for home.' And the king was content that he should do so, and gave orders to prepare for their journey.

Now in his heart the king cherished a deadly hate towards the poor young man whom he had tried to kill, but who had returned to him living, and in order to do him hurt sent him on a message to some distant spot. 'See that you are quick,' said he, 'for your friend will await your return before he starts.' The youth put spurs to his horse and departed, bidding the prince farewell, so that the king's message might be delivered the sooner. As soon as he had started the king went to the chamber of the prince, and said to him, 'If you do not start immediately, you will never reach the place where you must camp for the night.'

'I cannot start without my friend,' replied the king's son.

'Oh, he will be back in an hour,' replied the king, 'and I will give him my best horse, so that he will be sure to catch you up.' The king's son allowed himself to be persuaded and took leave of his father-in-law, and set out with his wife on his journey home.

Meanwhile the poor friend had been unable to get through his task in the short time appointed by the king, and when at last he returned the king said to him,

'Your comrade is a long way off by now; you had better see if you can overtake him.'

So the young man bowed and left the king's presence, and followed after his friend on foot, for he had no horse. Night and day he ran, till at length he reached the place where the king's son had pitched his tent, and sank down before him, a miserable object, worn out and covered with mud and dust. But the king's son welcomed him with joy, and tended him as he would his brother.

And at last they came home again, and the queen was waiting and watching in the palace, as she had never ceased to do since her son had rode away. She almost died of joy at seeing him again, but after a little she remembered his sick friend, and ordered a bed to be made ready and the best doctors in all the country to be sent for. When they heard of the queen's summons they flocked from all parts, but none could cure him. After everyone had tried and failed a servant entered and informed the queen that a strange old man had just knocked at the palace gate and declared that he was able to heal the dying youth. Now this was a holy man, who had heard of the trouble the king's son was in, and had come to help.

It happened that at this very time a little daughter was born to the king's son, but in his distress for his friend he had hardly a thought to spare for the baby. He could not be prevailed on to leave the sick bed, and he was bending over it when the holy man entered the room. 'Do you wish your friend to be cured?' asked the new comer of the king's son. 'And what price would you pay?'

'What price?' answered the king's son; 'only tell me what I can do to heal him.'

'Listen to me, then,' said the old man. 'This evening you must take your child, and open her veins, and smear the wounds of your friend with her blood. And you will see, he will get well in an instant.'

At these words the king's son shrieked with horror, for he loved the baby dearly, but he answered, 'I have sworn that I would treat my friend as if he were my brother, and if there is no other way my child must be sacrificed.'

As by this time evening had already fallen he took the child and opened its veins, and smeared the blood over the wounds of the sick man, and the look of death departed from him, and he grew strong and rosy once more. But the little child lay as white and still as if she had been dead. They laid her in the cradle and wept bitterly, for they thought that by the next morning she would be lost to them.

At sunrise the old man returned and asked after the sick man.

'He is as well as ever,' answered the king's son.

'And where is your baby?'

'In the cradle yonder, and I think she is dead,' replied the father sadly.

'Look at her once more,' said the holy man, and as they drew near the cradle there lay the baby smiling up at them.

'I am St. James of Lizia,' said the old man, 'and I have come to help you, for I have seen that you are a true friend. From henceforward live happily, all of you, together, and if troubles should draw near you send for me, and I will aid you to get through them.'

With these words he lifted his hand in blessing and vanished.

And they obeyed him, and were happy and content, and tried to make the people of the land happy and contented too.

[From *Sicilianische Mährchen*, Gonzenbach.]

CLEVER MARIA

There was once a merchant who lived close to the royal palace, and had three daughters. They were all pretty, but Maria, the youngest, was the prettiest of the three. One day the king sent for the merchant, who was a widower, to give him directions about a journey he wished the good man to take. The merchant would rather not have gone, as he did not like leaving his daughters at home, but he could not refuse to obey the king's commands, and with a heavy heart he returned home to say farewell to them. Before he left, he took three pots of basil, and gave one to each girl, saying, 'I am going a journey, but I leave these pots. You must let nobody into the house. When I come back, they will tell me what has happened.' 'Nothing will have happened,' said the girls.

The father went away, and the following day the king, accompanied by two friends, paid a visit to the three girls, who were sitting at supper. When they saw who was there, Maria said, 'Let us go and get a bottle of wine from the cellar. I will carry the key, my eldest sister can take the light, while the other brings the bottle.' But the king replied, 'Oh, do not trouble; we are not thirsty.' 'Very well, we will not go,' answered the two elder girls; but Maria merely said, 'I shall go, anyhow.' She left the room, and went to the hall where she put out the light, and putting down the key and the bottle, ran to the house of a neighbour, and knocked at the door. 'Who is there so late?' asked the old woman, thrusting her head out of the window.

'Oh, let me in,' answered Maria. 'I have quarrelled with my eldest sister, and as I do not want to fight any more, I have come to beg you to allow me to sleep with you.'

So the old woman opened the door and Maria slept in her house. The king was very angry at her for playing truant, but when she returned home the next day, she found the plants of her sisters withered away, because they had disobeyed their father. Now the window in the room of the eldest overlooked the gardens of the king, and when she saw how fine and ripe the medlars were on the trees, she longed to eat some, and begged Maria to scramble down by a rope and pick her a few, and she would draw her up again. Maria, who was good-natured, swung herself into the garden by the rope, and got the medlars, and was just making the rope fast under her arms so as to be hauled up, when her sister cried: 'Oh, there are such delicious lemons a little farther on. You might bring me one or two.' Maria turned round to pluck them, and found herself face to face with the gardener, who caught hold of her, exclaiming, 'What are you doing here, you little thief?' 'Don't call me names,' she said, 'or you will get the worst of it,' giving him as she spoke such a violent push that he fell panting into the lemon bushes. Then she seized the cord and clambered up to the window.

The next day the second sister had a fancy for bananas and begged so hard, that, though Maria had declared she would never do such a thing again, at last she consented, and went down the rope into the king's garden. This time she met the king, who said to her, 'Ah, here you are again, cunning one! Now you shall pay for your misdeeds.'

And he began to cross-question her about what she had done. Maria denied nothing, and when she had finished, the king said again, 'Follow me to the house, and there you shall pay the penalty.' As he spoke, he

CLEVER MARIA

started for the house, looking back from time to time to make sure that Maria had not run away. All of a sudden, when he glanced round, he found she had vanished completely, without leaving a trace of where she had gone. Search was made all through the town, and there was not a hole or corner which was not ransacked, but there was no sign of her anywhere. This so enraged the king that he became quite ill, and for many months his life was despaired of.

Meanwhile the two elder sisters had married the two friends of the king, and were the mothers of little daughters. Now one day Maria stole secretly to the house where her elder sister lived, and snatching up the children put them into a beautiful basket she had with her, covered with flowers inside and out, so that no one would ever guess it held two babies. Then she dressed herself as a boy, and placing the basket on her head, she walked slowly past the palace, crying as she went :

'Who will carry these flowers to the king, who lies sick of love?'

And the king in his bed heard what she said, and ordered one of his attendants to go out and buy the basket. It was brought to his bedside, and as he raised the lid cries were heard, and peeping in he saw two little children. He was furious at this new trick which he felt had been played on him by Maria, and was still looking at them, wondering how he should pay her out, when he was told that the merchant, Maria's father, had finished the business on which he had been sent and returned home. Then the king remembered how Maria had refused to receive his visit, and how she had stolen his fruit, and he determined to be revenged on her. So he sent a message by one of his pages that the merchant was to come to see him the next day, and bring with him a coat made of stone, or else he would be punished. Now the poor man had been very sad since he got home the evening before, for though his daughters had promised that nothing should happen while he was away, he had found the two elder ones married without asking his leave. And now there was this fresh misfortune, for how was he to make a coat of stone? He wrung his hands and declared that the king would be the ruin of him, when Maria suddenly entered. 'Do not grieve about the coat of stone, dear father; but take this bit of chalk, and go to the palace and say you have come to measure the king.' The old man did not see the use of this, but Maria had so often helped him before that he had confidence in her, so he put the chalk in his pocket and went to the palace.

'That is no good,' said the king, when the merchant had told him what he had come for.

'Well, I can't make the coat you want,' replied he.

'Then if you would save your head, hand over to me your daughter Maria.'

The merchant did not reply, but went sorrowfully back to his house, where Maria sat waiting for him.

'Oh, my dear child, why was I born? The king says that, instead of the coat, I must deliver you up to him.'

'Do not be unhappy, dear father, but get a doll made, exactly like me, with a string attached to its head, which I can pull for "Yes" and "No."'

So the old man went out at once to see about it.

The king remained patiently in his palace, feeling sure that this time Maria could not escape him; and he said to his pages, 'If a gentleman should come here with his daughter and ask to be allowed to speak with me, put the young lady in my room and see she does not leave it.'

When the door was shut on Maria, who had concealed the doll under her cloak, she hid herself under the couch, keeping fast hold of the string which was fastened to its head.

'Senhora Maria, I hope you are well,' said the king when he entered the room. The doll nodded. 'Now we will reckon up accounts,' continued he, and he began at

MARIA & THE KING

the beginning, and ended up with the flower-basket, and at each fresh misdeed Maria pulled the string, so that the doll's head nodded assent. 'Whoso mocks at me merits death,' declared the king when he had ended, and drawing his sword, cut off the doll's head. It fell towards him, and as he felt the touch of a kiss, he exclaimed, 'Ah, Maria, Maria, so sweet in death, so hard to me in life! The man who could kill you deserves to die!' And he was about to turn his sword on himself, when the true Maria sprung out from under the bed, and flung herself into his arms. And the next day they were married and lived happily for many years.

[From the Portuguese.]

THE MAGIC KETTLE

RIGHT in the middle of Japan, high up among the mountains, an old man lived in his little house. He was very proud of it, and never tired of admiring the whiteness of his straw mats, and the pretty papered walls, which in warm weather always slid back, so that the smell of the trees and flowers might come in.

One day he was standing looking at the mountain opposite, when he heard a kind of rumbling noise in the room behind him. He turned round, and in the corner he beheld a rusty old iron kettle, which could not have seen the light of day for many years. How the kettle got there the old man did not know, but he took it up and looked it over carefully, and when he found that it was quite whole he cleaned the dust off it and carried it into his kitchen.

'That was a piece of luck,' he said, smiling to himself; 'a good kettle costs money, and it is as well to have a second one at hand in case of need; mine is getting worn out, and the water is already beginning to come through its bottom.'

Then he took the other kettle off the fire, filled the new one with water, and put it in its place.

No sooner was the water in the kettle getting warm than a strange thing happened, and the man, who was standing by, thought he must be dreaming. First the handle of the kettle gradually changed its shape and became a head, and the spout grew into a tail, while out of the body sprang four paws, and in a few minutes the man found himself watching, not a kettle, but a tanuki! The creature jumped off the fire, and bounded about the room like a kitten, running up the walls and over the ceiling, till the old man was in an agony lest his pretty room should be spoilt. He cried to a neighbour for help, and between them they managed to catch the tanuki, and shut him up safely in a wooden chest. Then, quite exhausted, they sat down on the mats, and consulted together what they should do with this troublesome beast. At length they decided to sell him, and bade a child who was passing send them a certain tradesman called Jimmu.

When Jimmu arrived, the old man told him that he had something which he wished to get rid of, and lifted the lid of the wooden chest, where he had shut up the tanuki. But, to his surprise, no tanuki was there, nothing but the kettle he had found in the corner. It was certainly very odd, but the man remembered what had taken place on the fire, and did not want to keep the kettle any more, so after a little bargaining about the price, Jimmu went away carrying the kettle with him.

Now Jimmu had not gone very far before he felt that the kettle was getting heavier and heavier, and by the time he reached home he was so tired that he was thankful to put it down in the corner of his room, and then forgot all about it. In the middle of the night, however, he was awakened by a loud noise in the corner where the kettle stood, and raised himself up in bed to see what it was. But nothing was there except the kettle, which seemed quiet enough. He thought that he must have been dreaming, and fell asleep again, only to be roused a second time by the same disturbance. He jumped up and went to the corner, and by the light of the lamp that he always kept burning he saw that the kettle had become a tanuki, which was running round after his tail. After he grew weary of that, he ran on the balcony, where he turned several somersaults, from pure gladness of heart. The tradesman was much troubled as to what to do with the animal, and it was only towards morning that he managed to get any sleep; but when he opened his eyes again there was no tanuki, only the old kettle he had left there the night before.

As soon as he had tidied his house, Jimmu set off to tell his story to a friend next door. The man listened quietly, and did not appear so surprised as Jimmu expected, for he recollected having heard, in his youth, something about a wonder-working kettle. 'Go and travel with it, and show it off,' said he, 'and you will become a rich man; but be careful first to ask the tanuki's leave, and also to perform some magic ceremonies to prevent him from running away at the sight of the people.'

Jimmu thanked his friend for his counsel, which he followed exactly. The tanuki's consent was obtained, a booth was built, and a notice was hung up outside it inviting the people to come and witness the most wonderful transformation that ever was seen.

They came in crowds, and the kettle was passed from hand to hand, and they were allowed to examine it all over, and even to look inside. Then Jimmu took it back, and setting it on the platform, commanded it to become a tanuki. In an instant the handle began to change into a head, and the spout into a tail, while the four paws appeared at the sides. 'Dance,' said Jimmu, and the tanuki did his steps, and moved first on one side and then on the other, till the people could not stand still any longer, and began to dance too. Gracefully he led the fan dance, and glided without a pause into the shadow dance and the umbrella dance, and it seemed as if he might go on dancing for ever. And so very likely he would, if Jimmu had not declared he had danced enough, and that the booth must now be closed.

Day after day the booth was so full it was hardly possible to enter it, and what the neighbour foretold had come to pass, and Jimmu was a rich man. Yet he did not feel happy. He was an honest man, and he thought that he owed some of his wealth to the man from whom he had bought the kettle. So, one morning, he put a hundred gold pieces into it, and hanging the kettle once more on his arm, he returned to the seller of it. 'I have no right to keep it any longer,' he added when he had ended his tale, 'so I have brought it back to you, and inside you will find a hundred gold pieces as the price of its hire.'

The man thanked Jimmu, and said that few people would have been as honest as he. And the kettle brought them both luck, and everything went well with them till they died, which they did when they were very old, respected by everyone.

[Adapted from *Japanische Mährchen*.]